The Choice
of War

Recent Title in
The Ethics of American Foreign Policy

The Arrow and the Olive Branch: Practical Idealism in U.S. Foreign Policy
Jack Godwin

THE CHOICE OF WAR

The Iraq War and the Just War Tradition

ALBERT L. WEEKS

The Ethics of American Foreign Policy
David A. Welch and Robert G. Patman, Series Editors

PRAEGER SECURITY INTERNATIONAL
An Imprint of ABC-CLIO, LLC

A B C **❖** C L I O

Santa Barbara, California • Denver, Colorado • Oxford, England

Library of Congress Cataloging-in-Publication Data

Weeks, Albert Loren, 1923–
    The choice of war : the Iraq War and the just war tradition / Albert L. Weeks.
        p. cm. — (The ethics of American foreign policy)
    Includes bibliographical references and index.
    ISBN 978–0–275–99111–1 (hard copy : alk. paper) — ISBN 978–0–313–08184–2 (ebook)
1. Iraq War, 2003– —Moral and ethical aspects. 2. War on terrorism, 2001– —Moral and
ethical aspects. 3. United States—Foreign relations—2001–2009. 4. United States—Military
policy—Moral and ethical aspects. 5. Just war doctrine. 6. Bush, George W. (George
Walker), 1946– —Political and social views. I. Title.
DS79.764.U6W43   2010
956.7044'31—dc22   2009039041

14 13 12 11 10   1 2 3 4 5

This book is also available on the World Wide Web as an eBook.
Visit www.abc-clio.com for details.

ABC-CLIO, LLC
130 Cremona Drive, P.O. Box 1911
Santa Barbara, California 93116–1911

This book is printed on acid-free paper ∞

Manufactured in the United States of America

Contents

Preface

Now, let me also address the issue of Iraq. Unlike Afghanistan, Iraq was a war of choice that provoked strong differences in my country and around the world. Although I believe that the Iraqi people are ultimately better off without the tyranny of Saddam Hussein, I also believe that events in Iraq have reminded America of the need to use diplomacy and build international consensus to resolve our problems whenever possible.
—President Barack Obama, Cairo, June 4, 2009

As the midterm elections approached in 2004, signs of deepening public dismay over the war in Iraq appeared in the polls. President George W. Bush for the first time admitted that the Iraq War had been miscarried. In a late August 2004 interview with *The New York Times*, Bush stated that he had "miscalculated" in thinking that a "swift victory" could be achieved in the war in Iraq that the Administration had chosen to start in March 2003.[1]

After 2004 the occupation phase of the war continued to drag on as American casualties mounted. By the time of the election in November 2008, a number of top Bush officials had resigned. They included CIA Director George Tenet (2004); Donald Rumsfeld and his assistant in the Defense Department (DoD), Paul Wolfowitz (in, respectively, 2006 and 2005); another Rumsfeld war architect in the DoD, Douglas Feith (2005); Colin Powell, Secretary of State (2005); Scooter Libby, Vice President Dick Cheney's Chief of Staff (2007); Lawrence Wilkerson, Chief of Staff to Powell (2005); and Scott McClellan, Administration Press Secretary (2008). Some of these departed officials strongly criticized Bush Administration policies on the war while others continued to defend them.

By the end of Bush's first term in 2004, a watershed had been reached. At the end of Bush's second term in 2008, a majority of Americans considered the war to have been a mistake, with less than 20 percent of the population showing approval. This public sentiment seemed to echo the views of Colin Powell. He described his performance before the U.N. Security Council in 2003, when he produced alleged evidence of weapons of mass destruction (WMD) in Iraq, as "the worst day of my life." It was, he said, a "blot" on his record.[2]

The candidate who was elected president on November 4, 2008, had pledged in his campaign to break with the mistaken policies of his predecessor. President Barack Obama soon began a process of setting dates for extricating U.S. combat troops from Iraq while rectifying abuses (e.g., torture) of detainees that violated the Geneva Conventions. The new president pledged to shut down the detention center at Guantanamo Bay and never to countenance the use of torture against captives.

After initial hesitation as to how to cope with the previous administration's condoning of torture used against captives held at the various detention centers located and run by the CIA at home and abroad, the Obama administration in late August 2009 adopted a policy of actively investigating such past practices of prisoner abuse.[3]. Attorney General Eric H. Holder Jr. designated a seasoned federal prosecutor, John H. Durham, to determine whether crimes had been committed by harsh, inhumane treatment of prisoners. The investigation appeared to be aimed at resurrecting principles of jus in bello (justice in war fighting) that were evidently violated by CIA interrogators and agency contractors.

This book provides a compendium of the underlying, mistaken ideology for initiating full-fledged war against a weak Iraq in 2003. It catalogues the serious mistakes that were made during the central years of the war and occupation. The book assesses the way in which the former administration's ideology, sometimes characterized as the "Bush Doctrine," clashed with venerable, long-standing principles of just war—*jus ad bellum* and *jus in bello*—as well as with the Geneva Conventions pertaining to the waging of war and the humane treatment of prisoners.

The passing of the Bush era and the election of Obama in 2008 opened the way to a thoroughgoing reexamination of U.S. war and peace policies and strategy, as promised by the winning candidate. It is hoped that policymakers henceforth will give deep thought to the past violations, which are canvassed in this book. Moreover, it is hoped that General Powell's much-touted three guiding principles for military strategy will be borne in mind. Namely, that specific, realistic moral-political goals will be clearly stated; that overwhelming ground forces will be brought to bear instead of relying excessively on small numbers of occupying Special Forces or on bombings by the Air Force; and, finally, that in any future conflict a clear exit strategy will be developed.

In short, the new administration in Washington must find ways to repair the damage made to American prestige worldwide during the preceding eight years. In future war planning, the policymakers must restore the "mainstream" American principle of fighting defensive wars rather than waging an ill-conceived, preemptive "war of choice" that lacks a moral foundation while violating the country's best traditions.[4]

September 2009

Introduction

> But if the cause be not good, the King himself hath a heavy reckoning to make, when all those legs and arms and heads, chopp'd off in a battle, shall join together at the latter day and cry all, "We died at such a place"—some swearing, some crying for a surgeon, some upon their wives left poor behind them, some upon the debts they owe, some upon their children rawly left. I am afeard there are few die well that die in a battle; for how can they charitably dispose of anything when blood is their argument? Now, if these men do not die well, it will be a black matter for the King that led them to it; who to disobey were against all proportion of subjection.
>
> —Shakespeare, *Henry V*, Act IV, Scene 1

As American servicemen and women and U.S. civilian employees continue to die on an almost daily basis in Iraq, serious doubts about the justness and the wisdom of the war continue to arise. A majority of the American public and the international community now believe that America's invasion and occupation of Iraq were not based on an "imminent" threat to U.S. security and that the war was unjustifiable as well as a tragic mistake.[1]

Current debate rages on as it becomes clear that more is at stake than how or when victory can be proclaimed over an enemy whose very identity and whereabouts in latter-day counterinsurgency struggle within Iraq are problematical. Meanwhile, with bitter irony the Iraq population has become increasingly anti-United States as Iraqis call for American and coalition troop withdrawals. Moreover, large numbers of American GI's, who are themselves deployed to the region, give mounting evidence of appearing to be in favor of a U.S. withdrawal.[2]

The most poignant of all questions concerning the Iraq War is its moral justification. It boils down to asking two key questions: Was the Iraq war just? Was it fought in a just way?

As Shakespeare's character, Williams, suggested in Henry's fire-lit camp the night before the start of the Battle of Agincourt, any battle or war has *moral dimensions*. These measures mark the war as either just or unjust, as viewed by the soldiers and the civilian population. It will go down in history with a favorable or unfavorable verdict. The "heavy reckoning" as to the rectitude and legitimacy of the cause and strategy behind the Iraq War is being weighed today. The reckoning is likely to continue long after the war is over.

The rationale for the war—any war—is central and crucial. It is a matter, after all, of justifying the whole enterprise. Since March 2003 until the winter of 2008, casualties mounted to over 3,000 killed and some five times that number in wounded American servicemen and women, some permanently so. Some sources have placed the figure for Iraqi deaths at 100,000 or more, and this number continues to climb.[3] These sacrifices further focus the discussion on the justification of the war.

In the history of Western thought and literature worldwide, the heavy reckoning over the reasons for going to war has led men and women traditionally to categorize wars as being either just or unjust. Since the time of Homer, poets and playwrights, philosophers and theologians, as well as legal scholars have grappled with the issue of whether the ultimate sacrifice in human lives in a certain war was justifiable and "worth it." Whether in the West or in Far Eastern countries, this literature is rich and informative. In surveying it, one can begin to orientate oneself on the moral rightness of a given war, and the Iraq War in particular.

As we review the well-entrenched tradition of classifying wars in this way, we will see that these insights have not lain inert on the pages of ancient manuscripts and latter-day treatises. From ancient times to the present day, the relevant concepts and criteria for making moral judgments about warfare have been canvassed and reworked. In the end, they were cast into tangible laws, rules, and sanctions. The answers regarding the purpose of war and how it is fought and terminated have become guidelines that are inscribed in universally recognized treaties and conventions. These principles are also embodied in the charters of international organizations, such as the United Nations. Moral principles and rules for waging wars were no less viable in 2007 than they were in past centuries and millennia. No state today, in fact, can justifiably avoid acknowledging the viability of moral considerations without becoming an outlaw or a pariah. The people of a nation that is planning war or is at war want to know, for example, whether there was a just cause in taking up arms. They wonder if the war-maker's intentions were pure, good, and rational. They also wish to know whether the authority (i.e., government) that sent the soldiers into combat was legitimate. Was the decision to make war guided by broadly based discussion and reasoning? Were the chances of ultimate victory in war carefully weighed? Above all, were all other means for resolving differences between the combatant states exhausted in such a way that war became the only feasible, last resort?

In reviewing these and other questions and relevant moral concepts and criteria, we may agree that such moral issues concerning war are not confined to philosophical or legal writings alone. The pros and cons of a war also raise technical questions of tangential relevance to morality. The professional military's study of armed combat as conducted in the discipline of military science itself accords a dominant place to such questions. One need only read the writings of the well-known Prussian military strategist, Carl von Clausewitz, in order to understand how applicable to war are moral and, as he termed them, "political" principles. He also addressed the issue of how a war strategy will have political and moral consequences. As Clausewitz wrote in *On War* (*Vom Kriege*):[4]

> Moral factors cannot be ignored in war ... Moral elements are among the most important in war. They constitute the spirit that permeates war as a whole ... The will [in battle] is itself a moral quantity ... Since war is not an act of sense-less passion but is controlled by its political [that is, moral—ALW] purpose, the value of this purpose must determine the sacrifices to be made for it in magni-tude and also in duration. Once the expenditure of effort exceeds the value of the political purpose, the purpose must be renounced and peace must follow.

The ancient Chinese strategist Sun Tzu (c. 500 B.C.) likewise laid great stress on the moral aspect of war. This factor was reflected in war, he wrote, by the war's justness as perceived by the soldiers and the population. The people and the soldiers, he wrote, must feel and be "united in purpose." Yet he also insisted that it is always preferable "to subdue the enemy *without fighting*," which, he said, "is the acme of skill."[5]

In other words, both of these "technicians" of the art of warfare fully appreciated what was at stake in applying bloody means to reach (so they trusted) justifiable ends. Despite their in-depth study of this bloody business, or perhaps because of it, they were fully cognizant of the "sacrifices," as Clausewitz put it. Sun Tzu and Clausewitz, who are echoed in modern writ-ings about war, thought it was crucial to make certain that war fighting was absolutely necessary as a last resort. As Sun Tzu wrote, defeating the enemy "without fighting"—in today's terms meaning via diplomacy, deterrence, containment, and other nonmilitary means—is the most skilful, or as we might say, the most humane way of containing and ultimately defeating the adversary. Under certain circumstances this can be achieved by minimal military means or via diplomacy or containment.

Condemnation of taking life for unjustifiable reasons is, of course, a prevalent theme in Western as well as Eastern thought. In Chapter 3 we will explore the various contributions made—pagan, Jewish, Christian, Muslim, Buddhist—to the discussion of just and justifiable war. We will examine the distinction that is traditionally made between moral versus immoral war, legal versus illegal war making, and the advantages of peace and the avoidance of war whenever possible.

The "present interest" in developing such a study should be as obvious as it is urgent. Consider today's world and the weapons of mass destruction (WMD), whose proliferation hangs like a Damoclean sword over populations worldwide. Also, consider the tangible menace of terrorist networks like Al Qaeda and the states that might harbor and encourage terrorist violence perpetrated against innocent civilian noncombatants in other countries. In fighting against contemporary terrorism, as typified by the acts committed on American soil on September 11, 2001 and the terrorist acts perpetrated against urban populations in the United Kingdom, Spain, Russia, Saudi Arabia, Somalia, and elsewhere, counterterror forces must not only use effective, forceful means against such enemies. *They must also remain true to the moral standards for waging this struggle.*

Holding the moral high ground is no less crucial than seizing the "commanding heights" in combat. Any flouting of the venerable principles governing the rationale and justification for going to war, the way in which it is fought and terminated, as well as how enemy prisoners of war are treated must be considered counterproductive, immoral, and ultimately dangerous. Moreover, neglect of such principles weakens the moral fiber of the war-makers while lowering their prestige among other nations. Any country that does not honor this collective tradition is open to the claim that it is no better than the enemy. As a result, it may find itself isolated from the rest of the civilized world.

No nation-state, even the world's number-one superpower engaged as it is with other states in a legitimate fight against the terrorist enemy, can afford such isolation. It should not allow the loss of allies in the common struggle because it put aside moral and legal principle in waging the struggle.

Clemenceau once remarked that war is too important to be left to the generals. It might also be said that it is too bloody a matter for any state to ignore basic principles. This can be capsulated as follows: *When it is not absolutely necessary to go to war, it is necessary not to.* When it is unnecessary, such a war is likely to be immoral as well as illegal.

In singling out the Iraq War as a test case for remaining true to the time-worn traditions of morality that should govern war fighting, the author of this book finds that the Bush Administration has failed to fully honor this legacy of thought and international law. In fact, as this book will show, beginning in 2002 the war planners in Washington had deliberately set about violating any number of accepted, traditional standards for legitimizing the waging of war under warranted conditions as interpreted by the web of international law and custom. In so doing, the administration in Washington managed to set an unfortunate precedent in American history and the American tradition of rationalizing and waging any war in which it is a participant, let alone the initiator of combat. This book will catalog other unwise decisions and actions by the Bush administration that sullied this nation's reputation and will also discuss how such decisions radically departed from American tradition and in some ways encouraged the kind of militancy that the post-9/11 "war against terrorism" was supposed to discourage and suppress.

As we proceed to consider the various principles for waging just war and terminating it with just means, we will weigh the Iraq War point-by-point against moral and legal standards. We will closely examine these political and moral principles and show how they should guide any legitimate struggle against perceived enemies.

Part One canvasses the tradition—in philosophy, theology, law, and *belles lettres*. These writings classified wars according to their moral and legal rectitude. Part Two uses these long-established principles and criteria of *jus ad bellum*—justice of war—as they apply to the U.S.-initiated Iraq War. Part Three evaluates the Iraq War according to the criteria of *jus in bello*—justice in war.

This book will detail how from the start the administration tried to justify its war of choice against Iraq in ways that struck a contrast with the war it was waging in Afghanistan as a "war of necessity."[6] We will investigate the validity of its rationalizations for the former on the eve of the invasion of March 2003. Namely, was the claim that Iraq under Saddam Hussein posed an "imminent threat" to the United States a valid one; did Iraq possess an arsenal of ready-to-use WMD; was Iraq collaborating with Al Qaeda; and was Saddam Hussein an evil dictator who committed crimes against his own people in ways that made an invasion and occupation of Iraq a necessity?[7] Moreover, we will take note of how by 2004 and 2005 the original rationale was amended, with the emphasis being put on the war's principal aim of converting Iraq into a peaceful, pro-U.S., democratic, Middle Eastern polity. This left the administration vulnerable to rising public nonsupport of the war, since above all it was the alleged imminent threat of Iraq to U.S. security that had been used as the justification for waging war. As the occupation proceeded, the administration's various flawed methods and rationalizations for coping with the pacification of Iraq seriously damaged America's image abroad. As of 2005 and 2006, if not earlier, even in Iraq itself a majority of its population thought the war and occupation had been a "bad job."[8] The call among Iraqis for the occupiers to leave their country continued to rise throughout 2006 and into 2008.

No less relevant to our examination of the wisdom of the war against Iraq is the consequent weakening of the Iraqi state in the face of a threatening neighbor to the east—namely, the theocratically ruled, terror-exporting Iran. In the 1980s U.S. policy viewed Iraq under Saddam Hussein, a Sunni, as a countervailing force against Shiite Iran within the framework of the balance of power in the Middle East. U.S. military aid was duly extended to Baghdad. By destroying Saddam's regime and weakening the state of Iraq, however, the United States thereby lost an important counterweight to Iraq's old enemy, Iran. The latter, in fact, has become the leading menace in the Near East.[9]

Furthermore, the likelihood that an eventual Shia regime in Baghdad would close ranks with a Shiite-dominated regime in Tehran cannot be ruled out. General Wesley K. Clark, former Supreme Allied Commander, Europe, as well as other observers have made this eventuality the centerpiece of their analyses of the U.S.-led occupation of Iraq.[10]

Finally, former Director of the National Security Agency from 1985 to 1988, Lieutenant General William E. Odom, U.S. Army (Ret.), made this comment about the war:[11]

> The invasion of Iraq may well turn out to be the greatest strategic disaster in American history. In any event, the longer we stay, the worse it will be. Until that is understood, we will make no progress with our allies or in devising a promising alternative strategy.

As we sort out the evidence, it may be agreed that America, by its own history, traditions, and principles, should not go to war without a clear and present danger that concretely and directly threatens its security. The United States does not traditionally espouse a military policy or strategy for waging offensive or "preemptive" (or "preventive") war.[12] Neither noble-sounding rhetoric nor a crusading spirit in putative defense of peace and democracy can alone justify planning and executing preemptive or preventive war against a sovereign nation-state, whatever its type of regime. If the state represents no tangible, aggressive, or clear and present military threat to other states, we must rule out, all things being equal, the justifiability of an invasion and occupation of that country, its tyrannical nature aside.

Jus ad Bellum and *Jus in Bello*

1

The Human Habit of War

In determining the justness of the rationale for waging war, the long-standing concept of *"jus ad bellum"* is central to the discussion. The term can be loosely translated as "war justly motivated." The concept concerns the rectitude of the arguments that are given by the war-maker for entering into *or* initiating a war. An inquiry is made using various criteria, or touch-stones, to determine whether and how these reasons can be described as just.[1] On the other hand, *jus ad bellum* is distinguished from *jus in bello* in that the latter connotes the justness of the way in which violent means are applied in war—*in bello* (i.e., in actual war). This concept also involves the way in which a war is terminated.

Jus ad bellum analyzes the idea of the just *cause and intention* in making war. It also weighs the factor of the *legitimacy of the political authority* that decided on these extreme, violent means as a last resort. It is only to be employed against a clearly perceived, palpably threatening, or aggressively attacking enemy. Also involved in the concept is whether a given war is feasible. That is, it should be capped by tangible victory, thus precluding continuous mayhem that could be described as a war of attrition with no clear end in sight. Modern insurgency war is particularly apt to present just such a quandary to the counterinsurgents in their attempt to bring about a determinate conclusion to the fighting. In that type of guerrilla warfare, the "battle lines," or "fronts," are difficult to ascertain. There is no formally declared truce since the guerrillas intend to continue fighting within the population indefinitely.

The justness of rightly conceived war by a governing authority is diametrically opposed to a war undertaken by an unjust war-maker's fabricated or falsely described enemy or enemy threat. Such falsification may be used as a mere pretext for waging war for some narrow, self-serving purpose. Falsification could result from faulty intelligence about the enemy's intentions and/or malfeasance by those who initiate war. These two concepts will guide the discussion throughout the book. In Parts Two and Three, we test their applicability to the Iraq War.

DERIVING MANKIND'S WAR MAKING

Any discussion of the making of war, whether just or unjust, must consider the factors in general that make for war within humankind—a unique species when it comes to killing its own kind.

Over the six millennia of human history, the civilized world has seen by some counts 14,000 major armed conflicts that have taken dozens of millions of lives. In the past two giant World Wars alone, 1914–1918 and 1939–1945, the death toll added up, respectively, to 21 million and 50 million persons. Imagine if added to this list were the numbers of casualties—maimed and wounded—that have mounted merely in the past century. Adding together all such casualties, there would be enough corpses and maimed bodies, ghoulishly speaking, to fill several New York-sized cities. Given the phenomenon of war making that haunts mankind, someone once lamented that "war would end if the dead could return"[2]—and pace in a ghastly way among the living.

Given this grim fact, we need to explore mankind's proclivity throughout recorded history to resort to war as an extreme means of settling disputes between parties (in modern times, between nation-states). We must determine how these wars have been regarded in various writings in the past, whether in philosophy, theology, or *belles lettres* (epics, plays, or poetry). In making this survey, we can gain insight into the often deep, reflective thinking about war that has critiqued bloody fighting over the centuries. This heritage amounts to a body of thought that has led to mankind's consciousness of war's disadvantages and unsuitability in resolving disputes. As the philosopher Kant wrote of war making and its preparations:

> We have to admit that the greatest evils which oppress civilized nations are the result of war—not so much of actual wars in the past as of the unremitting, indeed ever-increasing preparation for war in future.[3]

It might be objected that war is only one of several man-made causes of death. Indeed, one gets another awesome statistic for the twentieth century alone when totaling up the deaths of people—wars aside—from the genocidal *domestic* policies of tyrannical, totalitarian, or authoritarian regimes. The Communists, Italian Fascists, German Nazis, Japanese militarists, and other dictatorships since 1900 spawned their own hideous homemade death tolls, as such regimes still do in the twenty-first century in latter-day templates of absolute power. These occur in slave labor and death camps, filthy prisons and torture chambers, on "killing fields," or in aggressively motivated civil wars. Some scholars put that particular bloody figure for domestic mayhem over the past century at 60 million victims.[4]

How, then, do we explain all this death—of humans, by humans? Was a lethal sidetrack taken in evolution when man came onto the scene? It is sobering to think that if previous species of mammals had done each other in violently the way humans do, would evolution and the "ascent of man" have been halted altogether? Not even ferocious beasts, the "lower animals," go about killing within their own species or against other species as humans are wont to do on such a grand scale. As Thomas Jefferson put it:

> What is called civilization seems to have no effect on [man] than to teach him to pursue the principle of *bellum omnium in omnia* on a larger scale ... to engage all quarters of earth in the same work of destruction. When we add to this that as to other species of animals, the lions & tigers and mere lambs compared with man as a destroyer, we must conclude that it is in man alone that nature has been to find a sufficient barrier against the too great multiplication of other animals and of man himself, an equilibrating power against the fecundity of generation.[5]

We must wonder, if there had been no checks on humans killing humans, would our race have even survived? Philosopher Bertrand Russell once pondered if man were perhaps a "maladaptive organism doomed to self-extinction."[6] Other writers, like Arthur Koestler, have wondered whether the advent of man might have been "one of evolution's mistakes."[7] Humans, after all, willfully choose to engage in intra-species killing in lethal ways that are virtually absent among the lower mammals. A semanticist might wonder that if other, nonhuman animals could invent a lexicon, whether they would need to include in their dictionaries so many words ending in the suffix –cide, or its equivalent in other human languages. Throughout evolution, the human brain—cerebral cortex—grew large enough for hominids to think up all kinds of reasons for going to war. Humans also acquired the capability of developing new technology in the form of tools to make war as lethal as possible. Language, too, has been a great asset in this process since it could be used to rationalize, legitimately or not, the taking of life for a designated cause.

The famous pacifist, Norman Cousins, once put it that the danger of war will keep increasing as the effectiveness of the instruments of war increases.[8] Better swords, he thought, will not be beaten into plowshares. Instead, they will be thrust at or dropped as bombs on the nearest adversary. Cousins has a point. An ascending line describing the development of war technology arches far above a parallel line lying below that designates man's ability to control the lethal instruments he has invented. This "lag" demonstrates mankind's inability—including its moral sense—to cope rationally with the technology for making war. In other words, we have allowed the killing-machines invented by humans to get the better of us by virtually suppressing our so-called instinct to survive. Moreover, the momentum throughout history to wage war ever more effectively and lethally seems unstoppable. International efforts at curtailing WMD proliferation are not proving effective. The geographic scope of war-instilling tensions—the "arena"—also keeps enlarging. Witness in this respect the two world wars of the twentieth century and the looming "Third World War" in the thermonuclear age throughout the latter half of the last century.

As to the cause of this –cide penchant in humankind, some thinkers point to man's flawed "psycho-social" makeup. Whether from "nature" or from "nurture"—i.e., whether because we're human or because of the way we humans are "brought up," or conditioned, by society—mankind shows over and over that it has a blood-red, belligerent streak running through it. Psychologists, like Sigmund Freud, went so far as to say that regardless of nurturing—no matter how peaceful the intentions of family, society, or country—humans will still need an "outlet" for their "inborn ... instinctive" aggressiveness, as he analyzes this tendency in *Civilization and Its Discontents* and his other writings. We humans are simply inherently aggressive, claimed Freud. It was as if he had singled out a secular "Original Sin" in the form of the inherited Oedipal Complex, aggressive traits, and a so-called "death wish"—yet without his setting this phenomenon originally in any Garden of Eden where the "sin" was consummated.

On the other hand, other observers such as Albert Einstein, in a famous correspondence with Freud in the early 1930's, agreed less with Freud than with earlier "rationalist" philosophers as to curtailing the war-making proclivities within mankind.[9] There may or may not be, Einstein suggested, any such congenital belligerency that is biologically imbedded in humankind. Instead, hatred is taught and learned. Einstein spoke in favor of the remedial effect of reeducating mankind. He thought a web of effective international law embodied in a world organization (e.g., the League of Nations) would provide such a cure-all. His was a "reasoned" approach, in contrast with Freud's "psychotherapeutical" approach. Einstein and others insisted that the way to direct human societies and government into peaceful pathways is to develop social and educational programs and laws that do just that: conduce people and nations to think about peace, not war, and to develop sanctions that criminalize those who break the peace.

In other words, these thinkers insisted, as some others do today, that mankind is not irremediably homicidal. Perhaps our species can be "trained" to live in a more civilized way, even to eliminate war altogether. Humans can do this by learning tolerance and love for their fellow man. At the same time, when the perceived need to wage war—but only *defensively*—arises, it must be based on just principles. In other words, nations must develop the international means to sanction those—whether they are individual leaders, stateless terrorist organizations, or governments—who refuse to live by the rules in a civilized manner. Above all, it is necessary that governments and their governed be conscious of the rules, abide by them, and set an example by their own policies and actions. No nation-state should think of itself as an exception or that it can choose to wage war whenever it alone decides, regardless of world opinion.

In the midst of the Iraq War, such ideas about collectively reforming and reeducating humanity and making war illegal remain alive. Yet some people nevertheless ask whether such reform ideas are *realistic*. Are they merely recipes for pie-in-the-sky pacifism? Above all, can such ideas have any deterrent or remedial effect on humankind's apparently chronic disposition to make war and to settle disputes in a lethal way?

Assuming mankind is not "fated" to indulge in intra-species killings on a massive scale, it is time to ask whether we can find in the twenty-first century realistic ways to stop war making. This effort is especially urgent as we see war-fighting becoming intolerably sanguinary with the use of various forms of WMD.

The feeling that some method must be found to change man's bad habit of making war arose a very long time ago. Immanuel Kant (1724–1804), in some ways the father of modern and contemporary philosophy, became an ardent and rational spokesperson for finding remedies for this human condition. As he pointed out in *Perpetual Peace*, a classic writing on the dangers and counterproductivity of war, it is especially incumbent upon *democratic* states (tyrannies, he said, are incapable of such restraint) to resist the temptation to settle disputes between states by military means. Kant regarded war as humanity's ultimate folly. It is, he lamented, the principal brake on human progress. The "possession of power [by states] inevitably corrupts reason's free judgment," he wrote, and leads them to resort to war.

At the same time, Kant dismissed as repugnant those politicians, the "political moralists," as he called them, "who forge a morality to suit the statesman's advantage" and who proffer war as a putatively moral cause.[10] Such "moralizing politicians" who invent pretexts for war making, wrote Kant, make progress toward peace impossible. "Act," Kant advised, "so that you can will that your maxim ought to become a universal law no matter what the end might be." Rationalizing war while ruling out other possible means to keeping the peace, he insisted, violates this maxim.

Finally, Kant insisted that in the end war "becomes not only a very artificial undertaking, so uncertain is the outcome for both sides, but also a very dubious one given the aftermath that the nation suffers by way of an ever-growing burden of debt"—and the sowing abroad of hostility.[11]

WARS' HISTORY AND THE RISE OF MORAL CONSCIOUSNESS

Wars first took place in history at the very birth of civilization around 5,000 B.C. In most cases, they were little more than mindless, bloody contests between cities and empires. Today we might describe them as utterly senseless, just as we do many of the wars that followed in later centuries up to the present. What motivated these bloody contests was little more than greed, at best defense fought by one greedy power against an equally greedy attacker.

Amazingly, between 5,000 B.C. and the birth of Christ, scarcely any poet, philosopher, or historian, as far as we know in the West at any rate, ever penned a bad word against wars of any type, whether defensive or aggressive. Nor, for that matter, did anyone generally speak out against other forms of brutality perpetrated by humankind. In those distant, yet early so-called "civilized" times, armed combat on the level fields of combat or in the Coliseum in the form of public amusement led to needless bloodshed, torture, and prolonged, agonizing death. Although the Romans introduced the word "*humanitas*" into Indo-European speech, the ancient Greeks had no equivalent word. Yet, Greek choruses groaned of "*agonia*," unrelieved agony, that is associated with human turmoil. Yet as to specific inhumane excesses existing in their societies, they were silent. Nor did the Romans show much respect for this word they added in Latin to their lexicon, *humanitas*. In any case, humanitarianism was never fully addressed by the ancients specifically in the context of condemning war.

On the contrary, in ancient societies people eagerly (as far as we know) prepared to wage war under the leadership of revered god-kings and god-emperors and of courageous archons and consuls. They prepared en masse for war that resembles the way aspiring athletes train today for the bloodless events in Olympics competition. Nor did it ever seem to enter people's minds, apparently even the minds of literate thinkers and writers in those times, to raise serious moral questions about the justifiability of any given war, let alone war's overall inhumanity. For the leaders and subjects of ancient empires—between the Tigris and Euphrates Rivers and beyond eastward and westward to the Sumerian, Babylonian, Egyptian, Persian, Hebrew, Greek, and Roman civilizations—war-fighting was an ever-present occurrence that was all but taken for granted. Painful issues of war that are felt so deeply by the public in modern times—such as defining which side starts a war or which side is to blame for hostilities, death, and destruction—were not seen as a *moral* problem in ancient times.

WRONG REASONS FOR WAGING WARS

The aim of ancient wars consisted mostly of conquest for its own sake. Alternatively, it meant winning war booty and territory as a prize for military victory. The "nobility of war" consisted largely in its demand for heroism and sacrifice. The "cause" was victory, pure and simple. In this, there was no room for "antiwar" sentiment or humanitarian sentimentality. Nor was the justness or unjustness of any given war ever at issue.

Much later after Christ in the fourth and fifth centuries, St. Augustine (354–430 A.D.), writing in Books XIX and XV of his monumental *City of God*, condemned the fierce, what he termed "plundering," wars of his time and earlier. He viewed them merely as mass mayhem, as genocide that honored "pillaging" and marauding. Wars were acts of mere "brigandage," he wrote, that established grounds for empty, meaningless heroics. The advent of the Christian era, he hoped, would change this attitude. In fact, Augustine insisted in the *City of God* that the fall of the Roman Empire indicated God's plan to see this type of inhumane civilization replaced by a merciful one.

As the heroism of the brave warriors and the spoils of conquest were celebrated—with scores of bodies interred or cremated—it was never asked, as Augustine implicitly inquired, "Was it worth it? Was it humanitarian?" At the same time, war as an onus of mankind was by no means taken lightly by sensitive minds. Writers did not propose remedies, but they did express horror at the mayhem. Poets, dramatists, and chroniclers —like Homer, Hesiod, Herodotus, and Thucydides—together with a number of Greek playwrights and Roman writers, such as the Stoic Seneca, were by no means numb to the tragedy and sacrifice in lives consumed by war. Perhaps such writers were reflecting, or refracting, the reactions and sentiments of ordinary men and women in those times, especially the surviving loved ones of the warriors who fell in the bloody contests. (Alas, the writing of history seldom includes description of the feelings of common folk.)

A large number of such hoi polloi were the people, after all, who made up the audiences of performances staged in the huge outdoor theaters of ancient Greece and Rome. Literate people, that tiny minority in ancient times, must also have been affected by what they read from the pens of those few writers of the "intelligentsia," who found killing in war to be repugnant. By contrast, one never found an expression of *humanitas* in the detailed chronicles of ancient wars as in, say, Julius Caesar's journal, *The Gallic Wars*, or in Polybius's *Histories*. Such sentiment was absent altogether.

Nevertheless, it must be noted that the poet Homer together with some of the more "socially conscious" souls among ancient Greek poets and playwrights (as in the writings of Hesiod and the historians Herodotus, Thucydides, and even occasionally of Polybius's *Histories*) had meditated, if only in tangential ways, on the crass, tragic "other side" of war. As they listened to dramatic recitations and readings of such literature or the "singing" of the poetry of the epics *Iliad* and *Odyssey* or of the Roman Virgil's *Aeneid* or in reading the epistular essays of Nero's Stoic adviser, Seneca, ancient audiences or readers might indeed have felt pity for the fallen heroes and their survivors. They may have even felt sympathy for the vanquished as they sensed the meaninglessness of wars, especially those that seemed to have been fought with no clear moral aim whatever.

HINTS OF ANTIWAR FEELING

Indeed, at times there were such hints that suggested that ancient writers—poets and dramatists—despised war altogether as a way of life. Yet, we cannot be sure that they ever felt a deep sense of the inhumanity of war in general. Nor did they develop any such "antiwar" thoughts systematically. Ratcheting up of such public consciousness was to be the yeoman work of later Christian theologians. However, between the lines so to speak, even Homer occasionally seemed to convey a sense of the horror and abominable terror of war and bloodshed. This is felt in many episodes of his account in the *Iliad* of the Trojan War, which was triggered, one might say outrageously, by revenge for Troy's alleged abduction of the beautiful Helen. Perhaps, too, in parts of his poetry, Homer together with the others who built upon his epic and those of Hesiod's verses, reflected the feelings of common people. After all, it was they at whom the poets and dramatists aimed their verses and speeches. Perhaps in this way they subtly expressed their own antiwar sentiments.

In rereading Homer or viewing latter-day feature films about his two epics, it is easy to be overwhelmed by the unrelenting, unrelieved cruelty and willful vengefulness that take place in his verses. The brutality is unspeakable as told in horrific ways by the poet. For instance, the funeral for Achilles's friend, Patrocles, turns into a vile, bloody massacre—notably without comment from the poet. Early in the war, Agamemnon declares that every Trojan will be killed, be they children, pregnant mothers, or innocent bystanders. The Athenian general pledges that the hostile "race" of Troy will be completely liquidated. There will be, he cries, "no one left to shed tears." With all this, of course, no pity is expressed. Nor is any apology or condemnation of war offered from the poet.

At same time, however, Menelaus, brother of Agamemnon, can speak sympathetically of the people "who grow weary of it all, even of sleep and love, of sweet music, the perfect dance—all things that take far longer than a battle to make a man cry out, 'Enough!' "[12] Another character, Antenor, a Trojan elder, wonders remorsefully as to what it would have been like if Troy had only shown a willingness to compromise so that hostilities might end. He thus says plaintively, "Let us end it now and give Argive Helen back to the Atreidae together with her property. By fighting the way we do, we make ourselves offenders of Right (in Greek, *dikianon*; in Latin, "*jus*").

As far as I can see, no good can come from this." Hector himself had spoken similar misgivings about the war.

Such a plaintive, questioning spirit occasionally crops up even in the war-rife *Iliad*. In one memorable scene, the function of a physician is contrasted with that of a soldier. "A surgeon," voices the Homeric reciter, "who can extract an arrow and heal a wound with his ointments is worth a regiment." In *Odyssey* such moderation and "refinement" are even more obvious. Captives, it is suggested, could instead be ransomed and freed. Moreover, material compensation, as a kind of bribe to avoid war, might be substituted for the spilling of blood. In the epics, any failure to show a degree of mercy was at times seen as sacrilegious, deserving condemnation by the gods. For his part, Ajax is depicted as showing a conciliatory spirit in contrast to his kinsman, Agamemnon. Homer interjects this lamentation in the *Odyssey*: "In no way was anyone prudent or just." At one point, Zeus himself, the chief god, is heard to protest to Ares, the god of war: "Most hateful to me art thou of all gods that hold Olympus, for ever is strife dear to thee, and wars and battles."[13]

Historian Gerardo Zampaglione opines that the harsh attitude of Agamemnon has been tempered by Ajax because Agamemnon "reflected the views of a pre-Homeric aristocracy [while] the mildness of the latter was in line with the thinking of later generations."[14]

In the widely attended plays of Aeschylus, Sophocles, Euripides, and Aristophanes, there are elements of what Zampaglione calls peace-minded "refinement." As he explains, an undercurrent of morality is detected as the playwrights occasionally assign moral motives even to the perverse, violent-prone chief god, Zeus. In their tragedies, the suffering of mankind, expressed through violent episodes into which men are thrown, is treated at times sympathetically but always "monumentally" as a form of noble sac-rifice (as in war). For instance, in Aeschylus's *The Persians*, even the victors suffer pangs of remorse and pity for the surviving loved ones of slain soldiers, even on the enemy side. At the same time, in many of the penned tragedies war was viewed as inexorable and "capricious fate" (*moira*—fate—even intimidates the gods). The pain is not compensated by the fact that victory in war may have benefited the community. Death and chaos were lamented, if not implicitly scorned.

As Zampaglione notes, the unmistakable feature of so much Greek tragedy was the thought that "war throws its own shadow on the cities, poisoning their existence and hampering their progress." The problem is dealt with not only from the angle of the pain caused to individuals, but also from that of the hardships suffered by communities as a whole who are robbed of their young men.

Mixed messages about war likewise come from the writings of Greek philosophers. Heraclitus, for instance, could all but accept war by describing it as universally the "father of all things." In his "dialectical/antithetical," yin-and-yang view of the world as a play of opposing forces, he reasoned that if war were eliminated, so would be peace.

For his part, Plato suggested in *Republic* that war, at least when fought between Greeks, should in some way be regulated and subjected to rules. Was this perhaps an anticipation of the modern, Geneva Convention approach to regulating and moderating the effects of war?

2

Judaeo-Christian
to Modern Views of War

The coming of Christian thought saw a significant shift from the former, generally amoral, pagan indifference to war. This watershed marked the start of a many-century addition to the discussion and classification of war that remains relevant to events in the present day.

Christian writers, together with writers representing other world religions, condemned war and other forms of organized misanthropy as found in pagan societies. From the Christian point of view, such abominations as the brutal Roman circuses and the many wars of ancient times stemmed from what theology saw as derived from the "original sin" of "fallen Man." The fall of man in *Genesis*, which some modern thinkers regard as allegorical, was the stain of sin that resulted from Adam and Eve in the garden. It led to Cain's murder of his brother, Abel, and to other homicidal and genocidal acts down through history.

Besides the idea of man's "inborn" penchant to be disobedient and to use violence, Christian thought also developed the notion that there were positive ways that humankind could be reformed. For the first time on a large scale in the way that people in ancient society viewed the human condition, the new, Christian message of love and humanitarianism became a pervasive as well as persuasive message. It was a message of both of love and peace. It was remarkable that this pattern of thought could begin to take the place amid the old, heroic, and noble postures of hatred and killing.

This moderating influence remained true of the intended effect on society of Christian teaching despite later fanatical, bloody crusading, and bloodletting heresy hunting against "infidels" and among Christians themselves.

The newfound religious message was as much Jewish as it was Christian. Much fighting and killing, it is true, characterize accounts in the Old Testament. God's punishment can be extensive and brutal. Yet, in the Jewish scriptures it is the peacemakers who are the most revered. The point is that the firmly implanted Judeo-Christian concept of the all-good, monotheistic God—a God who scorns evil and rewards the good on earth and in the after-life—amounted to a radical departure from the ways of paganism. As philosopher Ernst Cassirer points out, there was a "radical, world-historical shift" in people's perception of religion, especially as it affects thought and behavior in this world, including war. Cassirer observes in *An Essay on Man*:

> Man's whole existence, physical and moral, [had been] smothered under the continual pressure of [the primitive taboo system and paganism]. It is here that [Judeo-Christian] religion intervenes. All the higher ethical religions—the religion of the prophets of Israel, Zoroastrianism, Christianity—set themselves a common task. They relieve the intolerable burden of the taboo system [and paganism. Instead,] they detect ... a more profound sense of religious obligation that instead of being a restriction or compulsion is the expression of a new positive ideal of human freedom.[1]

In the spirit of the new thinking about the inviolability of the human right to promote life and scorn violence, Bishop Clement of Alexandria (c. 150–211–215 A.D.) condemned the pagans' armed contests in stadiums. He lamented their unmitigated rivalries, vengefulness, and commission of atrocities in war. As the bishop viewed it, the pagans did such violence so as to "glut themselves to the full with human blood."[2] Of the Roman penchant for cruelty and inhumanity, historian Lewis Mumford wrote in *The Human Condition*:

> The Greek philosophers had praised temperance, courage, prudence, and wisdom: they had sought to discipline the flesh and fortify rational judgment. [By contrast] Jesus gave love a social mission and political province. Who was one's neighbor? Anyone who needed one's help. The parable of the Good Samaritan is a condemnation of every form of isolationism.[3]

Of Judaism's influence, Mumford wrote:

> Essential to Christianity's survival were its Jewish foundations ... From Israel came a most radical theological conception: the belief that the Will of God is worked out in human history: that every historic event is a judgment of God upon man's understanding of the Divine Will and his readiness to cooperate with it. [Any contemplative withdrawal] was at odds with the prophetic

tradition of passionate struggle and involvement with the evils of earthly existence.[4]

The Middle Ages saw the deepening of religious consciousness. Nevertheless, little by way of taming humanity was achieved in medieval times despite religious pressures (such as with "Peace Days"). In the battles between knights as well as the four Crusades, much bloodshed was needlessly spilled. Extreme mysticism and intolerance within the church itself was responsible at times for needless violence. The medieval crusade, with its often bloody accompaniments, was viewed by its participants as fulfilling what men, women, and children on those long, dangerous, and essentially futile pilgrimages to the Holy Land regarded as God's will.

What of wars between the larger fiefdoms, and later between nation-states? Can they, too, be viewed against moral criteria as being either good (justified) or evil (unjustified and offensive, or "offencist")? How can such belligerence be justified according to humanity's interpretation of God's will? Moreover, what if such wars were waged between *Christian* nations? This occurred, for instance, between England and Spain in the sixteenth century, between France and England in the nineteenth century, and between Christian England and Christian Argentina in the Falklands War of 1982 in the twentieth century.

Such moral issues as these arising in war were confronted head on. They became the subject of long, thoughtful dissertations by theologians and philosophers of law and politics through the Middle Ages and into the Renaissance—and, indeed, up to the present time. These discussions contributed to the heritage of sorting out wars according to their justness or unjustness. These works have also exerted an influence by condemning war in general as an unacceptable way of resolving differences between peoples, states, and rival political or religious groups. Today, the pitched controversy of a moral type over the war in Iraq is proof enough of the way religious/moral-*cum*-international–law criteria are involved in current discussions about war.

As we determine the justifiability (justness) versus the unjustifiability (unjustness) of war in modern times, we should bear in mind what Ernst Cassirer called that "radical shift" in human thinking that came with the incorporation of Judeo-Christian thought. (Statistically at over 2 billion worshippers, Christianity is currently the dominant faith among the world's assorted religions.) This Christian-religious influence in the West was dominant even in the secular-minded, humanist-inclined centuries of the Renaissance at the time of Machiavelli and the Borgias 500 years ago.

It is this *second "radical shift"*—i.e., *the thinking of inter-state relations in moralistic ways*—that still affects international relations so deeply today. The contribution from religion remains no less influential. By being mindful of the inheritance of theory and practice, both religious and secular, we weigh the pros and cons of modern wars against established criteria. The U.S. policy of preemption (or "preventive war") as applied to the war in Iraq is an instance of weighing the justice of initiating war and the methods applied in waging it.

JUST VERSUS UNJUST WARS: CHRISTIAN/PAGAN DIFFERENCES

Blessed are the peacemakers, for they shall be called children of God.
—*Matthew* 5:9

You do not know what manner of spirit you are of; for The Son of Man came not to destroy men's lives but to save them.
—*Luke* 9:54f, as glossed by later manuscripts

For so good is peace that even where earthly and moral affairs are concerned no other word is heard with more pleasure, nothing else is desired with greater longing, and finally nothing better can be found.
—St. Augustine, *City of God*

Let's take a closer look at the religious endowment within the framework of the just-war tradition and specifically the concept of *jus ad bellum*.

In the opening centuries after Christ, the church Fathers emphasized the advantages of peace while scorning the bestiality of war in human society. The fourth century Bishop of the North African town of Hippo (near today's Casablanca), Augustine started the thought process of systematically weighing—on moral scales—different types of war. He encouraged a line of thought that would promote peace within the "sinful" human society of the "worldly city." This was the beginning of the contemporary distinction that is made between wars that are seen as just *versus* those that are condemned as unjust.

By raising as he did the distinction between just war versus unjust war, Augustine established a lasting tradition. It influenced and was reflected in the writings of later theologians (e.g., St. Thomas Aquinas). It also influenced secular international law, such as in the writings of the seventeenth-century Dutch legal scholar, Hugo Grotius (1583–1645). These premodern theologians and philosophers set a golden precedent that led to establishing nonreligious, secular laws against war and the rules for waging war when it was absolutely necessary. In other words, these were writings that ruled out offensive, aggressive wars. By the time nation-states came onto the scene in the seventeenth century, a vast legacy of thought about war and peace was already in place.

Jurists in various parts of Europe wasted no time imbedding such thinking into the categorization ("typology") of wars. They distinguished the illicit wars from the allegedly necessary, legitimate ones. They established the rules by which wars should be fought. They laid out strictures for fighting wars as briefly and painlessly as possible. This tradition has made it possible to fix criteria for the justness *versus*. unjustness of wars up to the present day. Without this legacy, wars would be viewed in a moral vacuum.

For his part, Augustine argued that given the fact that the "earthly city" is ruled by imperfect men—unlike the future "heavenly city" of eternal peace and justice as anticipated in *Revelations*—it was the duty of the church to prepare citizens of this world for their "pilgrimage" into the next. Therefore, the church should extend its influence upon temporal rulers. It should impart to them the Christian message of peace and goodwill toward men. A "just republic," if it is to be truly such on earth, wrote Augustine, must align all of its worldly actions with justice. This process included establishing sound, just reasons for going to war as well as the ways in which war was conducted. In the secular city, Augustine warned, "Who can really say whether in a time of peace it is a good or evil thing to reign or serve, or to rest or die, or in time of war to command or fight, to vanquish, or get killed?"[5] Any war, wrote the bishop, must be viewed as an "instrument" occasionally used by Almighty God to interfere in human affairs. Sovereigns and nations are victors or vanquished according to God's will. Yet, wars are not specifically "ordered" by God, albeit they are "authorized" by him since they are part of his design: "All power derives from God, Who sometimes commands, sometimes allows," he wrote.

Making distinctions between "good" and "bad" wars was no scholastic's exercise. These distinctions and rules played, and still play, a key role in those parts of international law and multinational conventions that bear upon the root questions of war in modern times.

Finally, Augustine wrote, any war must be defined "by its *purpose, authority, and the way it is conducted*." Augustine asked what constitutes a just war. He answered that when rulers lead their peoples into war, their motivations should be *exclusively those of defense as the well as a rapid return to peace*. Rulers use war to defend their citizens against harm. A just war seeks to "right wrongs" in the name of defense and the restoration of peace. Merely wreaking vengeance makes any war unjust. Thus, it is the *intention* of the war-makers that is crucial. "The passion for inflicting harm, a cruel thirst to wreak vengeance, an unpeaceful, relentless spirit of belligerency, the fever for revolution, the lust of power," Augustine wrote, "all these are rightly condemned in war."

CHRISTIAN/PAGAN DIFFERENCES

It is revealing to see how the Christian message of peace was received by those who rejected Christianity on pagan grounds—that is, by those who leaned in the direction of the "old religion" of mythology and the cults. Most of this discussion took place within the first centuries of the acceptance of Christianity by increasingly large portions of Greco-Roman society.

In this early period, one of the themes in anti-Christian, pagan writings (as found, say, in Julian Apostate's [331–363 A.D.] letters and essays of the fourth century) was that Jews and Christians had rejected war out of cowardice or from "false ethics" derived from Jesus's ministry. Julian accused Christians of "atheism." For instance, in the writings over the centuries of Celsus, Porphyry, and Julian Apostate, among others, accusations against Christians ran along lines of their alleged unrealistic and unpatriotic pacifism. Such writers complained of Christians' "exclusiveness" within society and their tendency to put their God above all secular considerations instead of showing undivided loyalty and respect to the secular rulers and citizens' duty to fight in wars.[6]

Pagan polemicists renounced, for instance, the message of *Ephesians,* 4:17–20: "They are darkened in their understanding and separated found in the Platonic-Socrates, by the Christian teaching of "humility" and "turning the other cheek." All of which, Celsus, an anti-Christian polemicist, said, simply proves Christian ethics are an "inferior system." Christ, the alleged Son of God, protested writers of pagan persuasion and brought a message that scorned the heroic Greco-Roman gods and the secular traditions of authoritarian consuls, emperors, and warriors. Christians, who so often refused not to participate in wars, were to such pagan minds abominable.

In all this criticism leveled against the Christians, it was especially directed at their impermissible (by pagans) Augustinian "divided worlds" concept. This was the idea, as discussed earlier, in which the peaceful, heavenly city is vastly superior to the fallen, terrestrial city by which the Christian message of peace and goodwill toward men was thereby thrown into positive relief. Anti-Christian polemics succeeded, ironically, in showing how magnetic the Christian message was. It strongly asserted peace and love above war and misanthropic hatred. Writing in the nineteenth century, the American pragmatist philosopher Charles Peirce thought that in the form of virtual "survival of the fittest" between contending religious ideas, the Christian religion and its message had won out over rival creeds and disbeliefs because it harmonized with mankind's innermost thoughts and desires in favor of peace and tranquility.[7] Paganism, a rejected design for living, argued Peirce, was historically winnowed out analogously in the way "unfit" organisms are weeded out in the evolutionary process of Darwinian "natural selection." Paganism did not "fit" with the basic, peaceful strivings engendered in humanity.

ST. THOMAS ON JUST WAR

With the medieval writings of St. Thomas in the thirteenth century, the discussion of rightful versus wrongful war was further deepened and refined. Thomas Aquinas offered three criteria for the justness of any war. (These distinctions are redolent in any discussion today of just war, as canvassed in Part Three.)[8]

First, according to Thomas, the war must be duly authorized by the legitimate powers-that-be—that is, the lawful government.[9] Violence perpetrated by rogue, non-state groups and pirates do not fall under the heading of "legitimate war." Theirs is mere banditry, a description that is also found in Augustine's *City of God*. This is worth keeping in mind today as Al Qaeda and other terrorist gangs, with no popular or legal mandate commit murder on a global scale (see Chapter 4 on this point).

Second, the cause—purpose or motivation—for the war must be just. Above all, the aim should be near-term restoration of normal peace (the "*status quo ante*").

Third, the fighting must be well intentioned, not waged vengefully or as violence for the sake of violence. As seen in today's Al Qaeda Manual, contemporary terrorists wage violence in the name of inciting more violence and instability. As Thomas wrote: "Those who are attacked"—that is, counterattacked following their initial acts of violence—"should be attacked because they deserve it on account of some fault." Refining further this point about "fault," which he viewed as an aggressive motivation in the attacker, Thomas insisted that, above all, war should be terminated rapidly. The conduct of hostilities should reduce combat brutality to a minimum. Today's "carpet bombing" of populated areas, for instance, would likely fall under the category of "needless brutality," as would "countervalue" (aimed at populated centers) nuclear bombing.

Unnecessary violence, said Thomas, stemmed from ignorance of God's message of peace and goodwill. Above all, it stems from a "hardening of their hearts." On the other hand, wrote the Christian-baiting Celsus in presenting these proscriptions against war, Christians "distorted" the ethical teachings of Greek philosophers. Furthermore, the civilian assets of the enemy against which the war is being fought, said Thomas, should not be reduced vengefully to rubble (which is an important element in *jus in bello*). The war-waging society should not be "poisoned," he wrote, by rampant fighting. If an enemy's resources were so decimated, *restoration of peace— the main rationale for fighting*—would be delayed. Moreover, this should be viewed as sinful. As he insisted:

> If the Christian religion forbade war altogether, those who sought salutary advice in the Gospel would rather have been counseled to cast aside their arms and to give up soldiering altogether. If he (St. John the Baptist) commanded them to be content with their pay, he [therefore] did not forbid soldiering.[10]

Thomas argued further that St. Paul had given those in secular authority the right to punish "by the sword" internal or external disturbers of the society's peace. It is the government's duty, lawfully and morally, to use arms *defensively* against a commonwealth's external enemies. By "enemies" he meant those "disturbers of the peace [and] evil doers" against whom war is waged in the first instance.

Meanwhile, the fifth biblical commandment, "thou shalt not murder," is sometimes considered an injunction against inter-person homicide, not against wholesale war or penal capital punishment. Jesus had rearranged the ranking of this Old Testament commandment against killing. He placed it first, in his reputed words specifically "in order to restore peace" (*Mark* 10:19). For his part, Thomas Aquinas regularly employed Scriptural passages to define just war while also occasionally in the *Summa Theologica* citing secular sources.

REFORMING MANKIND: RELIGION'S CONTRIBUTIONS

As we saw, the issue of humanity's belligerent nature began to become focused after Christ's short ministry 20 centuries ago. This was when a wholly new way of looking at mankind arose and began to seize much of Western man's consciousness and imagination. The same concern was not absent, either, in the preceding centuries of Judaism. It was also present in succeeding centuries when Muslim religious thought appeared in the world.

Beginning by the second century after the Jesus Christ's preaching as related in the *New Testament* and in Paul's Epistles, Christian thought on war and peace began a long process of establishing a rich tradition about man and his nature and his habit of war and violence. In religious and later nonreligious versions and glosses, this legacy and tradition of thought about war has remained intact until today. It helps point the way toward honorable peace and against needless, unjust, or illegitimate war.

On their part, Christian thinkers claimed that mankind, although "created in the image of God," became flawed with "original sin" because of men's own prideful willfulness. The "mark of Cain," Christians said, was engraved on every human's "forehead." Yet, as the doctrine also insisted, humankind is not thereby fatally doomed to being cruel and brutal. Man can be reformed and redeemed (Jesus is known, of course, as the "redeemer"); man is not incorrigible. Men and women, the doctrine said, having been created in God's image, could be "saved" through divine grace. The latter was deserved and won by man through his own willed actions in this world. As taught by Christian theologians, mankind, unlike lower animals, is equipped with a thinking, rational "soul." This organic fact sets humans apart from mere beasts in the jungle with their instinctive "bloodied tooth and claw."

Whether this partly fabulous biblical account is viewed as a story, a metaphor, paradigm, or allegory (as it actually was by early commentators on

Scripture), the Judeo-Christian idea and the theology about the sacredness of mankind and the "redeemability" of imperfect men and women—who can be led into peaceful ways if they so will it—marked a major departure from the skeptical views commonly held by ancient Greco-Roman pagan thinkers.

BRINGING ANTI-VIOLENCE DOWN TO EARTH

The church—itself not always peaceful either within itself or towards others (as in its later militant heresy-hunts, Crusades, and Inquisition)—continued to deepen the Christian arguments against avoidable killing in general and against avoidable war in particular. Such thought was not argued on purely fantastic grounds but was rather reasoned through discourse. Over time it penetrated the "public conscience," even that of rulers. As temporal rulers, the latter feared papal or bishop condemnation (excommunication) and consignment to an afterlife in hell if authorities disobeyed biblical injunctions. "Peace Days," observed throughout the year, were the rule during the Middle Ages. Even the exalted Charlemagne, crowned emperor by the pope in the A.D. 800, would periodically retire into a monastery for spiritual renewal as a show of moral and political probity. Lesser princes did the same. Religion permeated the public mind and conscience, albeit with mixed success.

By the church-decreed Peace Days together with the later humanist philosophies of the Renaissance and Reformation—that is, by 1500–1600 A.D. —a new crop of thinkers appeared on the scene in Western Europe. They were armed with *secularized* Christian doctrines against war. Yet even as they wrote, the duration of armed battles lengthened. Improved technology for making war progressed as the sheer size and increasing power of city-size republics, later nation-states, grew. After the Protestant revolts, which divided peoples and lands (nations and principalities) into rival camps, Catholic *versus* Protestant, there followed vicious wars, including those that arose over religion. They raged across the continent. This bloody fighting, which included wholesale massacres, were in violation, of course, of basic Christian principles. Yet with the support of rival camps of clerics (Christian states fighting other Christian states under the same cross), the religious wars that especially bloodied the sixteenth and seventeenth centuries were in part mitigated by the religion-inspired Treaty of Nantes (1685). This treaty established the idea of religious toleration, but its main motivation, following an era of interminable strife and war, was the essential Christian one of peace. The impulse for the agreement was moral.

At the same time, new thinking about the human condition increasingly merged with the old Christian message of "peace on earth, goodwill toward men." These ideas began to be discussed together with the practical problem of how the age's enlarged countries (the emerging nation-states of the 1600s) could flourish by escaping war against each other. At the same time, ideas began to circulate as to how to cope with a situation in which empires and countries sometimes perforce were*obliged* to wage war—i.e., legitimately—in order to defend themselves. Thinkers, religious and secular, pondered the question of how modern war might be considered just and necessary as opposed to wars that should be considered unjust and aggressive. In the beginning, nation-state size and dimension along with their larger, longer wars were not viewed as an intolerable curse. After all, before the Renaissance and Reformation—that is, going back to when feudalism arrived by the eleventh and twelfth centuries—fighting to the death had become an early form of what we might call today "local wars." They had often been waged on a relatively small scale between semi-autonomous units of a country (as in France and Germany). Significantly, wars fought by the knights of a castle-town against knights in another town with the emerging national boundaries were not always sanctioned by the king or emperor (as, say, in the Germanic Holy Roman Empire). This illustrated the disunited, chaotic way places were "governed" centuries ago. Above all, it showed how decentralized political control and government, especially under feudalism, contributed to the absence of orderly peace and tranquility.

The Roman Catholic Church generally condemned such random fighting. The kings, like the church with its bishoprics and monasteries, mainly sought unity and internal security. They abhorred anarchy and turmoil while also occasionally instigating wars themselves. Yet they were largely powerless to maintain order, at least in the earliest feudal period of the Middle Ages. The church at first also lacked the authority and power to bring peace and tranquility. However, by the high Middle Ages as cities grew (among them many proud "cathedral cities") and commerce and trade became part of life (one of the few positive spin-offs from the several Crusades to the East), kings, those sceptered "lords" of the realm, became equipped with fresh power. This greater command was buttressed by centralizing their acquisition of gunpowder and new technology as well as the funding (through taxation) to wage war. As neighboring political entities and potential adversaries arose, the urge to further unify correspondingly strengthened. The people united into nation-states. Governments collected tax monies from the rich and poor. These revenues were used, putatively, to defend the nation's subjects against other, newly formed, large-scale polities that entered into the play as competing nation-states. The kings and princes most often showed loyalty to the church, of course. It was the bishops and the pope, after all, who had helped sanctify and "enrich" the monarchs' worldly power.

The church-officiated coronation oath gave the king or queen legitimacy. Significantly, however, it also subordinated him or her to rule "under the law and God." This, in turn, obliged the monarch to act as a "prince of peace"—on the model of Jesus's Sermon on the Mount. This was the two-edged sword that kept, and ideally still keeps, the secular power within moral, symbolically "hypostatized" (transcendent) bounds. Analogously, in modern times the same duality made the people's "God-given rights" sacred and free of temporal oppression. Religion succeeded in spreading a purple moral cloak over the king's policies—that is, when it could. To be crowned and wield their kingly power and to be "legitimized" by bishops or the pope in Rome were indispensable to the monarchs' hold on power. As late as the nineteenth century, even Napoleon found such legitimization indispensable when he, too, became a papally-endowed emperor.

For all this sanctification and legitimizing of secular leaders, the church exacted a price. Sometimes this took the form literally of a payment to the First Estate, the clergy, in the form of land and other emoluments. Moreover, indulgences were paid the church by the king's lords and subjects in order to assure for themselves a place in heaven. This was part of the bargain in exchange for sacerdotal (from *sacerdotium*) support to the "secular" power (*imperium*). In all this, the church viewed itself as the highest representative of Christ on earth. It was so empowered through the "Vicar of Christ," the pope, in the Vatican. As the First Estate, the church, above all, represented the guardian of the "soul" of the nation, of its rulers, and of its subjects. The symbolic metaphor used at that time was that the government was metaphorically viewed as the Moon that shines by reflected light. By contrast, the church was the Sun shining by God's intrinsic power. (Plato's famous "Allegory of the Cave" with its metaphor of the Sun as the symbol of truth is implicit here.)

In acting as the public's—and the government's—conscience, the church was thus in a position to assert itself as society's moral teacher and guide. By this means, it could carry on its mission of encouraging peace and goodwill. Its authority extended to all areas of secular life, thought, and behavior. Besides blessing (or not) the secular order, the church ran schools and provided help to the poor, diseased, and disabled. The church administered nurseries, charities, and institutions that in those times acted as hospitals, which included tending the wounded in battle. Therefore, church attendance and following the sacraments through all phases of one's life were universally recognized as primary duties for everyone in society of all rank and station.

By the ripened Middle Ages into the 1200s, the church had become an extremely powerful and influential institution. Even in the more secularized, worldly, post-medieval eras that followed, the shadows cast over the European landscape, metaphorically speaking, by cathedral spires were still long and deep. As its authority was viewed as extending "over souls," religion's moral status continued to match, even transcend, the king's secular power in the most vital—that is, spiritual and moral—sphere. Kings and princes ruled citizens' bodies, it was said; it did not rule their souls. Upon the latter, political power had no right to impinge.

The fates of those sacrilegious kings who did impinge on the power of the church were well known—as with the notorious case of the English King

Henry II's arranged "murder in the cathedral" of Archbishop Thomas à
Becket in the twelfth century. Thomas became a saint while Henry was
scorned and disowned and barely able to recover his former authority. Other
kings and emperors were likewise kept in line, even humbled by the church,
sometimes by the pope himself. In one case, a Holy Roman Emperor, no less,
was reduced to kneeling and shivering in the snow to beg the pope's
forgiveness. (Ironically, however, in that case the prince wrought revenge
on his "papal oppressor" by having him unseated as pope.)

Despite religious teaching against war and religious demands to show
goodwill toward and within human society, the show of ill will through
armed hostilities and bloody wars continued. In some cases, kings and princes were excommunicated and severely sanctioned because of their brutality
toward their own people and other peoples or because of their show of
disrespect toward the church. Even tyrannicide—the killing of brutal
leaders—was sanctified and endorsed by the Jesuit Order and by other
religionists of the late Middle Ages.[11]

WHAT HAPPENED TO THE CHRISTIAN MESSAGE?

In the end, it appeared that the secular (earthly) power had essentially won
the struggle for citizens' minds and bodies when the Middle Ages came to an
end. The Protestant Reformation led to the separation of church and state,
but also to the increased power of the secular leaders. Yet, was it not, rather,
that the church/state standoff had turned into a draw? After the Reformation,
it is true that the church was steadily separated from the state and that sectari-
anism had fractured beyond recall Roman Catholic unity. Nevertheless, did
this not mean that each side reserved in itself a potent sphere of authority
and power while religion embraced the "better part" of men's lives? In other
words, the separation did not lead to a withering of religious consciousness.
Just the opposite, in fact, occurred. The merging religions following the Reformation affirmed *individual* religious feeling and expression. If anything, this
sectarian development was more efficacious both to the individual and to society than the previous, often enforced unity had been.

Eventually, this process led to representative government in which the
popular will, expressing an arithmetic sum of individual wills in a majority
way, would assert itself in major decisions made by government. War was
viewed as one of these popular decision-making issues.

By the post-Reformation arrangements throughout Europe and in the
New World, kings, presidents, and prime ministers to the present day were
seen as ruling "under God" and not by their own fiat. In modern times,
if not a coronation oath, at least an inaugural ceremony conferred on the
new head of state legitimacy—in the United States by swearing on the Bible
and in other countries by swearing on the Constitution or a written oath.
Such ceremonies, particularly in authentic democracies symbolically and

concretely through the "fundamental law" of the constitution along with a time-tested political culture of separation of powers succeeded in circumscribing, at least in theory, a leader's authority. Implicit in these democratic rituals was the medieval idea *that the secular leader was bound to respect the realm of "higher law" arching above his authority*. His signed declarations, his drafted civil and criminal laws or promulgated decrees, his actions as "commander-in-chief"—all these were circumscribed by "hypostatized" (transcendent) law. This together with God was also seen as the ultimate source of the people's rights.[12]

As far as war making was concerned, this hierarchical view in turn led to *constitutional restrictions on earthly power* that were to become embodied in constitutional prescriptions and legalistic procedures regulating the making of legitimate, and *only legitimate*, war.

In other words, religion in the long term can be viewed as having won the battle for power between "church and state." It did this by retaining its moral hold over decisions affecting people's lives and property, and for the religious-minded, their souls. This meant, above all, those decisions and policies that affected war and peace viewed the relationship between citizens and the government, as the philosopher Immanuel Kant might say, "as if" there were two spheres: one that viewed men's souls and individualities as inviolable versus the governmental sphere which must respect this "presupposed" distinction. By the time of John Locke (1632–1704), the modern philosopher of democracy whose writings inspired the American Founding Fathers, one's mind, or soul, was viewed as inviolable "private property" in the person.[13] Kant was inspired by Locke's and Jean-Jacques Rousseau's endorsement of legislative power as used to defend a people's life and property, to protect legislative power from encroachment from the executive side, and in advancing the notion (in Kant) that viable expression of popular will in government is more likely to lead to peace than to war.

OTHER RELIGIONS ON WAR AND PEACE

Among the world's religions, is Christianity alone the dispenser of a message of peace to its adherents? Curiously, whenever and wherever humanity develops religious thought, religious thinkers invariably come up with *parallel ideas* that favor peace and endorse life while opposing animosity and needless killing. These religious beliefs, as we saw with Christianity, are bound to influence secular laws and customs, including attitudes toward war. The blatant exceptions, seen among a minority of rabid fundamentalists of whatever faith, merely prove the rule. Such fanatics do their hateful work as a relatively small number of deviants. Like the Al Qaedists vis-a-vis Islamism, the radical fundamentalists lack the support of the mainline adherents of the given religion, be it Muslim, Jewish, Christian, Hindu, or some other, and their principal interpreters.

We learn from studying other, non-Christian religions, including Judaism, that a certain "ecumenism"—universal consensus of interlocking concentric (Venn) circles of agreement—emerges between them on the believer (his struggle to serve Allah); the other is external in the *unforced*, missionary sense of extending the faith to those who are willing to accept it. Still, a strain of superiority is seen by some historians of religion to run through this faith. Islamists at times consider their religion to be the latest as well as the "truest" form of religion as taught militantly by Muhammad, himself a warrior. It is said by some imams to combine all the best element of earlier religions, like Judaism and Christianity, while adding significantly new verve to both faiths and the worship of God.

Note that in the Koran, jihad largely connotes an internal, personal struggle. Muslims are taught to make an effort to understand, to bring themselves in line with God, and submit to him. True, jihad can also mean a determined, militant struggle to extend the faith or, more often, to defend the faith. This might be construed to mean simply that Islam contains the same crusading spirit as do other religions. However, the missionary spirit, according mainstream Islam, must not take the form of Palestinian suicide bombers or of pilots flying planes into buildings. Such actions, in fact, are universally and severely condemned by the mainline interpreters of the Koran as well as by faithful rank-and-file Muslims worldwide. It is a fact that all religions have a "crusading" or "missionary" spirit. Does this imply, however, that the adherents favor exporting the cause on the tips of swords or on the noses of rockets or aircraft that kill people vengefully? Rationally speaking, "struggle" against a nonbelieving opponent surely cannot mean killing him. Converting corpses to the faith is quite impossible, after all.

Just after 9/11 and the Yankee Stadium speeches about the Qaeda attacks, *Christianity Today* Magazine, like other religious publications, discussed the matter of Islam's fundamental views on the use of violence, in the context of September 11, 2001.[14] A report in this journal quoted a Muslim scholar at the University of Virginia, who wrote that he "felt embarrassed at the thought that it could very well be my fellow Muslims who had committed this horrendous act of terrorism. How could these terrorists invoke God's mercifulness and compassion when they had, through their evil act, put to shame the entire history of this great religion and its culture of toleration?" Every judgment about Islam, all reactions to Muslim doctrine, and each Muslim-Christian encounter, might now be cast in the light of the events of that dreadful day, he lamented.

The magazine, quoting Muslim clerics and ordinary Muslim believers, noted that three interpretations are often given by Muslims of the events of September 11 and for other acts of Islamic violence. The first is the insistence that terrorist acts do not represent mainstream Islam. As President George W. Bush had said, "Islam is a religion of peace."

One of the Muslims widely familiar to other rank-and-file believers of that faith is Yusuf Islam, the well-known pop-music star in London who now helps promote Muslim education in England. "Today," he wrote in a London newspaper, "I am aghast at the horror of recent events and feel it a duty to speak out. Not only did terrorists hijack planes and destroy life; they also hijacked the beautiful religion of Islam."[15]

During the broadly-viewed TV-recorded and CD-recorded interfaith ceremony at Yankee Stadium on September 23, Imam Izak-El M. Pasha urged in his address that Muslims honor their faith and not betray the teachings of the Koran. In-depth study of other religions, Islam included, exposes the wrongheaded, prejudiced opinions voiced against these religions that claim that religious faiths congenitally preach violence and war. As part of this ecumenism to the contrary, Muslims, for instance, consider the Jewish prophets, going back to Abraham, to have been holy and who carried a message that Islamists, too, embrace. In a sense, what the Old Testament teaches, Muslims likewise accept as truthful.

As to Islam, consider the meaning that orthodox followers of that religion attach to "*jihad*." The term may denote "holy war," but not of the type that wantonly kills people. Yet jihad carries a double meaning. On the one hand, it denotes an internal struggle for perfection within the believer; on the other, the external struggle of the faith in defense of Islam:

> Do not allow the ignorance of people to have you attack your good neighbors. We are Muslims, but we are Americans. We Muslims, Americans, stand today with a heavy weight on our shoulders that those who would dare do such dastardly acts claim our faith. They are no believers in God at all.

Christianity Today canvassed the major Muslim organizations throughout North America, including the Council on American-Islamic Relations, the Islamic Society of North America, and the Muslim Students Association. The publication found that these organizations had strongly denounced the violence of the terrorists and repudiated this form of terrorist warfare as a legitimate form of "jihad." The events of 9/11 became the occasion for Muslim organizations worldwide to speak out in mainline Islam against wars, violent jihads, and acts of terrorism purportedly waged in the name of that religion. The powerful American Muslim Council issued a press release on September 11, stating:

> [We] "strongly condemn this morning's plane attacks on the World Trade Center and the Pentagon and express deep sorrow for Americans that were injured and killed and send out its condolences to all the families of the victims of this cowardly terrorist attack.[16]

Iranian sources (e.g., *Iran Today*, September 24, 2002) also condemned the type of terrorism that was consummated by Al Qaeda on 9/11:

Iran has vehemently condemned the suicidal terrorist attacks in the United States
and has expressed its deep sorrow and sympathy with the American nation.[17]

Moreover, the governments of the Arab countries Bahrain, Egypt, Lebanon,
Oman, Pakistan, Palestine, Qatar, Saudi Arabia, Turkey, United Arab Emirates, and Yemen all expressed similar sentiments.

Discussion of Islamic militancy often revolves around two questions.
First, how much of Islamism as practiced by fundamentalist Muslims is
prone to lead adherents to violence and/or is allegedly rooted in some "dark
side" of the teaching and practice of the prophet Muhammad? Second, do
violent, so-called jihads of the pre- and post-9/11 period find any support
in the Koran, or for that matter in the teachings or practices of the first
Muslim leaders?

The prophet Muhammad himself engaged in many military battles and, it
is said, could be merciless to his enemies, even those who simply attacked
him verbally. His original sympathies with Jews and Christians as "Peoples
of the Book" gave way to a harsher treatment when they did not follow
Islam.[18] In one episode, Muhammad cut the heads off hundreds of Jewish
males of the Beni Quraiza tribe who did not side with him in battle.
"The sword," said the prophet, "is the key of heaven and hell; a drop of
blood shed in the cause of Allah, a night spent in arms, is of more avail than
two months of fasting or prayer: whosoever falls in battle, his sins are
forgiven, and at the day of judgment his limbs shall be supplied by the wings
of angels and cherubim." Yet, the Koran includes the famous passage in
Surah 2:256: "Let there be no compulsion in religion."[19] This verse fits
well with other Koran verses in which *jihad means personal and communal
spiritual struggle or striving.*

True, the Muslim holy book also employs the term *jihad* to mean waging
"holy war," and the language is occasionally strong. To wit, Surah 5:33
reads, "The punishment of those who wage war against God and His Mes-
senger, and strive with might and main for mischief through the land is: execution, or crucifixion, or cutting off of hands and feet from opposite sides, or
exile from the land: that is their disgrace in this world, and a heavy punishment is theirs in the Hereafter."[20] The direction of this teaching appears to
be against those who would use violence against Muslims, yet it is also arguable that Islam's earliest, bloody expansionism was justified through original
Islamic law that divided the world into two realms: *Dar al-Harb* (the land of
war) and *Dar al-Islam* (land under Islamic rule). Paul Fregosi's *Jihad in the
West* and Jewish scholar Bat Ye'or's *Decline of Eastern Christianity Under
Islam* document the reality of Muslim crusades long before the notorious
Christian crusades of the Middle Ages.

Out of these realities emerge two strongly contrasting perspectives among
modern Muslim interpreters. A minority of violence-prone Islamists consider their terrorist actions to be a true, "holy war" against infidels and the

enemies of Islam. They believe it is right to target America, "the great Satan." For his part, Osama bin Laden claims that the Koran supports his campaign, that the prophet would bless his cause, and that Allah is on his side. However, the vast majority of Muslims believe that nothing in Muhammad's life or in the Koran and the Hadiths , the authoritative bearers of Islamic law, justifies terrorism.

Islamic scholar Yahiya Emerick notes that the prophet Muhammad specifically outlawed the killing of noncombatants. "[He] never allowed any Muslim soldier to harm women, children, or the innocent. The trouble with bombing a bus or library is that soldiers are not the ones who are killed. Thus, people who engage in this type of attack are going against the teachings of Islam." According to the Koran (5:32), notes Emerick, " 'If you kill a life unjustly it is as if you killed all life.' " As to suicide, the Koran speaks of it this way: "Whoever kills himself with a weapon will have that weapon in his hand, and will kill himself forever in the fire of Hell." Emerick added, "This is exactly what these men do when they detonate bombs strapped to their bodies."

Writing in *The Wall Street Journal*, Bernard Lewis, the noted historian of Islam, explained that throughout history Muslims have given *jihad* both spiritual and military meaning.[21] Lewis stresses the legal traditions in Islam concerning what constitutes just war. After noting the many limitations placed on military jihad, he writes:

> What the classical jurists of Islam never remotely considered is the kind of unprovoked, unannounced mass slaughter of uninvolved civil populations that we saw in New York. For this there is no precedent and no authority in Islam.

In "The Clash of Civilizations," Samuel Huntington analyzed the competing ideologies of our time. He drew particular attention to the potential clash between Islam, but without noting that Islam cannot be regarded as a monolith without existing factions, and that there are clashes *within Islamic civilization* itself.[22]

For their part, anti-Semites, who can be found even among fundamentalist-minded Christians, allege that the Judaism of the Old Testament teaches, above all, warmongering, an "eye for an eye, a tooth for a tooth." However, that simply isn't true of mainline Judaism. Nor has it been taught for centuries, and still taught, by rabbis and their holy texts. On the contrary, Judaism's message is essentially peaceful and charitable. (In fact, it was the ancient Hebrews who invented charitable works.) For instance, the command to "love your enemies," lest some Christians forget, is found in several books of the *Old Testament*: namely, in *Genesis, Deuteronomy, Leviticus*, and *Exodus*. Recall that Jesus remarks in the Sermon on the Mount (*Matthew*, 43–48) that "you have heard that *it was said ...*" He was referring to what was found in Jewish Law going back to Moses. Following the opening of this sermon, Jesus then recalls and reiterates the main lessons derived from Jewish teaching. Among them is "love your enemies" and "thou shalt not kill."

Following the spirit of the Sermon on the Mount, it might be agreed that Jesus's message—that is, the Judeo-Christian message—amounts to the affirmation, to paraphrase, that since God made the world so that "sunshine and rain are bestowed" upon all people and peoples, good or evil, we, too, should copy this model by showing tolerance and understanding toward our reputed enemies—that is, toward the evil as well as the good. Paul and succeeding Christian theologians added that such forbearance should be shown toward alleged enemies—in Paul's words, "wherever and whenever possible." Speaking of Paul, in his Epistles, the Christian missionary refines this basic message of peace. He speaks, for example, of humans wreaking vengeance on other humans as forbidden by Jewish and Christian teaching. It is God alone, he says, who retains exclusively the right to mete out deadly punishment (*Romans*, 12:19). As *Revelations* states, "They that take up the sword shall perish by the sword." For his part, Paul preached, "If possible, so far as it depends on you, live peacefully with all men" (*Romans*, 12:18).

Was Paul of Tarsus referring only to individuals or did he mean whole communities and states in their relations to each other? According to a number of interpreters, his statement probably can be construed in the latter, broad "international" sense.

Other religions, among them Buddhism, also a carry message of peace, brotherly love, and understanding The fundamental thrust of Buddhism, in fact, is one of peace, both individual and communal. The Buddha taught that once people understand the road to peace by understanding what can bring it about, persons are then empowered to use their reason to realize a tranquil life, for themselves and for others. Yet, if we do not first address the fundamental issues, then all peaceful actions will come to naught. Buddhism teaches that all forms of life participate in an identical spiritual source. Buddhist thought does not condone intra-human struggle to the death—that is, "artificial" death before natural death. The latter is seen as part of the divine cycle of death/rebirth, which we should not attempt to interdict. Buddha teaches that minds at peace lead to peaceful actions. Peaceful minds make the world peaceful. The Buddhist method is to get people to liberate themselves from the "unnatural" storm and stress of worldly life that can only lead to unpeaceful thoughts, speech, and hostile, deadly actions, such as wars.

In short, Buddhists believe in reducing or, if possible, eliminating violence altogether throughout the world. The Buddhist doctrine of *karma* teaches that force and violence, even to the level of killing, never solves anything. Killing only generates more fear and anger (as Kant also showed), which in turn leads to more killing, more fear, and more anger in a vicious cycle without end. Moreover, in some Buddhist teaching, if you kill your enemy in this life, he is reborn, seeks revenge, and kills you in the next life. When the people of one nation invade and kill or subjugate the people of another nation, sooner or later the opportunity will present itself for the people of the conquered nation to wreak their revenge upon the conquerors. Hinduism provides another example of a widely influential religion that preaches nonviolence. In his book, *Gandhi and King: The Power of Nonviolent Resistance*, Michael J. Nojeim notes:

> Philosophical adherents to nonviolence are found among all the major world faiths, Christianity, Islam, Judaism, Hinduism, and Buddhism. Nonviolence for these people is not just a matter of choice. It is an undeniable and inviolable way of life that springs directly from their religious beliefs. It is their covenant.[23]

In conclusion, we might agree that religion has acted and still acts as a much-needed fountain of moral condemnation of needless violence, killing, and war. It is a spiritual brake that attempts to halt the human habit of killing. Atheists contend that religions are not successful in "taming" belligerence in humans. On the contrary, say some writers of atheist persuasion, who argue that religion actually fosters mutual enmity. They cite the Christian religious wars of past centuries as well as the contemporary tensions between various religions, Muslim, Jewish, or Christian. Others argue that the religious factor in struggle is simply a cover, or rationalization, for territorial expansion, power, and greed.[24] For their part, religionists claim that the belligerency is not the fault of religious beliefs but of the underlying factors in the human makeup. Religion, they insist, remains a powerful inhibitor of atavistic tendencies, habits, and "instincts" in human beings.

Jus ad Bellum and the Iraq War

3

"Just Cause" and the Iraq War

The launching of a war against Iraq, if it were to be considered moral, legitimate, and legal, had to be based upon the concept of *just cause*. This generic criterion divides itself into several clear touchstones that cover the following questions regarding the United States as the "initiator" of that war:[1]

- Was the danger of war by an aggressor state *clear and present* and enough to warrant and justify initiating a war against the perceived threatening state?

- Was the massive resort to force based on a *justifiable intention* on the part of the side initiating the war? Put another way, was the danger truthfully construed by the war initiator?

- Was the initiator's war policy and actions based on *legitimate authority*? In democratically-ruled states, this should mean a broad, clearly expressed consensus on the necessity of using arms in defense of the country's tangibly endangered national security.

- Depending on the degree of threat posed by the designated enemy, were *all nonmilitary means exhausted* for reducing or eliminating the perceived threat? War and the tragic sacrifices it exacts are considered traditionally and understandably in modern times to be necessary only as a "last resort." In the international political environment of post-September 11, 2001 and through 2002, were other viable options, short of war, thoroughly exploited by the U.S. Government in order to preclude the alleged "necessity" of waging war against Iraq?

- Assuming, finally, that the war was indisputably necessary, was the possibility present of *achieving a clear victory* in the massive military undertaking of invasion and occupation and was victory able to be clearly defined? If no discernible victory was possible—either because the initiator lacked the means to achieve it or because of the elusive nature of the situation—was the risk worth taking if a virtually interminable occupation by the initiator of the war was necessary?

"IMMINENT THREAT"

Let's consider the Iraq War under the first criterion within the rubrics of just cause. In 2002, did the state of Iraq under dictator Saddam Hussein present palpable evidence of the *imminence of the threat of its waging aggressive war*? Was the danger of Iraq's aggression such as to be legitimately described as clear and present to U.S. security as well as an "imminent" threat? Following are some of the many statements made by U.S. government officials, including the president, about the putatively grave, imminent danger posed by an allegedly threatening Iraq:

> The Iraqi regime is a threat of unique urgency ... The Iraqi regime is a serious and growing threat to peace. ... The Iraqi regime is a threat to any American.
> —President George W. Bush,
> in statements made respectively on October 2, 2002,
> October 10, 2002, and January 3, 2003

> Even at this eleventh hour, we have the time to do this Right with the greatest possible international support.
> —Sandy Berger,
> in a speech to the Harvard Law School, March 13, 2003,
> criticizing America's going to war in Iraq

> This is about imminent threat.
> —White House spokesman Scott McClelland,
> February 10, 2003

> Absolutely, an imminent threat.
> —White House Spokesman Ari Fleischer,
> answering a query on whether Iraq was an imminent threat, May 7, 2003

> Intelligence gathered by this and other governments leaves no doubt that the Iraq regime continues to possess and conceal some of the most lethal weapons ever devised.
> —President George W. Bush,
> televised address to the nation on the eve of the war,
> March 17, 2003

Before assessing the position of international law and custom on the matter of defining an imminent threat as a justifiable reason for going to war, consider the argument mounted by the Bush Administration in the winter of 2002 and 2003.

In an ABC News/Washington Post survey taken in midsummer 2005, a majority of Americans believed that the Bush Administration had "intentionally misled" the country into war. As the 2002 Downing Street memorandum put it, intelligence information was misleadingly "fixed" around the already-determined policy to wage a "preemptive" war against Iraq in order to topple Saddam Hussein.[2]

When President Bush and members of his administration were laying out the case for war to the Congress and the people, accusations arose that they had been lying. With the Senate Intelligence Committee report of summer 2004, it was at very least evident that faulty intelligence information had led to a false impression and to an exaggerated presentation of Iraq's alleged "direct threat to American security," or as the president had put it, "to any American."

The possibility that the president of the United States would intentionally mislead American citizens, the Congress, and the media for the purpose of inducing them to support a preemptive war on false pretenses is an extremely serious charge. Yet, past presidents no doubt on occasion have withheld information from the public or tampered with the truth. For instance, in 1960 President Dwight D. Eisenhower publicly denied that CIA spy-plane pilot Gary Powers was the airman whom the Soviets claimed they had shot down over the Ural Mountains and whom they had captured after Powers had bailed out and landed alive on Soviet territory. Given long-standing secrecy surrounding U-2 flights over the USSR, Ike might be excused for telling this "white lie."[3]

The faking of evidence within the Lyndon B. Johnson Administration over the "Tonkin Incident" of autumn 1964 is another case of rigging the evidence. In this example the fabrication was related to U.S. involvement in war. It seems clear, however, that the United States would have been drawn into a war in Vietnam regardless of the details of the Tonkin incident. For one thing, North Vietnam had crossed the 18th Parallel in regiment strength by late 1964. This intrusion in strength by the North Vietnamese Army may have been reason enough for Washington to decide to honor its treaty obligations with South Vietnam to help defend it if attacked.

In the grave matter of whether or not to send young men and women into war, any deception or exaggeration of a enemy threat on the part of the White House is clearly out of line as well as dangerously self-defeating. Was there *intent* on the part of the Bush Administration to dissemble?

On January 3, 2003, President Bush claimed in his words that the "Iraqi regime is a threat to any American ... a real threat." On March 16, 2003, Bush declared, "The dictator of Iraq and his weapons of mass destruction (WMD) are a threat to the security of free nations." On July 17, 2003, some three months following the invasion of Iraq and with Saddam Hussein "neutralized" and in hiding, the president declared that "we ended the threat from Saddam Hussein's weapons of mass destruction." On May 7, 2003, White House spokesperson Ari Fleischer described Iraq as "absolutely" an "imminent threat" ("imminent threat" had been used several times before by high Bush officials). Secretary of Defense Donald Rumsfeld, Vice President Dick Cheney, Deputy Defense Secretary Paul D. Wolfowitz, and National Security Adviser Condoleeza Rice all used the words "threat" or "serious threat" to the United States in the context of Iraq's alleged WMD. Cheney was particularly alarmist. He proffered claims that "uranium" was being pursued by Saddam for his WMD program. On "Meet the Press" in May 2002 and in several speeches later in the year, Cheney claimed that Iraq was "actively pursuing nuclear weapons at this time."

By September, in his address to the United Nations the president himself alluded to uranium in the context of Iraq. In the notorious "16 fateful words" in his State of the Union Address of January 2003, Bush erroneously claimed that Iraq had imported uranium "yellowcake" from Niger.[4] Bush advisers had simply ignored the U.N. International Atomic Energy Agency's warning that the documents supporting this farfetched claim were fakes. In October 2002 the National Intelligence Estimate had informed Congress, as it was considering a resolution that would authorize war against Iraq, that claims by British intelligence that Iraq was trying to obtain uranium from Niger were "highly dubious." This warning, too, was ignored by the Bush Administration. Given the available evidence, the accusation of lying about the threat posed by Iraq cannot be written off as mere mudslinging.

As to lying, the philosopher Kant made a distinction between intent and the effects of a good deed as well as the inadmissibility of lying. He inquired as to whether the allegedly good consequences that might flow even from a good deed would become sullied by the deed's having had bad motives. Was, he asked, "good will" missing? Was there an unassailable sense of duty and were there good intentions as motives for the deed? A person deserves disapprobation, Kant argued, if in committing a charitable act he has, in fact, performed it for egregious or selfish motives.[5] (This notion runs parallel to Jesus's admonition about sinning in one's heart.)

As to good deeds, suppose that a person shows generosity toward another in order to obtain some profit from his act. For Kant and many other philosophers going back to Socrates, one's self-interested motives cancel the alleged nobility of his action, no matter how superficially good its results may appear to be. The goodness of the deed has been ruined by the false note of its motivation. That is, instead of the person's having acted from sincere altruism or from disinterested duty, the falsely "generous" person has corrupted his deed because his intention was not truly altruistic. Rather, it was selfish.

Kant insisted, moreover, that the act of lying demands the same kind of rigorous examination. To lie, he wrote, is to "throw away" one's human dignity and to spoil his relations with others. One lie was as bad as another. There was absolutely no justification ever to lie. In a sense, lying, like doing good deeds, relates to *intention*. Lying and deception create a field of mistrust. Suppose one objected by saying that if the lie is for noble purposes, let it pass. A Machiavellian view toward lying "for the cause" construes deceit as a useful tool when used shrewdly by a prince in order to get into power or do in political competitors. If the effect of the lie is "helpful" in some respect—say, a physician sparing relatives of the fact of a sick patient's terminal illness—then such lying is—presumably—acceptable. Yet the philosopher Sissela Bok responds to this claim by insisting that no matter how lying is sliced, what is falsely presented as true is still an unpardonable lie. Its effect is harmful. Overstatement and understatement likewise bring in the onus of lying. Either may be done for impure motives.

Similarly, in the case of the administration's statements and actions before the March 2003 invasion, we can detect what would appear to be hidden intentions that were cloaked in misleading language. Here the president and his closest aides had deliberately used language that exaggerated the alleged threat posed to the United States as they went breezily ahead with their invasion plans. How do we know this?

We discover, for instance, that the president was very careful *for his own part to never himself use the word "imminent"* to describe the Iraqi threat.[6] He seems deliberately to have left that solely to his press-relations spokespersons. This intentional "omission" would indicate that the president knew that Iraq was not a threat that would permit his own use of the extreme description, "imminent." Otherwise, wouldn't he himself have used the term? After all, President Bush had shown no reluctance to depict the threat to its direst extent. So a suspicion lingers. Moreover, there were at least a dozen occasions when the president described the threat. This author examined every available instance of his reference to the Iraqi threat and found that not once did the president ever describe it as "imminent." Yet, as we saw, others under his supervision were authorized to do so on several occasions. They made these claims as White House and Defense Department spokespersons who have contact with the mass media.

So, if the president knew that the threat was *not* imminent, as it would appear he knew, why did he permit others to tell the "imminent" lie? Does that not inculpate him for permitting such baseless fear mongering to go out under his authority? The president can be seen as deliberately allowing fallacious exaggeration in the form of that crucial misleading expression, which would thereby affect the public in the way he wished. In the Niger yellowcake case—Bush's 16-word allusion in his 2003 State of the Union address to Iraq's alleged attempt to import this uranium ore used in the manufacture of nuclear weapons in which he asserted, "Iraq recently sought significant quantities of uranium from Africa"—the White House later recanted via Fleischer, on July 6, 2003. It admitted that the information had been untrue and that this error was known at the time it was inserted into the president's address. That sounds like an admission of lying.

In her reflective book, *Lying: Moral Choice in Public and Private Life*, philosopher Sissela Bok notes that exaggeration itself, by bordering on if not involving outright lying, cancels "the reliability of all knowledge."[7] Such deception contaminates the source from which the "managed" information comes and whichever office engages in such manipulation. In a crisis, such as war, manipulation of crucial data and information at the highest level can have a disastrous effect upon public trust.

It would seem obvious that such manipulation clashes with the concept of just cause and the stated intention of going to war under *jus ad bellum*. Such disapprobation applies especially to an official as highly placed as the president of the United States. This behavior can also harm public morale, not to mention the morale of soldiers fighting in the war when lying about the need for going into battle was involved.

Consider, too, that if a president *understated* a threat, the subsequent exposure of the truth would not necessarily impugn his later assertions. For instance, during a war or when an epidemic is raging, the president might well have to choose between keeping the population from panicking or fully informing the population. Thus, he might understate the danger. But what about *over*statement—as in the case of exaggeration or distortion? Had the president said that we had nothing to worry about from Iraq even when we did, this misstatement or understatement would have been incomparably more excusable than his actual overstatement of the threat, as he put it, to all Americans. The point is that overstatement may often lead to action since an exaggerated danger is more alarming and invites a reaction Understatement may be misleading by minimizing a tangible danger; "tangible danger," however, could not have applied to the weakened Iraq of 2002 and 2003. In any case, a disinclination to exaggerate a threat will not normally lead to action. By contrast, exaggerating a threat spurs a demand for action that makes overstatement vastly more incriminating than the latter.

In "Sincere Deceivers," *The London Economist* editorialized (July 17, 2004) that "such hyped-up salesmanship [in favor of war] was understandable. [Nevertheless] well-intentioned or not, *such salesmanship has made us all less safe and more vulnerable to terrorists because even now more people will refuse to believe (intelligence warnings)*" [author's emphasis]. By his apparent dishonesty, said *The Economist*, Bush must bear the responsibility for "having made things harder and more dangerous."

Through the ages, the editorial said, "grandmothers have advised that honesty is the best policy." One must agree that in the long run any form of lying is detrimental. It misleads people into false thinking and acting. It also pollutes the public's sources of information. In the case of the Bush Administration, the Government could be seen as having besmirched itself and the concept of *jus ad bellum*. As a result, public suspicion would surround any subsequent call by the Government to go to war to eliminate the source of an alleged "imminent threat."

It is noteworthy that much of the information concerning the presence of WMD and other military assets in Iraq had come from the Iraqi émigré group, the Iraqi National Congress, headed by Ahmad Chalabi, whom the Bush Administration called the "George Washington of Iraq." While still in London as a prominent (and wealthy) Iraqi exile, Chalabi was said to have had close ties to such neoconservatives as Wolfowitz and Defense Adviser Richard Perle, who in turn promoted him as a spokesman for leading the rebuilding of Iraq.

As it turned out, not only did these data supplied by members of his circle of émigrés turn out to be erroneous, but Chalabi himself personally fell out with U.S. officials as the appointed head of the first interim regime in that country. His funding was cut off when it was discovered that he had committed various misdemeanors, including counterfeiting. As a result, Chalabi's relations with the Pentagon utterly deteriorated. Yet as an influential Shiite political figure, he later moved on within Iraq, assuming various political positions in which he touted policies of the Shiites while criticizing U.S. policy. His nephew, Salem Chalabi, is a high figure serving on the tribunal that was formed to prosecute Saddam Hussein for various crimes against humanity. This man was once indicted by an Iraqi court for the alleged killing of a political opponent. Both Chalabis protested their innocence, claiming that the American "occupiers" were making groundless accusations against them.

After being ostracized by U.S. authorities, Ahmad Chalabi assumed blatant anti-U.S. stands that appealed to militant Shiite and other disgruntled forces inside Iraq. When U.S. officials attempted to recover secret documents that the Pentagon had shared with Chalabi in the pre- and post-invasion years, Chalabi claimed that the papers had been destroyed in a fire.

The Chalabi case had the overall effect of staining the credibility of the stated U.S. intentions. It seemed that Washington had relied on dubious, flimsy evidence in making its case for war. If not displaying outright lying, the case provides another instance of bungling by the Bush Administration on a vitally important matter touching on the just cause for war.

International law is quite clear on the point that a nation may defend itself if an attack against it is *looming and concrete*. Such defense qualifies it as a just cause for mounting war, as an instance of proper application of *jus ad bellum*. Writing in the *Michigan Journal of International Law*, the eminent

Dr. Michael N. Schmitt, Professor of International Law at the George C. Marshall European Center for Security, Gremisch-Partenkirchen, Germany, wrote an extended, heavily sourced analysis of the preemption issue.[8] Schmitt struck off the following points:

- Since the seventeenth-century birth of nation-states and the "Westphalian Order," attention to security and the national-sovereign interests of states may at times undercut "world-order" conceptions (e.g., as sketched out in Immanuel Kant's *Perpetual Peace*). Schmitt notes that Republican Party epigones like Henry A. Kissinger and Brent Scowcroft duly warn that preemption presents a "complicated option when applied to real-world events."[9]

- The law of self-defense, as stipulated in international law as a warrant for preemption, assumes that the preemption action will be undertaken because of an "imminent threat." The action will have to be adjusted as the nature of the threat changes," notes Professor Schmitt. But, he asks, "Is this an example of 'hyper-power' contorting international legal standards to its own purpose?" The answer, he says, would depend on the facts at hand in each individual case.

- Established twentieth-century norms for warfare, such as those found in the Kellogg-Briand Pact of 1928, while prohibiting warfare as a means of resolving international disputes, nevertheless reiterated self-defense as a legitimate reason for the use of force under certain circumstances. This remained the norm until Article 2(4) of the U.N. Charter, drafted in 1945. Under this article U.N. member-states are obliged to "refrain from the threat or use of force against the territorial integrity or political independence of any State, in any other manner inconsistent with the Purposes of the United Nations." Schmitt adds that the wording of this article suggests that while attacks against a nation-state as a whole are outlawed, it would appear that a preemptive attack against, say, a "weapons manufacturing facility with no intent to seize territory or affect the political process [in the nation-state] would not implicate a prohibition." Perhaps more to the point is the U.N. Charter's prohibition of threats to use force. As he wrote, "The years preceding the Second World War witnessed numerous such threats that contributed to the outbreak of global conflagration. Accordingly, the Charter drafters included [such] threats in the Article 2(4) proscription."

It is noteworthy, says Schmitt, that these U.N. Charter provisions warrant military action only in the presence of a clear, concrete "*threat*" to peace, not merely in the form of perceived "aggressiveness," past or present, by a state. Security Council Resolution 1441 of October 2002, which demanded Iraqi compliance with the U.N. weapons-inspection regime, known as UNMOVIC, included in its text the threat that noncompliance by Iraq would mean that the state would face "serious consequences" as a result of its continued violations of its obligations. It thus remained for the Security Council to define the extent and significance of those presumed violations, and which in turn meant that the U.N. body would develop its own definition of a warranted (presumably forceful, or military) response to Iraqi violations. The council would thereby define its intention to sanction against the offending state. No motion to apply sanctions was ever put before the Council. The United States had sounded out member delegations in January and February 2003 and determined that it lacked the necessary votes to apply sanctions against Iraq. Thus, the resolution was never put before the United Nations. Instead, the United States and the United Kingdom went ahead with the invasion of Iraq that was preceded by bombing attacks on strategic military targets in Iraq—raids that came to be known as the (illegal) opening "shock and awe" phase of preparing the invasion.

Clearly defining the meaning of "self-defense" has presented the world body and the U.S. Congress with no less a quandary than other slippery issues arising in interpreting the application of preemption under international law in the course of defining self-defense. In NSS 2002 and follow-up statements by the Bush Administration, the U.S. Government reserved the right, unilaterally if necessary, to define when self-defense applied. It had to decide on its own when to conduct anticipatory military operations. This is true when, as NSS 2002 explicitly states, there is "uncertainty as to the time and place of the enemy's attack." Threat assessment, in other words, is mainly up to the state itself to determine.

Yet, it could be contended that a state's sovereign right in this respect should not violate the spirit of international law and the rich legacy of the definition of when war is waged justly and when it is waged unjustly. The new U.S. approach in its defense strategy generally was supported by the Joint Congressional resolution that passed nearly unanimously in late 2002. The resolution had granted the president the authority to assess the threat, and he was given power on his own to develop necessary military measures to cope with any clear and present danger. It was obvious that the Congress was so minded to cooperate with the president in the tense aftermath of the events of September 11, 2001, and subsequent events of a threatening nature (e.g., the outbreaks of postal letter-borne anthrax). In Professor Schmitt's opinion, the legislative branch's resolution was "entirely consistent with the 2002 National Security Strategy." This is true. Yet that still left open the question of the moral rectitude of NSS 2002. It could be argued that the formulation invited abuses that would clash with the spirit of *jus ad bellum* especially in the case of the state, such as the United States, having strong presidential power stemming from its system of government.[10]

A further detailed definition of "self-defense" remains a moot question. It is subject to executive branch together with legislative branch definition and intervention via the Senate's power of "advice and consent." The latter power theoretically might in a sense "preempt" a president's role in enforcing security. The threshold for making such a determination in a democratic state that respects the separation of powers, as Schmitt argues, should remain very high. Still, the assertion of executive power depends on a number of factors—the nation-state's constitution and its political culture and practice. In America's case, the threshold is especially high because of America's strong presidential system of government, as opposed to the parliamentary form in which executive authority sometimes must yield to "real-time" legislative pressure. For instance, were the American system a parliamentary one, the "parliamentary" elections of November 7, 2006, as a new party took over both houses of Congress, would have meant a new "prime minister," or head-of-government. By contrast, in the presidential system the president continues in office even when the legislative branch is dominated by an opposing party. (This was precisely Princeton Professor Woodrow Wilson's principal objection to the American political system.)

Issues of legality of the war against Iraq continue to be debated. Consider the genesis of the U.S. invasion in 2003. The invasion began without the explicit authorization of the United Nations Security Council. A number of authorities on international law claim that the action violated the U.N. Charter.[11] In response to such criticism the Bush administration cited Security Council resolutions from the early 1990s (warranting use of force in some cases) as legal justification for its action in March 2003. Yet the resolutions did not clearly legalize the use of military action specifically against Iraq. On March 17, 2003, in his Address to the Nation, President Bush demanded that Iraqi President Saddam Hussein and his two sons, Uday and Qusay, leave Iraq. They were given 48 hours to vacate the country. The next day the White House withdrew this ultimatum. It stated that the United States would invade Iraq whether or not Saddam Hussein exited Iraq. U.S. military operations then began in earnest and were conducted under the name Operation Iraqi Freedom. United Kingdom military operations were known as Operation Telic, and the Australian operations were dubbed Operation Falconer.

Facing the coalition was a large yet poorly-equipped Iraqi military force. The regular Iraqi army was estimated at 290,000–350,000 troops. These included four Republican Guard divisions, each numbering 50,000–80,000 troops, plus the "Fedayeen Saddam," a 20,000–40,000 strong militia. The latter employed insurgent tactics both during and even after the invasion. There were an estimated 13 Iraqi infantry divisions, 10 mechanized and armored divisions, as well as some special forces units. (The Iraqi Air Force and Navy played a negligible role in the conflict.)

All were defeated by the U.S.-led coalition using state-of-the-art military technology. The Coalition occupation began after less than a month of fighting when the regime of Saddam Hussein and the Baath Party were terminated. Thereupon, approximately 260,000 United States troops, supported by 45,000 British plus the smaller occupation forces from other nations (known together as the Coalition of the Willing), began the occupation.

Arising in *jus in bello* is the issue of "proportional" response, known to jurists simply as "proportionality. This principle is also invoked in the discussion of *jus in bello* and is germane in the discussion of the normative (law-bound) application of preemption. If, for example, the putative military threat is minimal and if the factor of urgency-of-response to the threat is also minimal, then preemptive action should be so scaled down to conform to the "proportionality." How is this relationship determined so that the "punishment fits the crime"?

As Schmitt pointed out, this, too, is left up to the threatened party. For instance, in the case of Iraq's building of a nuclear reactor in 1981, Israel seemingly took "proportionate" action to eliminate the said reactor threat alone. Israeli Defense Forces did not invade Iraq. Israel merely took out the nuclear installation, which was under construction, by means of surgical air strikes. Schmitt notes that the Israeli raids were "skillfully conducted [by] discriminately targeting the source of a major threat to Israel and violating Iraqi airspace with only a handful of aircraft for a very short period." Nor were there any casualties. In other words, a preemptive response to a threat presumably need not necessarily involve cross-the-border engagement of the threatening state's armies, even when they are attacking. It might conceivably be just as effective to target in pinpoint fashion a hostile nation's assets in ways that would make its invading armies retreat or its policy moderated, thus reducing the aggressor's "cost-benefits" in continuing his hostile actions.

The factor of *imminence* likewise raises other crucial issues. When is a threat truly imminent? Who determines it? Once again, it is clear that by international law and custom prevailing between states it is the threatened state that will assert its sovereign right to define when a threat is imminent. As to objectively determining imminence, a host of problems arises. Does "imminence" mean, for instance, immediacy? That is, is there no time left for negotiation or deliberation to cope with the perceived threat? On this matter, Schmitt concludes, "It would be absurd to suggest that international law requires a state to 'take the first hit' when it could effectively defend itself by acting preemptively." Yet the implication is, as Schmitt indicates, that the threat is proven to be tangible, that it is clear and present. What, therefore, must be weighed in determining the legitimacy and legality of adopting the extreme course of preemptive attack are the *nature and immediacy* of the danger and the prospective preemptor's *exhaustion of all options—e.g., diplomatic—to preclude the necessity of undertaking preventive, or preemptive military actions.* Otherwise, the time-honored traditions for defining just war and just cause for going to war under *jus ad bellum*, especially waging war in an obviously offensive way, is ignored. Any state acting in this way invites the stigma of having violated traditional rules in waging just war.

As we now know, by 2002 Iraq constituted no such imminent threat to U.S. security or even to that of its immediate neighbors. It is doubtful that it represented even a long-term threat. Saddam's military machine had been decimated by the Persian Gulf War 10 years previously. Increasingly

tightened U.N. inspections and supportive testimonies about the effectiveness of the inspections (made by hard-line U.S. inspectors themselves) show
that by 2002 Iraq was in a severely weakened condition in the military sense
as well as in its damaged prestige internationally.[12] Moreover, the U.N.
Security Council unanimously-passed Resolution 1441 in October 2002
had put Saddam Hussein's Iraq on the spot, which further weakened it.
The governments of Germany, France, and Russia, which later condemned
the U.S. invasion, had by autumn 2002 indicated their strong intention to
see through a newly strengthened, thoroughgoing inspection regime in Iraq.
These powers supported the imposition of sanctions, presumably including
military ones, if the Baghdad regime ultimately refused to cooperate or if
weapons violations were discovered.

If the turmoil erupting in Iraqi society after the U.S. invasion in March
2003 and the chaos that has since ensued during the occupation are any indi-
cation, Iraqi society in the prewar years was clearly rife with intense religious, regional, tribal, and political discord. The authoritarian Baathist
regime itself may have been in the throes of collapse. Saddam Hussein himself was obviously conscious of the erosion of his power. He was suffering
severe loss of prestige at home and abroad. The dictator tried to compensate
for this by assuming an almost fantastically stubborn, imperious posture
through the period of focused U.N. Security Council consideration of the
Iraqi issue in the winter of 2002–2003. The Iraqi dictator seems to have
deliberately assumed this ridiculous pose as compensation for the fact that
his alleged arsenal of WMD was nonexistent, his overall power obviously
weakened. He thus used the alleged "Iraqi threat," so trumped up by his
enemies, the United States and the United Kingdom, as an imaginary ploy,
a tool of intimidation or "scare tactic."

Yet, by the time of the rigorously-worded Resolution 1441 in October
2002, the dictator's bluff was about to be called—by the Security Council
itself, which had passed this resolution that anticipated applying stern measures against an Iraq that defied the Council's will. It thus appeared that
without an invasion as planned by the United States that Iraq under the
Baathist regime had put itself into a highly precarious position. This, in turn,
meant that the way lay open for allied diplomatic pressure and action that
could have taken the place of a U.S.-initiated war. As we now surmise, the
Bush Administration was bent on war as a means of deposing Hussein while
attempting to find the locations of alleged Iraqi WMD.

BUSH ADMINISTRATION RATIONALE FOR WAR

Let's recall the major decisions made at the top of the Bush
Administration in 2002–2003 and the foreign policy philosophy that lay
behind it. This body of thinking is involved with the definition of just cause,
which is a function of government policy. International law is obliged to

allow a degree of elasticity in judgment concerning it and to specific conditions under which it is applied.

First, as to discerning the underlying thrust of President George W. Bush's foreign policy as it relates to determining just cause in rationalizing war, we must turn to the real-life policymakers who were chosen by him to be members of his administration team, which was assembled after the election of 2000. This was the neoconservative "brain trust" that rose to prominence in the Bush Administration. It became the center of intense criticism by those who opposed NSS 2002 and the preemptive war waged against Iraq.[13] This neoconservative group had begun to assemble under the George H. W. Bush Administration in 1992. Their views were presented in articles published in the neocon *The Weekly Standard*. The thrust of this early neocon argument was that:

- America should adopt a new, forceful, proactive political military doctrine that would permit the United States to take preventive measures against nations that it deemed to be an imminent threat to its security and world peace. The spokesperson for this view was Paul D. Wolfowitz, later to become President George W. Bush's Pentagon strategist. As then Defense Department undersecretary for policy, Wolfowitz had already, nearly decade before 9/11, made a name for himself in his drafting in 1992 of the document, Defense Planning Guidance. The gist of this far-ranging paper was "American "primacism." That is, that America's global, superpower military predominance equipped it and tasked it to "prevent any hostile power capable of challenging that primacy [and] endorsed a policy of preventive disarmament of rogue states seeking to acquire weapons of mass destruction." The document never went into effect because President George H. W. Bush was not reelected in 1992. Instead, the Wolfowitz advisory went into cold storage, only to be resuscitated in 2001.

- More than 10 years later, beginning even before the terrorist attacks of September 11, 2001, Wolfowitz together with other "neocon hawks" had succeeded in acquiring key positions within the Bush Administration. Besides Wolfowitz at the Pentagon there were also Douglas Feith and Richard Perle, both well-known preemptionists and U.S. "primacists"—that is, those who proposed that the United States should strongly exert its unique power worldwide by military means as deemed necessary by America alone. Within the White House itself, neocon Lewis ("Scooter") Libby became Vice President Dick Cheney's principal aide. National Security Adviser Condoleeza Rice, herself an outspoken "hawk," even coined a term for this militant group of proactivists and preemptionists, "the Vulcans."

Well before the election of 2000, these neocon partisans had become election campaigner George W. Bush's defense and foreign policy team. After the election and the dire effect of 9/11 on the president, other "Vulcans" were brought directly into this group around Bush and Cheney. (Secretary of State Colin Powell was significantly left out of this influential loop.)

For instance, Bush's speechwriter, Michael J. Gerson, the presumed inventor of the term "axis of evil" and a reputed Christian fundamentalist and "Christian Zionist," came to the fore. He was known to be strongly pro-Israel, a sympathizer of the strong measures employed against the Palestinians by Israeli conservative, Likud Party leader and Prime Minister Benjamin Netanyahu and later by Israeli Prime Minister Ariel Sharon, also at that time a leading Likud Party official. As Likudists, both Israeli leaders tend to cater to the fundamentalist-inclined Oriental Jews, pre-1948 native Israelis who seek a "greater Israel" and who oppose the creation of a contiguous Palestinian State. (Sharon had significantly tempered his views in this respect by 2005.)

In sympathy with Israeli policies in the defense of its security, as viewed in the widest perspective in terms of the whole Middle East, are also such influential figures in the neocon community as Irving Kristol and Robert Kagan, among others, who collaborated on the magazine, *The Weekly Standard*. Some were given official posts in the George W. Bush government, either at the State Department or in the Pentagon. They saw the defense of Israel and the overthrow of Saddam Hussein as two sides of the same coin. Gerson, Feith, and others in the Bush administration thus sympathized with the hard-line policies adopted at that time by Israeli Prime Minister Sharon. Two well-known publications, *Commentary* and *The Weekly Standard*, became influential vehicles for airing the views of the neocons, who contributed articles to them that, in turn, attracted the attention of persons close to George W. Bush. However, it is inaccurate to draw from this that all, or even most, Jews and Jewish commentators in America endorsed neocon policy or the Iraq War simply because it apparently dovetailed with Israeli policy.

As far as rationalizing a just war against Saddam Hussein was concerned, the neocon position along with that of the Israelis meant, above all, that Saddam Hussein, a tyrant and a threat to peace, must go. His ouster demanded a full-scale invasion by U.S.-led forces in which Israel would play no direct part.[14] Not forgotten among neoconservatives was the fact that it was Israel's bold, preemptive 1981 surgical strike that had destroyed Hussein's budding nuclear reactor at Osirak on the outskirts of Baghdad. While a surgical strike is not the same thing as a large-scale invasion of a country with armies positioned across a broad front, Israel's strike nevertheless was an action that anticipated the incipient wisdom of making a large-scale first strike against Iraq that would entirely disable an aggressor-nation, as had been suggested in Wolfowitz's 1992 policy paper.

Such bold action in the post-9/11 environment would likewise send a signal about the United States as a power that not only favored the spread of democracy worldwide but was willing to use military force to abet this process and to liquidate an alleged imminent threat to peace. This "active defense" policy clashed with the policies of the preceding Clinton

Administration, which at most had favored and carried out policies of "humanitarian intervention," as in Bosnia and Kosovo, but always with the cooperation of NATO allies and the United Nations. The Bush policy also represented a major departure from the Republicans' traditional "realist" philosophy adhered to by the George H. W. Bush Administration in the late 1980s. Going back further, the neocon position has roots within the Reagan Administration where, in fact, many of the "Vulcans" first got their taste of a messianic-style foreign policy (in the U.S.-Soviet cold war) that would not only proclaim democracy for the world but attempt actively where possible to put it in place in countries (such as Nicaragua, El Salvador, Grenada) that were ruled by illiberal regimes of the right (in El Salvador's case) or threatened by radical, Marxist guerrilla movements and regimes. The defensive aspect of the Monroe Doctrine was also invoked in blocking the spread of such Soviet-supported leftist regimes "south of the border."[15]

A key player in designing and rationalizing the Bush war policy and carrying it out was Secretary of Defense Donald Rumsfeld. He likewise sympathized with the views of the neocons in broadening the definition of just cause in the application of U.S. military power. Well before he was appointed Secretary of Defense by Bush in January 2001, Rumsfeld had promoted an American political-military policy that could best be described as "forward-leaning." In February 2001, more than six months before the terrorist attacks of 9/11, Rumsfeld had drafted a memo titled "Guidelines When Considering Committing U.S. Forces." Presented in it was advice to the President on how to get a new, "proactive" defense policy across to the public in the most candid, expeditious way—that is, by being "brutally" frank, as he put it. He did not say, however, the policy would be presented by exaggerating available intelligence on Iraq's alleged WMD and "imminent" threat.

In *Plan of Attack*, Bob Woodward related how the Bush Administration's explicit intention, even before the terrorist events of 9/11, was to use preemptive military measures. They were to be used not only against the Afghan Taliban regime. "Wolfowitz believed it was possible," writes Woodward, "to send in the military to overrun and seize Iraq's south oil fields [and] establish a foothold. ... The proposal was dubbed an 'enclave policy' ... Wolfowitz was like a drum that would not stop. He and his group of neoconservatives were rubbing their hands over the ideas, which were being presented as 'draft plans.'" By 9/11 the "plans" had become active preparations for war— at first against Afghanistan.

An article in the Army War College's journal written by a former staff member of the Senate Armed Services Committee, Jeffrey Record, observed that the Bush Administration was in favor of "shooting in the Persian Gulf on behalf of lower gas prices."[16] It also advocated, he wrote, "the acceptability of presidential subterfuge in the promotion of a conflict [while explicitly] urging the painting over of the United States's actual reasons for warfare with a nobly high-minded veneer, seeing such as a necessity for mobilizing public support for a conflict." In April 2001, General Tommy Franks, former commander of U.S. forces in the Persian Gulf/South Asia area, testified to Congress that his command's key mission was gaining "access to [the region's] energy resources." This posture conformed as well to the new "primacist" notion of the bold application of U.S. superpower strength abroad. Thus, the "war against terror" and the long-standing U.S. goal of protecting its access to oil became wedded.

In May the U.S. Central Command began planning for war with Afghanistan. *The Washington Post* later reported (August 21, 2001) that Thomas Donnelly, Deputy Executive Director of the Project for the New American Century, an influential neoconservative think tank, explained to the *Post* that the United States should embrace its role as an "imperialist, hegemonic" dominator of the world. He stated that he had found prominent politicians who were in agreement on this point—as, say, concerned Afghanistan. "There's not all that many people who will not talk about it openly . . . It's discomforting to a lot of Americans. So they use code phrases like America's the sole superpower. I think Americans have become used to running the world and would be very reluctant to give it up, if they realized there was a serious challenge to it."

Yet, ironically, these very types of interventionist policies had been repudiated in Bush's campaign oratory of 2000. The Republican candidate for president had voiced his disapproval of what he called "nation-building." (This, obviously, was before the neocon "Vulcans" had gained the high ground among Bush's closest advisers.) In the summer of 2001, Defense Secretary Rumsfeld's office sponsored a study of ancient empires— Macedonia, Rome, the Mongols—apparently in order to learn how they had maintained dominance (*The New York Times*, March 5, 2003). Some observers, indeed, refer to present-day assertion of American power abroad as a concomitant of an "imperial" presidency.

It should also be pointed out, as neocon publicist Max Boot did in *Foreign Policy* magazine, that whereas the neocons at Defense and State were influential, the decisions made along neocon lines ultimately belong to the president, Vice President Cheney, and the Bush Cabinet. As Boot, a contributing editor to *The Weekly Standard* and a *Los Angeles Times* columnist, observed: "The influence of the neoconservative movement . . . supposedly comes from its agents embedded within the U.S. government . . . [Yet] the neocons have no representatives in the administration's top tier. President George W. Bush, Vice President Dick Cheney, Secretary of Defense Donald Rumsfeld, Secretary of State Colin Powell, and National Security Advisor Condoleeza Rice: Not a neocon among them. Powell might be best described as a liberal internationalist; the others are traditional national-interest conservatives who, during Bush's 2000 presidential

campaign, derided the Clinton administration for its focus on nation building and human rights. Most of them were highly skeptical of the interventions in the Balkans that neocons championed."[17] Boot adds a note of
triumph:

> The ambitious National Security Strategy that the administration issued in
> September 2002—with its call for U.S. primacy, the promotion of democracy,
> and vigorous action, preemptive if necessary, to stop terrorism and weapons
> proliferation—was a quintessentially neoconservative document, the new
> standard bearer of the neoconservative cause.

The writer, moreover, acknowledged that a faction within the Republican
Party, if not the neocons alone, favor unilateral action above multilateral,
U.N.-endorsed action. "These traditional conservatives," he wrote, "believe
that the guiding principles of U.S. foreign policy should be [quoting columnist George Will] 'to preserve U.S. sovereignty and freedom of action by
marginalizing the United Nations. Reserve military interventions for reasons
of U.S. national security, not altruism. Avoid peacekeeping operations that
compromise the military's war-fighting proficencies. Beware of the political
hubris inherent in the intensely non-conservative project of nation-
building. Neocons, by contrast, are committed above all to U.S. global leadership ... Like most conservatives, neocons are deeply suspicious of the
United Nations, which they fear is animated by anti-Americanism."

After 9/11, the "second Pearl Harbor," the United States was certain that
Afghanistan's Taliban rulers were harboring Al Qaeda and Osama bin
Laden. This amounted to a threat arising from a "terrorist state." With the
help of the British and Australians, and indirectly even the Russians,
the President ordered the invasion and occupation of that sovereign country.
Later, most of the world's nations, including the Permanent Members of the
U.N. Security Council (or PM 5) and our NATO allies, by and large
endorsed America's war there. They agreed, if reluctantly, that it had largely
been justified.

By then, the Bush Administration had made an important addition to its
national security strategy. Abbreviated "NSS" and formulated into a doctrine almost exactly one year after 9/11, NSS 2002 was declared. It incorporated a military policy that permitted the United States to wage *preemptive
war*, to use the doctrine's term, when deemed necessary—above all, on the
authority of the president as commander-in-chief. Instead of "waiting to be
attacked," America would strike first at any enemy nation that it perceived
to be an imminent threat. "We must adapt the concept of imminent threat
to the capabilities *and* objectives of today's adversaries," read the new doctrine. "The United States has long maintained the option of preemptive
actions to counter a sufficient threat to our national security."

A few months later, the Administration employed its preemptive-strike-
first/ask-questions-later strategy again. The United States invaded and

occupied another sovereign country, Iraq. It had been targeted by the Administration in the President's State of the Union address in January 2002 as one of the three states composing a threatening "axis of evil." This second, preemptive war against Iraq, however, was disowned and repudiated by several of our major allies in Europe. Public opinion there was overwhelmingly against the war. It was not supported by a majority of the 15-member United Nations Security Council or by three of the veto-wielding Five Permanent Members (P-5) of that body. Only the United States and United Kingdom spearheaded it. Anti-U.S. feeling spread like a tidal wave across the globe, with the superpower United States being depicted as a world-dominator and a prosecutor of unjust, illegitimate war.

For their part, the Bush Administration and defenders of the preemptive war against Iraq (which included leading Democrats along with the Republicans) claimed that, as with Taliban-ruled Afghanistan, Saddam Hussein's regime in Baghdad seriously imperiled America's post-9/11 security by describing the threat that way. (See Chapter 1 on this point.)

Based on what it was told by the executive branch, and with U.S. Senators rushing to judgment with a 75-to-23 vote on the Iraq War resolution in the U.S. Senate on October 11, 2002, matched by a House vote of 296-to-133 the same day, the whole legislative branch, the nation's representatives together with most of the media editorialists thus gave the Administration virtual carte blanche to wage war and to do so when it chose to. The resolution required the President to declare to Congress either before or within 48 hours after beginning military action that diplomatic efforts to enforce the U.N. resolutions had failed. Senator Robert Byrd, D-West Virginia, attempted to mount a filibuster against the resolution. He was cut off on a 75-to-25 vote. Byrd had argued that the resolution amounted to a "blank check" for the White House. "This is the Tonkin Gulf resolution all over again," the Senator said. "Let us stop, look, and listen. Let us not give this president or any president unchecked power. Remember the Constitution." On the GOP side, Senator John McCain, Republican of Arizona, argued strongly in support of the resolution. He claimed that the United States needed to act forcefully before Saddam Hussein could develop a more advanced arsenal.

Meanwhile, Baghdad denied having weapons of mass destruction. It offered to allow U.N. weapons inspectors to return for the first time since 1998. Deputy Prime Minister Abdul Tawab Al-Mulah Huwaish called the U.S. allegations "lies" and offered to let U.S. officials inspect plants that they claimed were developing nuclear, biological, and chemical weapons. The White House immediately rejected the offer.

The timing to strike was put on the front burner by the fact that after spring 2003 the oppressive, semi-tropical climate of Iraq would hobble the U.S.-led war. Taking this factor into account, the Administration decided that the war "had to be" launched as soon as, or by March—as, in fact, it had so begun.

However, within weeks most of the Administration's arguments about Iraq's alleged "growing threat," as the President called it, began to fall apart. Iraq's purported collaboration with Al Qaeda; its supposed concealed WMDs (nuclear, biological, and chemical); its presumed, continued wholesale violations of U.N. resolutions; plus other alleged evidence that Iraq was a clear and present danger to U.S. security—all turned out to be false assumptions. Two years later, in December 2005, President Bush finally admitted that the war had been based on faulty intelligence.[18] Yet he argued that the war was just because a tyrant and a potential threat to peace had been overthrown. The President also stressed that by 2005 Iraq had become what it was not under Saddam Hussein: a haven for Al Qaeda and other types of terrorists. This still left unsettled the fact that no connection between Saddam Hussein and Al Qaeda had ever been discovered. Nor did the Administration ever admit that Saddam's form of secular Islamism bore no resemblance to Al Qaeda and its anti-Baathist, theocratic Salafist ideology, and that hostility and bad blood between Qaeda and Saddam's regime had long existed.[19]

The argument made in 2002–2003 in favor of a just war was steadily if belatedly weakened, as one piece of detailed evidence for Iraq's alleged imminent threat was discovered to be false or deliberately falsified by allegedly trustworthy informants among Iraqi exiles. Such falsified evidence included the Iraqis' alleged mobile killer labs; their alleged "tons" of stored chemical weapons; their development of unmanned aerial vehicles (UAV) to deliver chemical or biological weapons (CBW); imported aluminum tubing to be used specifically in atomic-reactor centrifuges (allegedly to be used ultimately for the making of nuclear weapons); their alleged attempts to obtain uranium ore and yellowcake from abroad (e.g., from Niger). Thus, whatever support existed for waging a just war based on a tangible, imminent threat and the justifiability of the Bush Administration's intention to eliminate it collapsed.[20]

Yet such misleading information was authenticated by CIA Director George Tenet, who called it a "slam dunk." The President and Vice President likewise accepted it as undeniably true. It was uncritically repeated in National Intelligence Estimate (NIE) reports. Some of the most crucial evidence originated with Iraqi defectors, like Dr. Ahmad Chalabi, a member of the original ruling group of mostly Iraqi émigrés in the immediate, post-Saddam regime. Chalabi later criticized the Bush Administration and was disowned by it. He was later reinstated, apparently with Administration support, as a popular party leader in Iraq. Some of these Iraqi informants later confessed to fabrication. Some were suspected of it *in medias res.* Yet incriminating evidence known to some CIA officials was apparently withheld from the legislators.[21]

The final nail was driven into the coffin of these specious arguments made for war when the U.S. Senate Intelligence Committee issued its 511-page report on July 9, 2004. The report found that the U.S. preemptive war against Iraq should be viewed retrospectively as having been unjustified. This was not only because the evidence turned out to be flimsy and exaggerated. The committee report alleged that the war had also appeared illegitimate in terms of long-standing international law, the U.N. Charter, and the traditional norms for waging legal, morally-just *defensive* war. Besides stating these unsupported reasons for war, the Administration subsequently bolstered its case for using preemptive war against Iraq by putting the emphasis on liberation of that country. Liberation had been mentioned earlier but was seen as secondary to the other arguments for going to war. The American-led coalition, it said, freed the oppressed Iraqi people from the brutal Baathist dictatorship of Saddam Hussein.

Much of the American public's initial support for the war had been based mainly on this very mission—of bringing freedom to that country. Iraq's threat to our security, its alleged links to Al Qaeda, its possession of WMD all came second, according to the people's ranking of the rationale for going to war.[22] It was now claimed that the lofty purpose of liberation made America's preemptive war, called "Operation Iraqi Freedom," as equally just and moral as "Operation Enduring Freedom" had been against Taliban-ruled Afghanistan. As in that war, noble ends were said to justified violent means.

The administration made a further claim as to the intention lying behind its use of preemption: By its liberating invasion and occupation and the prospective democratization of Iraq that was to follow, Operation Iraqi Freedom would inevitably usher in a process of remaking the entire Middle East in the democratic image. Once erected in Iraq, democratic dominoes would start falling all across the Middle East. Ultimately, Israel would no longer be the only democratic state in the region. As President Bush put it in a dinner speech in February 2003, "A liberated Iraq can show the power of freedom to transform that vital region, by bringing hope and progress into the lives of millions."[23]

What was overlooked was that this extravagant claim would scarcely be acceptable to the sheikdoms and ruling establishments, even to the peoples, of the oil-rich Middle East and beyond. Their Muslim populations by no means were eager—or prepared—for democracy, especially one imposed by the United States or any foreign power. Observant people in these countries were all too aware of the threat represented by internal Muslim radicals seeking to unleash violence in their societies. The terrorists' threat to their established order was and is real and ominous enough. Destabilizing these societies further with appeals for democratization would appear to be dangerous and intolerable. Such clarion calls could well prove to be disastrously counterproductive. They would doubtlessly lead to chaos and a power vacuum, opening the way to radical Islamism. Certainly, Washington was not about to *impose* a "democratic order" on them.

By late 2006, many people in the United States began to rethink what America had been doing in following the preemptive road map of NSS 2002 for the past two years. Mounting casualties and loss of life on the American side alone; expenditures in three-plus years of war of $300–400 billion-plus (a price tag that could surpass that of the nearly decade-long Vietnam War); the negative fallout and worsening of tensions amidst growing militant Islamism worldwide: All these worked to raise doubts in the minds of the American public about the wisdom of the government's war policy. People began to ask if the war was worth it. As for realizing the noble purpose of liberating and democratizing Iraq or any other Middle Eastern country, that seemed to lie at best far in the distant future. Radically changing the way of life in a dozen or more Muslim countries and the way they have governed their more than 1 billion citizens for centuries was a fantastic stretch. How realistic was it to think of changing such societies' deeply rooted political and religious culture by fiat and *foreign*, Olympian command? There is nothing that agitates hostility among Muslims more, after all, than an attack on Islam "from the outside." Memory of the medieval Christian Crusades fought against them on their Middle Eastern home grounds is only one of numerous such grievances felt by many Muslims.

Legitimate Authority
and the Iraq War

The concept of *jus ad bellum* is linked to the issue of the *legitimacy* of the organizational or governmental authority that orders troops into battle. For a war to be considered just, the "authority" that sent the troops into action must be considered legitimate. "It is not the business of a private individual to declare war," St. Thomas Aquinas wrote in Question 40, Of War, in *Summa Theologica*, "[nor is it] the business of a private individual to summon together the people, which is to be done in wartime [since] the care of the common weal is committed to those who are in authority." This traditional, Thomist criterion is always included in contemporary discussions of just war (see Chapter 1, Endnote 1).

The generic term "authority" is employed in the literature on this aspect of *jus ad bellum*. This point is raised because it is possible that war might be initiated illegitimately by any number of local, non-state sources. These include guerrilla or revolutionary movements and their self-appointed leaders, small subdivisions of a larger administrative-territorial entity (such as tribal or ethnic groups), breakaway political entities, or even religious groups.

The above, unauthorized sources of war-making are considered illegitimate, along with the fighting they perpetrate. An example of unauthorized war fighting are "national-liberation" fronts of the 1970s and later. They were fully capable of illegitimately initiating conflict, or "local wars," which, in fact, they did perpetrate. Osama bin Laden's "war" against civil society is another example of an authority that is organized as a terrorist gang, but on a global scale.[1]

In modern times the most common large-scale war maker, of course, is the nation-state. In democratic states, it is expected that the electorate and the institutions that represent the public and freely reflect its opinion *in various ways will play a key role in the critiquing of any major policy or activity of the central government*. In America the legislative branch is not only tasked to represent the will of the people. Both the House and the Senate on their own and through such committees as those dealing with the armed forces and intelligence critically investigate the execution of policy, including foreign policy. This power stems in part from the fact that by the Constitution the legislature holds the purse strings for funding any endeavors, including and especially war. In the most recent years as doubts have arisen over the wisdom of the Iraq War, these representative bodies have tended to strengthen their influence on the execution of policy if, lamentably, at times well "after the fact." This, despite the double legislative grants of extraordinary power to President George W. Bush in 2001 and 2002 in the tense, post-9/11 environment.

As to the authority to make war, the War Powers Act of 1973 seemingly strengthened, or at least codified, executive power in initiating or sending U.S. armed forces into war. This law was passed in the wake of several conflicts in which the United States participated in the post-World War II years. These conflicts (such as the Korean and Vietnam Wars) did not entail a formal declaration of war. As if to compensate for this "gap," the 1973 law that President Nixon vetoed but Congress overrode put a time limit on White House dispatch of the armed forces into combat. The law stated that the president must consult with Congress before introducing any U.S. armed forces into combat under conditions in which "imminent involvement in hostilities is clearly indicated." After such involvement the president must "consult regularly" with Congress until the armed forces "are no longer engaged in hostilities or have been removed from situations." Within 60 days, the president must terminate this involvement unless the Congress has passed a declaration of war or by law has extended the 60-day period.

By the 1973 War Powers, the Congress in a sense was thus empowered to "hem in" executive power in the above respects. In recent times, however, several presidents have exploited executive power granted by the law to initiate smaller-scale hostilities, especially "local" armed interventions of the ad hoc, "humanitarian" type—such as in Somalia and Haiti or in Panama and Grenada, the latter in the form of interventions intended to prevent the authoritarian regimes there from threatening their neighbors and, indirectly, the United States.

Despite the appearance of the law's enhancement of presidential power, however, it is also clear, especially in the wake of the costly Iraq War and the errors that President Bush himself admitted have accompanied it, that the legislative branch has seen its power enhanced. Relevant committees in the Congress have been energized in the most recent times to critique more carefully than in the past the use of executive power. The legislators of both political parties, although belatedly, now seem to be newly cognizant of the consequences involved by their too hastily permitting presidential deployment of the country's military forces. Such sensitivity and consensus have lately appeared even in the post-9/11 environment of alarming, color-coded "alerts" and the wars and occupations in Afghanistan and Iraq. At times, this legislative critique can occur close to "real time," as when the Senate Armed Forces Committee on March 1, 2005, called in U.S. commanders to testify on the course of the war in Iraq. Other such hearings held in 2005 and 2006 brought in members of the President's Cabinet and Pentagon officers with functions related to the military. Candid legislative-branch investigation and debate swirled around the administration's execution of the strategy and tactics used in the war as both House and Senate committees queried the officials on many issues relating to foreign and defense policy and execution. There seems little question that these televised hearings, moreover, contributed to public dismay over the war in Iraq.

This, in turn, was reflected in the midterm elections of November 7, 2006, in which the Democrats won both houses of Congress. In early 2007 there was speculation that the Congress might pass, as it were, "a vote of no confidence" in the President's plan for a surge of 21,500 troops into Baghdad. Yet it was acknowledged by observers that given the U.S. presidential system, Congress's only "weapon" against administrative authority in waging the present war in Iraq and the commander-in-chief's constitutional prerogatives is by cutting off war funding.

In light of these off-year election results, the Democrat-controlled Congress might further intervene in executive authority in continuing the Iraq War, namely by cutting off the funding of the war. This congressional "power of the purse" was what finally brought about U.S. withdrawal from the Vietnam War. It is a precedent that could arise again with the war in Iraq. It also possible that a no-confidence vote might create waves of opposition within the public at large against the President

At times a given U.S. congressional inquiry, of which there have been many in recent years, faintly resembles the British Parliament in the sense of the candor and timeliness of the discussion that takes place between the legislators on one side and, on the other, government officials responsible for executive actions. Unlike the parliamentary system, however, the head of government, the U.S. president, is not present in the given Capitol committee room as his policies are examined in the persons of his aides. He thus is not personally subjected to the type of direct questioning that a Prime Minister, such as Tony Blair, undergoes in Westminster. Nor in the American system is there any threat of a president being deposed because the Congress does not support his policies. The president's term is fixed.

In discussing the American political system in the context of the legitimacy of authority, it is necessary to canvass the traditions of that system. In the discussion that follows we focus on how they affect foreign and defense policy. This examination will help explicate this part of *jus ad bellum* that concerns the manner in which a country, the United States in particular, goes to war—that is, legitimately.

Jefferson, Hamilton, Madison, and others of the Founders strongly warned against leaving the decision to send U.S. armed forces into combat solely up to the executive branch or to any single agency of government. Whether a war should be "commenced, continued, or concluded," Madison wrote, is not for the chief executive to decide alone.[2] Vital policy-making and decisions about war and peace must be aired among the people's representatives and ultimately among the people at large. Least of all was it seen by the Founders as the president's exclusive function to initiate war. As commander-in-chief, he is empowered only to "administer" a war once it is "declared" by the people's representatives. (It seems that the Founders would be horrified by the War Powers Act and the growth of an "imperial" presidency in contemporary times.) In later interpretations of the tradition, war is declared or executed only after the Congress and the public have carefully weighed the pros and cons of whether or not to resort to war. As Jefferson wrote, "The people themselves are its [the government's] only safe depository ... I have great confidence in the common sense of mankind ... To introduce the people into every department of government is the only way to insure honest administration."[3] We citizens, as members of that "safe depository," should address the commonsense question: When is it just, legitimate, and necessary to start a war in the name of restoring peace?

Let us recall the major decisions made at the top of the Bush Administration in 2002 and 2003. The five-month run-up to America's and Britain's war against Iraq went through two major opening phases in which the Bush Administration:

- Sought congressional approval for its actions, not through a formal declaration of war but via special, enabling legislation that it won by a large 4-to-1 majority in both Houses.

- Conducted an information campaign that smacked of propaganda. The Administration sought to win allies abroad and public support at home for launching a war against Iraq. It attempted, if halfheartedly and impatiently, to secure agreement within the U.N. Security Council, the key organ of the world organization for undertaking substantive, collective action against an aggressor-nation. Gaining such support would have meant that the war would be fought under the U.N. flag, as the Persian Gulf War (1990–1991) was fought and before that the Korean War (1950–1953). Instead, the Administration opted for a virtual go-it-alone, U.S.-spearheaded war.

PHASE ONE: MAKING IT CONSTITUTIONAL

As it unwound, Phase One went through several stages. First, it was necessary for Congress to freshly empower the President to act in forceful, military ways "against terrorism." The President should be allowed to use authority beyond what he had been granted by Congress in the well-known resolution passed in the immediate, post-9/11 environment. New, post-9/11 legislation gave the President fresh authority to defend America in whatever ways he chose without further, special authorization by Congress. At same time, Congress, as usual, implicitly reserved the right to de-fund (cut off money) to be used for any military purposes.

This novel grant of power to the Chief Executive and Commander-in-Chief in autumn 2001 had gone significantly beyond the former War Powers Resolution of November 1973. By that resolution, the President would have had to get Congressional authority to continue military actions that extended beyond a set period of between 60 and 90 days. (Since then Presidents, whether Democrat or Republican, have tended to refuse to recognize this "resolution" as law and have regarded it as all but unconstitutional.)

It was on the basis of the post-9/11 resolution as well as a more specific one enacted by Congress in mid-October 2002, updating the one of the year before, that Bush was equipped to realize his and his neoconservative team's "proactive" policies. With both resolutions behind him and having "gone through the procedures," President Bush proceeded at full tilt to plan and carry out the war against Iraq.

By mid-2004, the period of the "main hostilities" having (allegedly) passed, protests began to be heard in Congress that these grants of power in 2001–2002 had by no means anticipated waging a major war in the Middle East. Yet once the war was underway, the Congress did not intervene. By the fall of 2004, some senators and congressmen had even apologized to the public for having given the president a "blank check." Some legislators, like Senators Levin and Kennedy, expressed dismay that the Congress had not more carefully examined the questionable intelligence data used by the Administration to justify the war and/or that the administration had not provided complete information to the legislators. More thorough submission and examination of relevant information would have entailed, among other things, a careful review by Congress of President Bush's autumn 2002 address to the United Nations, among other speeches, as well as Secretary of State Colin Powell's alarming reports made to the Security Council in 2002 and 2003.[4]

As to alleged links between Al Qaeda and Iraq, the President said bluntly: "You can't distinguish between Al Qaeda and Saddam when you talk about the war on terrorism. They're both equally as bad and his hatred and capacity to extend weapons of mass destruction around the world."[5] Later he added: "The liberation of Iraq is a crucial advance in the campaign against terror."

Also raised in summer 2004 were serious objections that the Administration, and administrators of the relevant intelligence agencies, had not acknowledged any possible flimsiness of their intelligence data. Yet such flimsiness was available and known to them. It became known later that a number of intelligence officials had in 2002 and 2003 expressed doubts about Iraq's putative possession of WMD. Skepticism within the intelligence community was not made available to legislators. Disregarding such doubters within intelligence agencies, administration officials had reported no incredulity toward the sources of intelligence findings. For instance, ignored was the fact that some of the émigré-Iraqi input had been fabricated—a fact that was known at the time that fallacious émigré information was put into National Intelligence Estimate (NIE) 2002. One such instance of fabrication involved Ahmad Chalabi, leader of the Iraqi National Congress, the principal Iraqi exile group (based in London) that won the confidence of top Administration officials. By 2004, this confidence had been withdrawn as Chalabi's formerly close relations with Administration officials began to sour. Besides Chalabi, there was the infamous Iraqi defector code-named "Curveball," who was also a source of misinformation.

PHASE TWO: MAKING WAR "NECESSARY"

By late 2002, Phase Two of the run-up to war saw the Administration unleashing its information campaign to justify going to war. NIE 2002, submitted to the White House in fall 2002 (parts of which are still classified), claimed that Iraq without doubt had WMD and that it was developing Unmanned Aerial Vehicles (UAV), which "are probably intended to deliver biological warfare agents." CIA Director George Tenet was said to have told Bush that the evidence was "slam dunk."[6]

For example, NIE 2002 insisted that imported aluminum tubing was being used by Iraq in its plans to build a centrifuge to produce fuel for nuclear weapons. Yet the U.S. Energy Department had questioned this assertion, an objection not mentioned by Secretary Powell when he made his case for war to the U.N. Security Council in winter 2002–2003. Moreover, in his State of the Union Address in January 2003 the President claimed—as it turned out, apparently falsely, despite British support for the veracity of the evidence—that yellowcake, used in producing nuclear weapons, was about to be exported from Niger to Iraq. This was proof, he said, that Saddam Hussein was on the way to developing nuclear weapons. Other claims found in NIE 2002 likewise were later disputed.

If Hussein's plans were not nipped in the bud, Bush suggested, the world would be faced with an aggressive Middle East country in possession of nuclear weapons and the means to deliver them.

Controversy soon erupted after the 511-page Senate Intelligence Committee report was issued in summer 2004. Questions were raised inside Congress and the media about an intended second report that would disclose how the erroneous intelligence had been fed to the White House, and possibly how it had been colored by White House influence. Namely, the issue was raised as to whether a follow-up report, which to date still has not been issued, would show that the Administration had put pressure on U.S. intelligence services to "make the case for war."

One of the committee's firm conclusions was that the Congress had been guilty of "groupthink," a herd-like tendency to agree uncritically with what the government had told the House and Senate. According to Senator John D. Rockefeller IV, cochairman of the Senate Intelligence Committee, such intrusive White House influence was present. "I think there was a lot of pressure," he said without providing evidence but perhaps revealing that the committee became aware of such influence. For his part, the Republican Chairman of the Committee, Republican Senator Pat Roberts, Jr., once a staunch supporter of the war against Iraq, said he was "not sure" whether he would have supported the war in the first place had he been aware of the "flimsiness" of the intelligence data that were used to justify it.

Moreover, the committee had found that there was "no evidence proving Iraqi complicity or assistance" in the Al Qaeda attacks of September 11, 2001. This had been a strongly-implied accusation made obliquely against Iraq in Administration statements since 2001. Even so, in the weeks following the report, Vice President Cheney continued to allege that the reasons for going to war remained valid, that Saddam Hussein had close ties to Al Qaeda, that Iraq was in serious violation of U.N. resolutions, and so on.[7]

Above all, the committee was critical of the failure to "accurately or adequately explain the uncertainties" behind the intelligence claims spelled out in NIE 2002. The latter had stated unequivocally that Iraq possessed an ongoing chemical and biological weapons program and that it was renewing its nuclear program. Photographs of alleged "wagons" carrying WMD gear proved later to be utterly false.

On the British side, an analogous report made by a committee within Parliament on July 2004 concerning the Blair Government's insubstantial intelligence turned out to be a much less detailed report than its American counterpart when it was submitted to the MPs. The report found that many errors had been committed by British intelligence. Yet it saw "no reason ... to question the Prime Minister's good faith." There was "no deliberate attempt on the part of the government to mislead," the British report concluded.[8]

Speaking of British intelligence, the Brits later determined (in summer 2004) that Iraq had been "negotiating worldwide" to obtain fissionable material, including yellowcake (*The New York Times,* July 16, 2004, page 10). But no solid evidence for this was offered. "Yellowcakegate" receded into the background, as no solid evidence was produced of Iraq's intention to import nuclear material from Nigeria.

"Part Two" of the Senate Committee's report about whether the President exerted pressure on government intelligence agencies, especially the CIA, to get the "desired" intelligence estimate was not expected to surface until after the November presidential election. (It still has not appeared.)

For his part, Republican Intelligence Committee member Senator. John F. Lehman, former Secretary of the Navy under President Reagan, seemed to speak for many people in his party as well as for independent voters when he complained about the Bush Administration's dissemination of misinformation. "The editorializing," he said, referring to Administration defense of its war policy, "has shrunk and shrunk and shrunk as the facts before us have expanded and expanded and expanded."

Just as the war was getting underway against Iraq, former Clinton National Security Adviser Sandy Berger was invited to give an address to the Harvard Law School (on March 12, 2003). Berger's observations just before the war actually commenced (on March 19, 2003) were both ominous and prescient. "I wonder," he said, "what can be achieved as the result of a confrontation that does not have international support. If we invade Iraq as an American-British enterprise, all of the risks are substantially greater. Even at this eleventh hour, we have the time to do this right with the greatest possible international support. There is a right way and a wrong way to confront Iraq, and I believe we have the time to do it in the right way."

Finally, Berger addressed the problems that would face the coalition occupiers in postwar Iraq. The United States and its partners, he said, would encounter "many problems" that will arise as hostilities officially end. "Think [of the war] as the Saddam phase and post-Saddam phase," he said. In the latter phase, which, he said, could last a decade, he warned, the United States would face difficulties in preserving Iraq's territorial integrity. He spoke further of the likelihood of civil war, of issues arising between the Kurds in the north and Turkey. (This latter warning turned out to be, it seemed, only partially valid. Yet as the Iraqi nation settles into its new constitutional order, it remains to be seen how well the ethnic groups work together. There are already signs of serious regional dissension.) The country, he continued, is extremely disunited and rife with Shiite and Sunni rivalries. America would have to face, he predicted presciently, the coming "harsh realities" of governing Iraq.

This latter prediction turned out to be on target. Reconstruction and nation-building that candidate George W. Bush in 2000 said, ironically, was not America's calling, had by late 2004 turned into a slow, agonizing process. The $18.4 billion approved by Congress in fall 2003 had barely been used. Less than 5 percent had been applied to rebuilding that country. Iraqi oil production, which was supposed to pay for much of the reconstruction costs borne by the United States, was not up to prewar levels. Production often fell well below them largely because of insurgent sabotage and a lack of security, with the result that only a fraction of Iraq's oil is being exploited as a source of national income. Oil production in Iraq by mid-2006 was well below pre-Iraq War levels.

Meanwhile, Iraq continued to suffer from a wide range of shortages through 2006. Revenue from the export of oil still lagged behind levels attained under Saddam Hussein. Water and electricity are supplied to the populace only sporadically, which has a predictably negative effect on public morale; it and other, similar problems increased public Iraqi animosity toward the occupation. To begin with, foreign civilian contractors, critics note, were not the best postwar reconstructors. They found themselves in an unfamiliar and insecure land. Years late in being applied, reconstruction funding still flounders while Iraq writhes in dissatisfaction, which in turn contributed to Iraqis' generally negative attitude toward the country's "occupiers." Such blundering was costly and was obviously not anticipated by the Administration's civilian war-makers.

Berger concluded his remarks with this cogent observation: "We have learned the dangers of going to war when the people don't have their eyes wide open. We have been alienating our friends rather than isolating our enemies."

The Administration's invasion of Afghanistan in 2001 and the ongoing occupation of that country up to the present by NATO forces, including U.S. troops, is sometimes contrasted with the war in Iraq. The former invasion, it is said, was legitimate since Al Qaeda and its leader, Osama bin Laden, were based there. In order to rid Afghanistan of the Qaeda presence, it was necessary to eliminate the Taliban regime in Kabul that gave sanctuary to these terrorists while engaging in domestic terrorism against the Afghan population. We need to examine the Afghanistan War and occupation in order to distinguish this war from that waged against Iraq.

Immediately after 9/11, it was discovered that Afghanistan's Taliban rulers were harboring Al Qaeda and its leaders. The suspicion that Al Qaeda and bin Laden were based in that country had already been suspected during the tenure of the preceding Clinton Administration. The latter had attempted, with rocket fire, to exterminate Qaeda camps located in Afghanistan. Now with the help of the British and Australians, and indirectly even the Russians, President Bush in late 2001 made a bold decision. He ordered the invasion and occupation of that sovereign Southwest Asian country and was able to convince several regimes in Central Asia abutting Afghanistan to the north (member states of the former USSR) to allow the United States Air Force to use their air bases.

On that occasion most of the world's nations, including the Five Permanent Members of the U.N. Security Council and America's NATO allies, largely endorsed the war. They agreed, if somewhat reluctantly, that given 9/11 and Al Qaeda's explicit involvement in the attacks on that day, a preemptive invasion to get at the nest of the terrorist gang had largely been justified. By then, too, the Bush Administration was already preparing a critical extension of preemption policy in the form of its National Security Strategy, or "NSS," to Iraq.

However, unlike the case presented by Afghanistan as an overt nest of Al Qaedists and with a regime that gave the terrorists a base, Iraq, as we saw, was a different case altogether. Almost exactly one year after 9/11, this new strategy, whose principle of preemption was virtually unprecedented in the history of overt U.S. military strategy, was formulated in NSS 2002 and issued from the White House on September 17, 2002. (See Appendix A). It instituted a doctrine that permitted the United States to wage *preemptive war* when deemed necessary. Instead of "waiting to be attacked," America would strike first at any enemy nation that it perceived to be an imminent threat. "We must adapt the concept of imminent threat to the capabilities and objectives of today's adversaries," read the new doctrine. "The United States has long maintained the option of preemptive actions to counter a sufficient threat to our national security."

A few months later, as the occupation of Afghanistan was settling into place, the Administration employed its preemptive-strike-first/ask-questions-later strategy once again. The Administration ordered the invasion of Iraq. It thus occupied a second sovereign country, Iraq having been targeted by the Administration in the President's State of the Union address in January 2002. It was deemed as one of the three states composing a threatening "axis of evil."

Unlike the war against Afghanistan, this second, preemptive war against Iraq was disowned and repudiated by several of our major allies in Europe. Nor was it supported by a majority of the 15-member United Nations Security Council or by three of the veto-wielding Five Permanent Members (P-5) of that body (i.e., Russia, China, and France). Only the United States and United Kingdom spearheaded it. The P-5 governments' non-endorsement of the preemptive invasion helped lend a quality of illegitimacy to the war against Iraq.

Particularly noteworthy were the Administration's tactics in relation to the U.N. Security Council. Instead of supporting an "enabling" decision by the Council, based on unanimity among P-5 to undertake substantively (by the U.N. Charter) the sanctions referenced in Resolution 1441, as requested by France and Germany, the United States acted outside the Council's framework. It did this after sounding out policy positions among

Council members, and especially within the P-5. After this sounding-out among Council delegations, Washington found that it lacked support for adopting near-term military measures against Iraq.

This lack of support for war not only arose within the P-5. It appeared that a majority of the Council's total 15 members likewise would not support such a war, at least not without an additional, supportive vote in the Council. Nor, just as significantly, did world public opinion endorse this "proactive" policy. On the contrary, anti-U.S. feeling spread like a tidal wave across the globe, with the superpower United States being depicted as a world-dominator.

For their part, the Bush Administration and defenders of the preemptive war against Iraq (which included some leading Democrats along with a majority of Republicans, who in turn were backed by a majority of the public, as shown in opinion polls at that time) claimed that, as with Afghanistan, Saddam Hussein's regime in Baghdad seriously imperiled America's post-9/11 security. White House spokespersons actually used the word "imminent" to describe the Iraqi threat. Bush himself and members of his Cabinet came very close to using that term. However, Bush had seemingly deliberately refrained from using "imminent," thus leaving it to press officers to exaggerate by describing the threat in the most alarming ways (Chapter 2 presents the specifics).

Based on what it was told by the executive branch, and with the legislators rushing to judgment in support of war with a 75-to-25 vote in the U.S. Senate, the whole legislative branch and most, but not all, of the media's editorialists gave the Administration virtual *carte blanche* to wage war and to wage it whenever it chose to, thus superceding the limitations stated in the 1973 War Powers law. The timing to strike at Iraq was put on the front burner since by summer 2003 the oppressive, semi-tropical climate of Iraq would have hobbled the U.S-led war. Thus, the war "had to be" launched by March, as it, in fact, was.

Soon, however, most of the Administration's arguments about Iraq's alleged "growing threat," as the President called it, fell apart. Iraq's purported collaboration with Al Qaeda, if not in its 9/11 operation per se; its supposed concealed WMD (nuclear, biological and chemical); its presumed, continued wholesale violations of U.N. resolutions, plus other alleged evidence that Iraq was a clear and present danger to U.S. security all turned out to be false assumptions. One piece of detailed evidence after another was eventually discovered to be false or deliberately falsified by alleged trustworthy informants. This evidence included the Iraqis' alleged mobile killer labs; their "tons" of stored chemical weapons; their alleged development of unmanned aerial vehicles (UAV) to deliver chemical or biological weapons (CBW); Iraq's imports of aluminum tubing allegedly to be used in atomic-reactor centrifuges, used ultimately in making of nuclear weapons; and Iraq's alleged attempts to obtain uranium ore and yellowcake from abroad (i.e., from Nigeria).

This and other information the CIA, the President, and Vice President accepted virtually uncritically, as outlined in National Intelligence Estimate (NIE) reports. As it turned out, some of the most crucial evidence originated with Iraqi defectors, like Dr. Ahmad Chalabi, a member of the original ruling troika of the interim, post-Saddam regime. Some of these informants later confessed to fabricating the so-called evidence. However, the fact that they did falsify the information was not reported to legislators. The same fallacious information was shared with the United Nations Security Council in Colin Powell's speech of February 5, 2003, which in September 2005 he described as a "blot" on his record.[9]

The final nail was driven into the coffin of specious arguments made for war in the U.S. Senate Intelligence Committee's 511-page report of July 9, 2004. The administration's preemptive war against that country was seen retrospectively as tantamount to having been unjustified. This was not only because the evidence turned out to be flimsy and exaggerated, but also because the war had looked illegitimate to the committee on the well-established grounds of international law, the U.N. Charter, and the traditional norms for waging legal, morally just *defensive* war.

In autumn 2005 it became an opinion widely shared among Republicans and Democrats in the U.S. Senate that intelligence on Iraq had been shared by the Administration only partially, in "filtered" form. Thus, Senators were as unaware of the fragility of the intelligence as qualified CIA analysts themselves. The implication was that the White House had winnowed out any doubts expressed within the CIA about the data it had on Iraq and its alleged possession of WMD. The relevant House and Senate committees dealing with intelligence and the armed forces were thus deliberately deprived of the complete picture. Had they been informed of the doubtful nature of some of the intelligence submitted to them by the White House, the committees might well have been less supportive of the war.

Besides stating these unsupported reasons for going to war, the Administration subsequently bolstered its case for using preemptive war against Iraq—almost as an afterthought—by shifting the emphasis from Iraq's alleged military threat to the United States to America's liberation of that country from the tyranny of Saddam Hussein. This became part of the Administration's nation-building plan to entirely make over that California-sized nation of Kurds, Sunnis, and Shiites into a democracy. The American-led coalition, it then said, had freed the oppressed Iraqi people from the brutal Baathist dictatorship of Saddam Hussein. Indeed, some of the American public's initial support for the war was based on this very mission of bringing freedom to that country.

Yet it was Iraq's threat to our security, its alleged links to Al Qaeda, and its possession of WMD that were uppermost among the reasons for waging war against Iraq. This is seen in the polls' ranking of the reasons for going to war, as shown in at least one public-opinion poll taken in 2003. The lofty purpose of liberation, it was now claimed, made America's preemptive war, called "Operation Iraqi Freedom," as equally just and moral as "Operation Enduring Freedom" had been against Taliban-ruled Afghanistan. As in that war, noble ends were said to justify violent means.

CRUSADE FOR DEMOCRATIZATION

The administration made a further claim. By its liberating war and the prospective democratization of Iraq that was to follow, Operation Iraqi Freedom would inevitably usher in a process of making over the entire Middle East in the democratic image. Once established in Iraq, democratic dominoes could be erected and start falling serially all across the Middle East. Ultimately, Israel would no longer be the only democratic state in the region. As President Bush put it in a dinner speech in February 2003, "A liberated Iraq can show the power of freedom to transform that vital region, by bringing hope and progress into the lives of millions."

This belated shift in rearranging and prioritizing war aims as justification for resorting to war also strained the criterion of legitimacy. After all, the nation's political institutions, media, and public opinion had been led to believe that the invasion had been principally motivated by the "war against terror" if not also Saddam's links to Al Qaeda and 9/11.

This was buttressed not simply by the fact alone that Iraq had a tyrannical regime. Had the prime motivation for sending America's armed forces into harm's way been illiberal regimes, several other of the world's unfree countries that are ruled by self-perpetuating authoritarian regimes and oligarchies—making up at least one-fifth to one-third of the world's governments—would have legitimately qualified as targets for "liberation." Among such regimes are those of Middle Eastern and littoral Gulf (or "Gulfie") states that are considered to be among America's allies and/or are recipients of billions of dollars in annual foreign aid. These include such Middle East countries as Egypt, Jordan, and Saudi Arabia.

It is doubtful, however, that the relevant committees in the House and Senate would have supported the war had they known that the prime motivation would become some war-exported form of nation-rebuilding. This was a policy, after all, that George W. Bush himself had disowned in his presidential campaign speeches in 2000.[10] The same is true of public opinion, which in fact began to decline from its previous support of the war to less than a majority. This change evidently came about once the people had become aware of the faulty intelligence and the errors committed in occupying Iraq. When the doubt sank in, it also reduced the President's standing among the people, as some polls showed a drop of some 25 points, or at one of the lowest levels seen for any president in his second term in office.[11]

What was overlooked in the administration claim of the war's aim of democratizing the Middle East was that this extravagant goal would scarcely be acceptable to the sheikdoms and ruling establishments, even to the peoples, in that oil-rich region. The Muslim populations give little evidence that they are eager—or prepared—for democracy. Indeed, some observers in these countries are all too aware of the threat represented by internal Muslim radicals, who seek to unleash violence in their societies or establish fundamentalist principles in their domestic and foreign policy. The terrorist threat to these societies' established order was and is real and ominous enough, as ongoing terrorist attacks in the Middle East show. Destabilizing these societies further with appeals for radical democratization (by their standards) would be dangerous and intolerable. Such rousing calls for deep political reform could well prove to be disastrously counterproductive. They could lead to chaos and a power vacuum that in turn would open the way to radical Islamism.

Moreover, in the politics of the region to date there have been no indications that the possibility of some sort of democratic rule in Iraq would unleash democratic reform in those countries. The two elections in Iraq—in January and autumn 2005—came and went with no rippling effect seen in the other states. Instead, Egypt, for instance, saw the reelection of President Hosni Mubarak to a fifth term while the leading opposition candidate, Ayman Nour, was jailed just after the election on what appeared to be trumped up charges. Other Middle East regimes limited political freedoms and perpetuated themselves in power.[12]

Thus, by late 2004 and throughout 2005 and 2006, many nonpartisan people and independent voters in the United States began to rethink what America had been doing in following the preemptive road map of NSS 2002 for the past two years. This was one of the reasons, apparently, why the White House itself decided to issue a revised, moderated strategy in 2005. Omitted in the new formulation, moreover, was any reference to preemptive war given the mounting casualties and loss of the life on the American side alone and expenditures rising to upwards of $350, or $250 million per **day**.[13]

This is a price tag that will far surpass that of the nearly decade-long Vietnam War. Add to this the negative fallout and worsening of tensions amidst growing militant Islamism worldwide, all of which were factors that worked to raise doubts in the minds of the American public about the wisdom of the government's war policy. It seemed to dawn on the public that the war and what has accompanied it had become a specter of unjustness and illegitimacy. People began to ask whether the war was worth it. As to realizing the ambitious purpose of liberating and democratizing Iraq as well as any other Middle Eastern country, that goal lay at best far into the distant future. Radically changing the way of life in a dozen or more Muslim countries and the way they have governed over a billion citizens for centuries was a fantastic stretch.

In addition, unresolved issues arose by 2005–2006 from a flawed constitution that included the lack of proportionate representation of the Sunni population in the political and economic spheres. Sunnis make up a good quarter of the population but as a group are generally not located near Iraq's main oil installations and thus do not have the economic clout of the Shiites and Kurds, who are so located.

Finally, there was simply no way of predicting which way a postwar Iraqi government would turn in its foreign policy in the years ahead. The unpopularity of the prolonged U.S. occupation of the country certainly could not be expected to result in the adoption of a pro-U.S. policy by any new, independent government in Baghdad.

Moreover, the attempt to extend the meaning of just war to include liberation clashes with the recent history of the processes of democratization seen, for instance, in former Communist-ruled eastern Europe and Russia since 1991. This experience seems to show that to be authentic and viable, democratic reform must be homegrown, not mechanically imported from the outside, if indeed it is realizable at all in some polities. A number of ex-Soviet republics, after all, had a democratic past, albeit of short duration (e.g., in the case of Georgia in the Caucasus). Nevertheless, even for them the transition has been bumpy with unpredictable consequences, as has been observed, for instance, in Ukraine, and, of course, in Byelorussia. Other ex-Soviet republics as well—in Central Asia in the cases of Uzbekistan and Tadzhikistan—simply adopted a new form of autocracy, a system that was very different from their becoming genuine democratic polities. By analogy, it would not be at all surprising to see Iraq itself revert to some new form of authoritarianism once the coalition's occupation ultimately ends.

In conclusion, a just war by the criteria subsumed under *jus ad bellum* must strictly adhere to the principle of legitimacy as to the way the "authority" adopted and executed its war policy. Because the Administration's intelligence policy had been so critically flawed and because the nation's representative governmental institutions, let alone mass communications, were not given the complete picture of Iraq's alleged threat, the war lacked a full measure of that particular criterion for just war. The issues of whether or not to go war were simply not fully aired. This is hardly a tribute to ideas and principles upon which American popular government is based.

Former Secretary of State Colin Powell's own remorseful consternation over having delivered his misleading speech to the U.N. Security Council on the eve of war is symptomatic and telling evidence itself that illustrates the illegitimacy of the methods employed by the Administration in going to war. For here was one of its leading officials, himself former Chairman of the Joint Chiefs of Staff during the Persian Gulf War, being misled, perhaps hoodwinked by his own colleagues. This, in turn, raises questions concerning the "loop" that develops around the Chief Executive. It raises suspicions of the way certain top officials will be left out of the consultation, especially if they disagree with policies that are made by a small coterie of officials in the White House. This, in turn, reduces the number of counselors that a president needs for well-rounded input in making policy or devising national strategy. This, in turn, detracts from the factor of legitimate authority in adopting a war policy and going to war.

It would appear that this is not what our Founders had in mind when they designed a republic-type government in which the will of the people and its representatives would be consulted and brought into the political process—especially in matters of life and death.

5

Feasibility Criterion and the Iraq War

A crucial touchstone under *jus ad bellum* relates to whether success in waging a given war is feasible. The reasoning within a moral context is based on the traditional rule that soldiers should not be placed in harm's way if there is little or no chance of their achieving victory, and if the risks are too great. Don Quixote may tilt at windmills, but no government— certainly no democratically elected one—should treat its fighting men and women like cannon fodder by sending them out on unrealizable military missions.

What this criterion of feasible success in just war must be based upon is a careful *assessment of the risk* that war planners must conduct lest they opt for an immoral choice of going to war with little chance of success. The authorities' reason for making this assessment is not only to avoid taking undue risks in the purely military sense. It is also motivated by the necessity to assure the people that its citizens, civilian and military, will not be forced into making a needless sacrifice of life in a hopeless situation in which victory for the war-making side seems either remote or ultimately unrealizable.

In the thirteenth century, Thomas Aquinas considered a war to be unjust if it was unduly "inordinate and perilous" for the combatants.[1] Michael Walzer writes that war planners must "weigh the importance of their target against the importance of their soldiers' lives."[2] Along with the moral considerations in making the risk assessment, a number of strictly military factors must also be weighed that, in turn, are of moral significance:

- Is the likelihood of victory diminished by certain basic advantages accruing to the enemy side: whether geographic (e.g., the area of the country, its topography, and climate); the relative amount of its manpower and depth of military reserves; its comparative military-industrial potential; its morale, whether strong or fragile; and the enemy's capacity to endure longer than the protagonist over a long period of time (by virtue of its economy, military power, fighting spirit, etc.)?

- Is the "end-game" (ultimate victory) clearly discernible, even given what Clausewitz called the inevitable "fog of war," so that the attacker can avoid protracted war and occupation—that is, a virtual, debilitating war of attrition with no discernible victory in the end?

- In the final phase of occupation of the targeted country, is there a danger of forfeiting victory following a successful initial phase? Will extreme disorder encountered in the occupation lead to failure to consolidate Iraqi rule and secure victory?

- Is there a danger of collapsing support for the war on the war-maker's home front? In a democracy such a collapse is always possible. It is, after all, the people's representatives in the legislature who disburse the funds to keep the war going; this decision ultimately depends upon popular support.

For its part, the American public's patience with prolonged war is notoriously short. For instance, by the second year of the Korean War (1950–1953), there were serious doubts expressed in Congress and in public opinion polls about the U.S.-led war on the Korean Peninsula. This disaffection was striking when it is considered how obviously just that war seemed to be when measured against *jus ad bellum* standards.[3] Moreover, the war against North Korea and its allies was endorsed by the United Nations and fought under its banner. It seems to indicate that there should be no doubts within the population about the justness or its ability to win a war. This is especially true of a war that did not have the obviously defensive, moral character of, say, World War II, a war that sought to eliminate the dire, tangible threat that the Axis and the Japanese clearly represented to American security. Without this urgency and clear and present danger, the possibility of popular disaffection with the government's war policy might arise. The consequences of this are obvious: a cut-and-run retreat, humiliation, and loss of prestige for the nation. For a superpower whose military strength and resolve also act as a deterrent to war, such a retreat would send a highly undesirable signal to potential enemies.

The gist of all of the above points can be summarized as follows: If the foregoing factors in assessing the risks of war are judged to be too great, then war must by all means be avoided, at least in a situation where an alternate, nonmilitary choice is possible. Obviously, a state that has been subjected to an Operation Barbarossa or a Pearl Harbor surprise attack has no choice but to pick up the gauntlet and fight no matter what the odds of victory may be. But where the choice exists because the necessity for going to war is not pressing—and in March 2003 Iraq did not represent a dire threat—the above risk assessment may dictate a more cautious, risk-free, nonmilitary course as the preferred way to deal with the situation. This policy would be considered moral as opposed to the unacceptable choice of a risky war and occupation. Additionally, the nonmilitary decision answers the touchstone in *jus ad bellum* of deciding on war only as a last resort and only after other feasible options have been exhausted.

RISKING A WAR AGAINST IRAQ

In the immediate pre-Iraq War years it was generally assumed that the United States could easily defeat Iraq in an invasion just as it had in the Persian Gulf War of 1991. Back then there were some doubters about what they perceived as risk-taking in launching a ground war against Iraq. The then Chief of the General Staff Colin Powell was reputed to have been among them.[4] He had supported the air war in Operation Desert Shield but was said to have opposed a ground war. This fear was expressed among conservatives like Pat Buchanan and among liberals like Senator Ted Kennedy.

By contrast, the doubters of the wisdom of waging war against Iraq in 2003 are of a different cast of mind. For one thing, among them are many who are experienced senior military officers. These include such officers as General Eric K. Shinseki, former Commander, Allied Land Forces Central Europe; Commander, NATO Stabilization Force in Bosnia-Herzegovina; Admiral William J. Crowe Jr., chairman of the Joint Chiefs of Staff, 1985–1989; Chief of Staff, United States Army, 1999–2003; General Anthony Zinni, USMC (Ret.), former commander of the Central Command, 1997–2000; General H. Norman Schwarzkopf, former chief of CENTCOM and Commander in Chief of the Central Command during the Persian Gulf War against Iraq, 1990–1991; General Wesley K. Clark, former commander of NATO, 1997–2000; Admiral Stansfield Turner, former Director of the Central Intelligence Agency, 1977–1981; General Merrill A. McPeak, former chief of staff, Air Force, 1990–1994; and Thomas E. White, Secretary of the Army, 2001–2003, who was fired by Defense Secretary Donald Rumsfeld in April 2003.

Few such critics of the second war against Iraq could be found who doubted the capability of the U.S. armed forces to subdue Iraq in the *invasion phase*. Moreover, there are specialists in military affairs, among them senior officers in the Pentagon and the Joint Chiefs of Staff—as well as among civilians in the CIA and qualified civilian observers outside government—who expressed serious doubt about the wisdom of assuming the risks of waging war and occupying Iraq. For the most part their hesitancy applied to the occupation of Iraq, a country with an area as large as California's.

CRITICISM BY MILITARY SPECIALISTS

The objections raised among qualified critics, especially those who were among military officers, concerned the number of forces that would be needed to invade and, above all, to occupy the country. These officials cautioned against a force that would be too small to subdue what they expected would be a prolonged period of chaos in the multi-ethnic, tribal Iraqi population.[5]

They also sensed that invasion and occupation might lead to the rise of homegrown or the intrusion of foreign criminal and hostile elements into a destabilized Iraq. Such armed intruders would be able to penetrate any thinly guarded Iraqi borders (such as those facing Iran to the east and Syria to the west). This, in turn, meant that a robust occupation force, perhaps numbering 200,000 troops or more, would be the best insurance against such penetration and the rise of eventual insurgency directed at the U.S.-led coalition occupiers and the post-Saddam provisional government. If such insurgents employed the guerrilla tactics of 4GW, which critics expected, the occupation regime, no matter how ubiquitous, would be even further challenged by gunfire and bombs unleashed by insurgents fighting guerrilla-style. This, in turn, might incur the additional risk of spreading violence and even civil war.[6]

A totally unexpected factor (by the administration war planners) was the injection of Al Qaeda elements into Iraq. This came to pass when Abu Musab al-Zarqawi joined his forces inside Iraq to the terrorist mission of Qaeda. The Jordanian Zarqawi had not been an Al Qaedist until he wrote a letter to bin Laden in which he advocated fomenting civil war in Iraq.[7] This meant that the anti–coalition insurgency operating in Iraq would be augmented by Zarqawi's thousands of armed terrorists, an unknown number of whom are not native Iraqis. Native Iraqi insurgents are composed of disaffected Sunnis, armed militias whether Shiite or Sunni, and outright native-Iraqi criminals who profit from arms sales to the insurgents. Rampant unemployment in the country, estimated at over one-third of the population, also encourages segments of the native populace to resort to crime.

WARNINGS ABOUT OCCUPATION

Few doubted in 2002 or 2003 that a U.S.-led invasion of a militarily-weak Iraq would encounter any great difficulties for the world's best-armed state, the lone "superpower." Nevertheless, warnings were sounded in high places in the United States about the *occupation* of a country with an area of 169,000 square miles with built-in ethnic, religious, tribal, and territorial divisions and rivalries. In February 2003, Army Chief of Staff General Eric Shinseki informed the Senate Armed Services Committee that a successful coalition occupation of Iraq would require "something on the order of

several hundred thousand soldiers."[8] According to Army Secretary Thomas
E. White, Deputy Defense Secretary Paul Wolfowitz responded to General
Shinseki's statement with a rebuke: "[Wolfowitz] was agitated that we in
the Army didn't get it. He did not give arguments or reasons. Their view
was almost ideological in nature—that it was going the way they said it
was going to go."[9] A few days later Wolfowitz himself appeared before the
committee. He described Shinseki's estimate of the required number of
occupation forces as "wildly off the mark."[10]

BREWING OCCUPATION CRISIS

In terms of the criterion of predictable success and the dispute over the
required troop levels for the occupation, the mistakenly unanticipated factor
of unduly straining American troop reserves is a recurring concern. The
deployment of reservists in Iraq since March 2003 has meant excessive rotation of military personnel to the region. A consequence of this is the danger
of lowering troop morale. Declining recruitment levels saw a minor turn-
around by 2005 but remains a problem. The Pentagon seemed to be caught
in a crunch with respect to current demands on manpower, especially if the
need for additional troops arose in Iraq (and Afghanistan). Just as important
is the strain the occupation and its unforeseen contingencies have placed on
the U.S. armed forces during the three years of occupation, with uncertainty
with respect to the situation in Iraq continuing into 2007.

By mid-2006, some 141,000 U.S. forces were deployed in the Iraq War.
The debate over what this means in terms of stretching overall U.S. troop
strength in the face of possibly other crises is intensifying. A subtext of this
discussion raises the issue of the administration's risky, initial underestimation of the requirements for occupying Iraq and for securing victory. This,
in turn, raises the moral issue of taking undue chances and failing to foresee
the consequences of the invasion and occupation. It overlooked the possibility, even likelihood (as some qualified observers and some in professional
military anticipated—but who resigned their posts under the Bush or were
fired) that the occupation would fail without a much larger commitment of
occupying forces than the administration was prepared to make. Yet officials in the Pentagon continued to claim that a manpower crunch in this
respect was not imminent. They responded that reorganization of the
Army's existing combat units into strong, fast, and more flexible brigades
would have the same effect as adding more soldiers.[11] This opinion was
disputed, for example, by former Assistant Secretary of Defense for
manpower and reserve affairs under President Reagan, Lawrence Korb.
"We cannot fight a long, sustained war without a larger ground force,"
he said.[12]

As to the factor of troop rotation, observers have been warning for years
that in maintaining an all-volunteer army, there are limits to the demands

that can be legitimately made on the soldiers and their families. There is the risk among the troops of exhaustion and demoralization, especially as the tour of duty extends beyond a year, as it has for so many active reservists. In order to sustain one active brigade of about 3,500 troops in Iraq, one or two additional brigades must be ready to replace it. As a result, the tours of duty in Iraq by these reservists were often extended, much to the dismay of their families and loved ones. The Congressional Budget Office has estimated that the military could not sustain more than 123,000 troops in Iraq for much longer.[13] Additional forces, it said, would require an increase in the size of nation's entire land forces. This would entail terminating other U.S. troop commitments abroad while stepping up the already strained rotation process. As Korb commented, "There isn't much more leeway for simply moving people around," and could the troops be adequately equipped?[14]

Adding more land forces in a "surge" (see Endnote 9) presents many problems. A RAND Corporation study has found that historical data on post-invasion occupation forces show that occupation levels must soar to at least 2 percent of the occupied country's population. Using this percentile in application to Iraq and its population of 25 million, occupation forces would require 500,000 troops. (U.S. plus coalition forces averaged about 160,000.) Could a force as large as a half-million troops, based on our volunteer system, have ever been mobilized for duty in Iraq absent universal conscription? According to Pennsylvania Congressman John Murtha, who said he had consulted the military on this point, such levels could not realistically have been deployed and sustained, especially not for two or three years after the invasion phase. Nor could the United States have expected more multilateral contributions in personnel on the part of other members of the now shrinking coalition for the purpose of establishing order in Iraq.

Former allies began pulling their forces out of the coalition. By 2009, the British had withdrawn all of their combat troops. In the meantime, both recruitment and retention rates in the armed forces were declining or barely maintaining the minimum necessary. Nor did there seem to be signs of a major upturn on the horizon, which could put the armed forces into a bind unless there can be a sizable reduction in the occupation forces in Iraq, which appears to be doubtful. Early in 2006, Secretary of Defense Rumsfeld and other officials had spoken of possible troop reductions in the war zone, but in only small amounts. These reductions, had they occurred, could not have been sizable enough to relieve the mounting pressure on U.S. military manpower that began to build in 2005 and 2006. Increasing challenges to the troops because of sectarian violence, or civil war, together with calls (e.g., by Senator John McCain) for increased numbers of troops became evident by late 2006. This was when insurgent attacks (especially suicide bombings) were taking unprecedentedly high monthly tolls in lives among military and civilian personnel in Iraq as well as among the Iraqi population (see Endnote 9).

So what seemed to lie ahead? Conscription, a draft? This appeared to be an option if the situation worsened in Iraq. Issues arose over maintaining and extending U.S. soldiers' military commitments abroad in the fight against terrorism and as servicemen doing "nation-building." Recall that candidate Bush had once disowned this type of mission in his campaign for president in 2000. Concern also arose over the "thinning" of our forces as new threats to security kept arising. Moreover, continuance of the crusade to spread democracy worldwide and fleshing this out with interventions sparked controversy. Some argued that far from encouraging democracy, the opposite had occurred in a number of countries in the region.

To accomplish all of the above, of course, would not only require the deployments of additional U.S. forces but would also put a strain on the ongoing fight against the Taliban in Afghanistan. It would also imply winning over additional allies. This, in turn, would mean a U.S. commitment to multilateralism in foreign and defense policy in place of the virtual go-it-alone strategy. Yet such a change was not central to the Bush Administration's agenda. Instead, its go-it-alone posture meant sidetracking the U.N. Security Council and ignoring input on policy from most of the major European powers. Yet the United States, notably, had once depended on such allies in the NATO military operations conducted in Bosnia and Kosovo in the mid-1990s. Since 2003, the administration has favored American unilateralism in defense policy, even if during the second year of the Bush second term (2006), this policy appeared to some extent to have been modified. Until recently, the Bush policy has tended to isolate the United States in the world community, if not help stimulate hostility in Muslim countries. This played into the hands of Al Qaeda and jihadist extremists. The Al Qaeda manual actually speaks of using the Qaeda tactic of dividing the antiterrorist allies.

Newly-elected President Barack Obama seemed determined to reverse the previous course. He indicated a willingness to work more closely and openmindedly with allies.

A serious moral issue arises in this context. If America intends to continue to ignore world opinion or defy the governments that make up the Security Council on matters touching their security as well as America's, the United States will find itself further isolated and vulnerable to charges of being a "world dominating" superpower. This could impinge on America's ability to close ranks with allies in meeting future crises throughout the world. Such isolation might well again put inordinate demands on the military in ways that would strain its capability to meet them—unless it resorted to a draft —and thereby endanger its success in fighting wars.

To paraphrase the poet John Donne, no state in today's world is an "island." Today's trend worldwide, in fact, is toward more and more interdependence and globalization. An isolationist trend in American policy or among the public, which is already detectable, is reactionary, counterproductive, and dangerous. It cannot be in America's national interests—or in defense of moral principle of fighting wars in which success is all but guaranteed—for the United States to allow its current unilateralist drift to continue.

There is a second dangerous side to the drift that concerns the common fight against terrorism and the moral fiber that maintains it. Without a solid, allied commitment on the part of the major powers to cooperate in the common struggle, the antiterrorist struggle will suffer and the bloodshed shall increase. All antiterrorist forces, meaning above all the governments whose societies are most threatened by terrorism, can succeed only if they are united among themselves. The war in Iraq took an unwelcome toll on American prestige and the world's respect for America. In the long run, this decline in America's standing becomes a liability for national security since an unfriendly attitude on a global scale is hardly helpful to any positive role to be played in the future as the world's leading military power and to its influence in international affairs.

Moreover, officials and spokespersons within the Bush Administration have not helped dampen down inimical opinion abroad. They have bitterly criticized or mocked the opinions that are held abroad. Defense Secretary Rumsfeld himself made an invidious comparison between what he called the "old" and "new" Europe.[15] By "old" Rumsfeld was alluding to western European recalcitrance over the U.S.-led war in Iraq. By "new" Europe he referred to the newly-established, postwar eastern and central European states that were former Soviet "satellites" and which had lent modest numbers of forces to the war coalition. Ironically, in both the geological and political senses, the "old" Europe to which Rumsfeld referred is actually "newer" historically than Eastern Europe The latter in civilized times, Before the Common Era, has a longer, richer history in the economic, political, and military sense than its counterpart to the west.[16]

The day after the midterm election in November 2006, Secretary Rumsfeld resigned. There followed speculation that the newly-appointed Secretary of Defense Robert Gates would be beholden to the findings of the Baker-Hamilton commission. The latter was expected to provide advice to the Administration on its conduct of the war in Iraq and the possibility of a near-term withdrawal of forces, or at least a sizable reduction in their numbers in Iraq.

PART III

Jus in Bello and the Iraq War

6

Fatal Mistakes Made in the Iraq War

When weighing the justness of the way a war is fought by the criterion of "just conduct in war," reference is made to the means used in waging it.[1] Here the criteria for *jus in bello* traditionally include lowering as much as possible the overall destructiveness of the warfare so as to avoid "needless damage" (known as the "proportionality principle") and protecting civilians' immunity from the military combat so that they are not deliberately targeted by enemy forces.[2] Prewar planning under the principles of *jus ad bellum* is also relevant because such planning affects the actual conduct of the war.

In the case of the Iraq War, this criterion arises: Did faulty planning and execution of the war cause casualties among the belligerents and the civilian victims that could have been avoided? Keeping in mind the unpredictable contingencies that arise in any war, American tactics in the Iraq War were accompanied by a number of avoidable mistakes and miscalculations that invited and led to dire results.

Primary and secondary literature on *jus ad bellum* and *jus in bello* has cited the ancient principle of limiting the scope and duration of warfare and restoring peace as quickly as possible. These are basic principles of *jus in bello*. It appears, however, that past discussion of war under just versus unjust war has not *systematically* considered *war planning and execution* as a function of just conduct in war.

However, several contemporary authors and military and civilian specialists, some with combat command experience in the Iraq War itself, have shown how the Bush Administration and the Defense Department miscalculated as it planned the invasion and occupation of Iraq. One of the most egregious errors was the Administration's underestimation of the number of forces that would be required in the invasion and especially in the occupation phase in Iraq, as we canvassed in a previous chapter.[3] Not only were mistakes made as to the number of forces required, but also the means used in terms of the choice of tactics and weaponry *in bello* seemed often not to meet the actual requirements on the ground in Iraq. In fighting the terrorist insurgents, for instance, neither high-precision bombing nor in-and-out raids against nests of insurgents around Baghdad or in the western provinces in 2005–2006 were capable of measuring up to the new demands of waging latter-day *counterinsurgency* warfare. (Unfortunately, the same is true in Afghanistan where "collateral" Afghan civilian casualties have resulted from U.S. and NATO aerial attacks.)

The ensuing casualties suffered on the coalition side, and especially by U.S. forces (whose numbers of troops far exceed all other members' contributions) from 2003 to the present may be attributed to a series of errors.[4] These errors, in turn, contributed to the way in which the principle of *jus in bello* was violated.

The mistakes are especially reprehensible when it is realized that they could have been avoided. A number of senior officers who had participated in both phases of the war in Iraq have testified and put on record (in addition to what had already been put on the record going back to 2002–2003) how they had recommended deploying a different, larger U.S. force than the one that had been deployed in Iraq in order to see through the invasion *and* occupation. These commanders left active duty in 2004 and 2005 largely in protest after their professional advice and better judgment were ignored by the higher civilian and military authorities under the leadership of Defense Secretary Donald Rumsfeld. (See Chapter 5 for a list of professional–military war critics.)

UNDERSIZED FORCES AND OTHER ERRORS

As we saw earlier, during the planning phase of the Iraq invasion in mid-2002, disagreement broke out at the top levels in the Pentagon and the Joint Chiefs of Staff (JCS) over the number of troops that would be required to invade Iraq. According to some military experts, the invasion and occupation force needed in Iraq should number in the "hundreds and thousands" of troops.[5] Authors Michael R. Gordon and General Bernard Trainor list seven additional major mistakes that they deem were made in Iraq.[6]

First, the Bush team failed to understand and weigh the significance of the many ethnic groups and cliques that compose Iraq, which itself could be described as an artificial entity cobbled together by the British after World War I as a multiethnic area that historically was perennially disunited. This "misreading" of the foe, as Gordon and Trainor call it, led to a repetition of mistakes that had arisen in the Persian Gulf War in 1991. This mistake could be summed up as exaggerating the importance of the enemy Republican Guard to the exclusion of other combat forces aligned against the Coalition in Iraq. These forces, such as the Fedayeen guerrillas, successfully concealed tons of explosives. The routing of the Guard aside, the Fedayeens were allowed to disperse themselves throughout the country, thus ushering in enemy insurgency warfare. The latter were joined by criminal gangs and foreign forces that were able to penetrate Iraq over the Syrian border in the west.

Further post-invasion chaos arose—for which the coalition was not adequately prepared—from armed Shiite (and Sunni) militias. U.S. commanders found themselves flummoxed by the location of these hit-and-run guerrillas who exploded their lethal car and road bomb devices (Improvised Explosive Devices, or IED). Since U.S. forces had not themselves infiltrated counterinsurgency fighters, the former were frequently caught off guard. They took casualties as a result. The incapacity to cope fully with this type of insurgency struck an ironic contrast to the fact that the U.S. military had, or so it was assumed, absorbed important lessons in fighting counterinsurgency battles from the Vietnam experience of the 1960s. Yet it appeared that this experience had not taken on importance for Pentagon planners. Instead, they chose to put the emphasis on high-precision/hi-tech war fighting, which was seen by critics as a mere extension of outworn World War II methods.

The second major error was the U.S. reliance on military-technological innovation and superiority per se, a justifiably proud achievement in the arsenal of the world's supreme superpower. As applied in Iraq in the positive sense, this factor did mean that U.S. forces could advance into Baghdad before the enemy could rally his defenses. As the authors point out, America's "improved reconnaissance and surveillance and precision munitions gave well-trained U.S. forces a decisive edge."[7]

However, after the fall of Baghdad in April 2003, the requirements for achieving and maintaining the upper hand in Iraq became radically different. It now became necessary to conduct counterinsurgency operations of the type that would thoroughly penetrate the ranks of the insurgents. It became crucial to seize and occupy major insurgent locations countrywide and remain in them as a pacifying presence. Occupying forces would also be tasked to win over the public so as to better stem the violence and become better informed on the location of enemy guerrillas within the local population. (Embedded media correspondents frequently reported, as did U.S. soldiers, the unreliability of the largely intimidated local population, among which insurgents freely operated because the occupying forces were too thin or dispersed to win the loyalty and confidence of the Iraqi civilians (which is a crucial corollary in fighting a counterinsurgency war). The situation worsened to the point where even friendly informants among the Iraqi civilians could not be trusted.

In order to saturate the country in this way, many more counterinsurgent forces obviously were needed on the side of the U.S.-led occupation than the civilian planners in Washington had projected. Counterinsurgency warfare cannot be waged "on the cheap" and without sufficient boots on the ground. Iraqi manpower, available for the purpose of providing security, was, of course, lacking, as it was untrained and unreliable. The thinness of counterinsurgent Coalition forces along with inexperience in using such methods meant that the United States would suffer casualties *in bello* that might have been avoided. The hi-tech bias had become canon in the U.S. method of subduing the enemy in Iraq, with the result that full-blown counterinsurgency was minimized. The failed battle of Fallujah in 2005, the authors note, became a "metaphor for post-combat failure in Iraq."[8]

The third mistake was marked by the failure to flexibly react to developments as they unwound on the battlefield. As the Americans encountered typically guerrilla "homemade" weapons and enemy infiltration tactics (some of which were seen in the Palestinian Intifada combat against the Israelis)—such as roadside bombs, ambushes, car and suicide bombs, insurgents targeting civilians, as well as cross-the-border intrusion of foreign jihadists into the arena—the U.S. commanders tried to make adjustments to cope with this form of warfare. However, as the authors note: [9]

> The American war plan was never adjusted on high. [General] Tommy Franks never acknowledged the enemy he faced nor did he comprehend the nature of the war he was directing. He denigrated the Fedayeen as little more than a speed bump on the way to Baghdad and never appreciated their resilience and determination ... Once Baghdad was taken, Franks turned his attention elsewhere in the belief that victory was his, never realizing the irregulars he maligned constituted the real military center of gravity, one that had not surrendered ... At best [Franks] had won the first round of the war thanks largely to his subordinate commanders, but neither he nor they had won the war.

Not that all military thinkers and commanders had ignored the necessity of waging thoroughgoing counterinsurgency. For many of the officers and civilian specialists, who were later to criticize administration tactics, September 11, 2001, had sounded a tocsin for the United States to rethink its military strategy and its military's force structure throughout all branches of service.

In meeting the challenge of 9/11, a number of competent military minds produced studies that paved the way toward effective change in the interests of American national security. One such work was the 2003 book by U.S. Army Colonel Douglas A. Macgregor of the Center for Technology and National Security, *Transformation Under Fire: Revolutionizing How America Fights*. In it the author presented a well-argued, thoroughgoing case for overdue "transformation" (reform) of U.S. military forces. Some of his sources include then active-duty officers, such as NATO commander General Wesley Clark and General Merrill McPeak, Chief of Staff of the USAF. The gist of Macgregor's argument and of those who support it was that the United States needed to make major changes in every aspect of its preparations for war, especially with respect to ground forces. In a nutshell, the United States had adopted a "World War II state of mind" that would lead us to neglect so-called "low-level" fighting capability. The latter (say, in urban settings) involves lighter equipment, yet, insisted Macgregor, with precision-guided ordnance strictly suited to urban and many other kinds of environments. At same time, the author maintained that these forces must be able to disperse and retain their fighting ability in case nuclear weapons were used. He criticized the present equipment being used by the U.S. Army as lacking the flexibility required for post-9/11 combat situations.

Macgregor further noted that in the NATO operations against Slobodan Milosevic in Serbia and Kosovo in the late 1990s, too much stress was put on air power and bombing. Too little attention was given to deploying NATO forces on the ground. Many bridges, electric power grids, headquarters centers, and unfortunately civilians were unnecessarily destroyed and killed in the NATO air attacks. Despite the hi-tech attacks, Milosevic and his forces were not deterred. It also seemed that contending decisions made at the top in Brussels led to confusion in the battle plans devised to unseat Milosevic as dictator-president. This lesson, Macgregor insisted, taught U.S. defense policymakers, and certainly a large share of the military officers who were on active duty in these operations, that profound change was necessary in the U.S. approach to a variety of combat challenges and settings in the modern world.

Needless to say, scattered elements of Al Qaeda worldwide became a particularly challenging danger. The Al Qaeda threat called for a new accent on Special Forces and the way they are equipped and tasked to fight counterinsurgency wars. As Macgregor put it: [10]

> Unlike innovation in private sector firms, innovation in military affairs is a life and death matter, and maintaining a degree of dynamic equilibrium inside the military establishment is very important in war ... The newer the technology or its application inside the army, the more important it becomes to design its use with the whole world in mind.

In order to avoid making such "life and death" miscalculations in the future, it would appear that more public airing of defense issues and problems needs to be encouraged. Congress must involve itself more deeply in these all-important matters. The preemption strategy and the many ways that it has backfired tragically in Iraq should act as a wake-up call for our legislators to educate and inform themselves and to act more forcefully as the arm of government in whose hands, as the Founders said, should rest ultimate approval of executive war-making.[11]

The fourth error singled out by authors Gordon and Trainor concerns what they term the "dysfunction" of the U.S. command structures. As they factually demonstrate, this shortcoming produced needless *in bello* casualties. The problem arose from the exclusive dominance in war planning of Secretary of Defense Rumsfeld and, for a time, Iraq War commander-in-chief Tommy Franks. Left out of this decision-making, they contend, was the JCS. The chiefs "were pushed to the margins and largely accepted their [subsidiary] role ... Even [the Chairman of the JCS] General Shinseki in his remarks to Congress did not press the issue [of the number of troops for Iraq] inside the JCS, according to former chiefs."[12]

This stagnating, monolithic dominance at the top could have been challenged by a highly powerful official, such as Vice President Dick Cheney. However, it was Cheney who uncritically supported the unrealistic planning supported by Rumsfeld and Franks. Secretary of State Colin Powell (a seasoned military adviser who himself had once been JCS chairman during the Persian Gulf War) later revealed that he had been "odd man out" in pleading for more troops. He told the President that "he considered the policy-making machinery [on the Iraq War] to be broken."[13]

At the lower levels in combat in Iraq, this problem became one of inattention to the demands of occupation. No military headquarters had been established specifically to secure postwar Iraq. As L. Paul Bremer entered the scene as Washington's appointee designated to oversee the occupation (as head of the "Coalition Provisional Authority"), tensions between him and the military commanders led to "distracting and diverting attention and energy from [securing occupation of Iraq]. This occurred at the precise moment when the insurgency was beginning to gain traction"[14] and as American service members began to lose their lives in increasing numbers.

The fifth basic error made in Iraq concerns the Administration's revision of the factor of nation-building as a dubious rationalization for entering into war. Intervention is sometimes lamely rationalized in this way. But outright war is not. Nation-building cannot be inserted into the concept of *jus ad bellum*.

Indeed, in the presidential campaign of 2000 candidate Bush had denigrated nation-building as an unnecessary and unworkable policy. He claimed that it had proved disastrous when it was applied by the previous Clinton administration. As he put it, "I don't think our troops ought to be used for what's called nation-building. I think our troops ought to be used to fight and win a war."[15] Yet, despite the president's triumphal "mission accomplished" announcement aboard the aircraft carrier *Franklin D. Roosevelt* in mid-2003 after the invasion phase in Iraq, it soon became obvious that the war was not over in Iraq. It became clear that building a whole new political infrastructure in the defeated country was of prime importance.

The administration obviously did not attend seriously to this need. For instance, it rejected appeals from State and Justice Department officials to build native police forces in Iraq. The Bremer occupation had disarmed and disbanded the 500,000-member Iraqi Army while widely de-Baathizing Iraq's civilian and military infrastructures. This, in effect, decapitated Iraq's administrative system. Despite this vacuum, senior Administration officials nevertheless decided that such extra Coalition forces would not be needed for the administration and occupation of Iraq, that in any case the occupation could be enforced by relying on the existing Iraqi "enforcement apparatus."[16] This was—literally—a fatal as well as an indefensible mistake that produced near chaos throughout that occupied country.

Nor was the error inevitable. Authors Gordon and Trainor note that the while the war planning had taken about 18 months, post-invasion planning had begun in earnest only a few months before the invasion in March 2003. The importance of the latter planning had obviously been underrated. The team of Bush, Cheney, and Franks had concentrated on the least urgent task—namely, of defeating the ragtag Iraq Army. Meanwhile, the urgent, if not essential task of restoring law and order in the "new Iraq" was neglected. As the authors assert:

> The result was a surprising contradiction. The United States did not have nearly enough troops to secure the hundreds of suspected WMD sites that had supposedly been identified in Iraq or to secure the nation's long, porous borders. Had the Iraqis possessed WMD and terrorist groups had been prevalent in Iraq as the Bush administration so loudly asserted, the U.S. forces might well have failed to prevent WMD from being spirited out of the country and falling into the hands of the dark forces the administration had declared war against.

Finally, it should be recognized that the failure to foresee the likelihood of post-invasion insurgency and the tragic events that flowed from it within Iraq are shocking.

Administration war planners and spokespersons had often repeated, after all, that Saddam Hussein's regime was in cahoots with bin Laden and terrorist organizations such as al-Zarqawi's. U.S. officials had said that they suspected that jihadists had infiltrated Iraq. Realizing this, the Administration logically should have made plans to wage a concerted counterinsurgency war to root out terrorists as soon as the invasion phase was completed. Lamentably, it did not.

CATALOGUING "MISTAKES" MADE IN THE WAR

Besides the appearance of several books that dealt critically with the war, by 2004 recently retired senior officers and civilian specialists, some of them former cabinet officers in preceding administrations, were speaking

out with increasing frequency against the war. As they did so, they catalogued what they perceived as the cardinal mistakes made by the
Administration in war planning and in the conduct of the war after the
invasion of March 2003. Such errors, of course, bore upon the justification
of war under the rubrics of *jus ad bellum* as well as *jus in bello*. A double
onus falls on the war makers if faulty planning dooms the war to an
ill-fated conclusion and if fatal mistakes likewise foreclose victory or
success, however defined.

In one of the first rounds of such criticism, seven retired military leaders
drafted a list of their criticisms, which were widely excerpted in the broadcast and print media.[17] To these senior officers, the mistakes revolved
around the following:

1. The occupying force was too small to stabilize the situation within Iraq.
   General McPeak accused the administration of thinking that Iraq could be
   easily converted into a "Denmark with oil" and blamed officials like
   Rumsfeld, Wolfowitz, and Feith for living in a "fantasy world" in thinking
   that Iraq could be all but instantly democratized.

2. Coalition occupation had alienated the Iraqi population, whose support, said
   Turner, "we had lost" because we had not provided the populace with
   adequate security nor restored the Iraq economy

3. General William E. Odom advised bluntly that we should plan to terminate
   the occupation. "This is the way we were fighting in Vietnam, and if we keep
   on fighting this way, this one is going to go on a long time too. The idea of
   creating a constitutional state in a short amount of time is a joke. It will take
   10 to 15 years, and that is if we want to kill 10 percent of the population."

4. For his part General Anthony Zinni criticized the civilian leadership for not
   having followed the professional military's advice as to the required number
   of troops that would be needed to occupy Iraq. As he put it, "When I was
   commander of CENTCOM, we had a plan for an invasion of Iraq, and it had
   specific numbers in it. We wanted to go in there with 350,000 to 380,000
   troops. You didn't need that many people to defeat the Republican Guard,
   but you needed them for the aftermath."

5. General Claudia Kennedy raised the issue of civilian supervision of the war
   not, of course, by denying the tradition of overall civilian decision-making.
   Rather, the general questioned the idea that the secretary of defense, as she
   put it, "would tell the Army how to fight. He doesn't know how to fight; he
   has no business telling them. It's completely within civilian authority to tell
   you where to fight, what our major objective is, but it is absolutely no one's
   business but uniformed military to tell you how to do the job."

6. General Wesley Clark singled out the Administration's weak rationalization
   of the war as well as the overall planning of the war on terrorism as a whole.
   As Clark said, "It wasn't until the last minute that they came up and said,
   'Hey, by the way, we are going to create a wave of democracy across the
   Middle East.' That was February of 2003, and by that time they hadn't

planned anything. In October of 2003, Donald Rumsfeld wrote a memo asking questions that should have been asked in 2001: Do we have an overall strategy to win the war on terror? Do we have the right organization to win the war on terror? How are we going to know if we are not winning the war on terror? As it has turned out, the guys on the ground are doing what they are told to do. But let's ask this question: Have you seen an American strategic blunder this large? The answer is: not in 50 years. I can't imagine when the last one was. And it's not just about troop strength. I mean, you will fail if you don't have enough troops, but simply adding troops won't make you succeed."

7. Former chairman of the Joint Chiefs of Staff Admiral William J. Crowe addressed the factor of the civilian war planners' recklessness of entering into war. The idea that a quick victory would merge into a smooth occupation was described by the admiral as "terrible assumptions." Military advice was "overridden," he complained, by Rumsfeld. Like the other senior officers, Crowe wondered where civilian authority should yield to professional military know-how and experience. Crowe made some dire predictions that were close to what actually transpired in the coming two years: 'If we [withdraw] . . . there will be turmoil in Iraq [and] the question to ask is: Is what we are achieving in Iraq worth what we're paying? Weighing the good against the bad, we have got to get out."

For its part, the Institute for Policy Studies (IPS) tabulated the various costs to the United States that the think tank claimed made the war against Iraq unjustifiable as viewed under the principle of *jus in bello*.[18] These included:

- The human costs to civilian Iraqis and to U.S. and coalition service personnel, which also included civilian contractors' and journalists' deaths, reached all-time highs by the end of 2006. As of autumn 2006, Iraqi civilian deaths totaled 3,709 in October alone. This represented an 11 percent increase in such deaths from the total of the preceding month in September. U.S. service personnel deaths in combat were likewise at a monthly high at that time. Since the war's inception in March 2003 until late 2006 total U.S. service personnel fatalities in combat totaled 2,335. Wounded service personnel numbered an estimated 22,000.[19]

- Terrorist recruitment and action have intensified. According to the London-based International Institute for Strategic Studies, Al Qaeda's membership is now at 18,000, with 1,000 members active in Iraq. The State Department's 2003 "Patterns of Global Terrorism" documented 625 deaths and 3,646 injuries due to terrorist attacks in 2003. The report acknowledged that "significant incidents" increased from 60 percent of total attacks in 2002 to 84 percent in 2003. In addition, Al Qaeda membership was seen to have increased in 2005–2006.

- Besides the consequences resulting from military errors, other dire consequences were seen by IPS as flowing from the ill-conceived war. These included worldwide damage to U.S. prestige and credibility as revealed by polls; the propping up and trusting of Iraqi exiles; and low troop morale and lack of adequate equipment. (For example, the Army failed to fully equip soldiers with bulletproof vests until June 2004, forcing many families to purchase them out of their own pockets). In addition, the economic costs of the war as of mid-2007 neared the $320 billion level, or at a rate from $6-to-$9 per month (excluding postwar social and veterans' medical compensation costs, including mental health costs). This represented a rise of 17 percent over the annual costs of the preceding year of 2005.[20]

- The IPS tabulation also included the as-yet unknown effects of depleted uranium stemming from the 1,100 to 2,200 tons of weaponry made from toxic and radioactive metal during the March 2003 bombing campaign.
  The health impacts of the use of depleted uranium (DU) weaponry in Iraq are yet to be known. Many scientists blame the far smaller amount of DU weapons used in the Persian Gulf War for illnesses among U.S. soldiers as well as a sevenfold increase in child birth defects in Basra in southern Iraq.

- Security costs include the rise in the crime rate in Iraq, with more cases of murder, rape, and kidnapping seen in Iraq from March 2003 through 2006,. Violent deaths rose from an average of 14 per month in 2002 to 357 per month in 2003, and to many more in the succeeding years. The rising crime rate was also exacerbated by rampant unemployment, which was estimated to rise to as maximum of 50-to-60 percent of the workforce in Iraq and that saw little relief from 2003 to 2007.

- IPS also referenced the manner in which the war detracted from ("disabled") international law and the prestige of the United Nations. At every turn, alleged the IPS report, the Bush Administration has attacked the legitimacy and credibility of the United Nations and undermined the world body's capacity to act in the future as the centerpiece of global disarmament and conflict resolution. "The efforts of the Bush Administration to gain U.N. acceptance of an Iraqi government that was not elected but rather installed by occupying forces," IPS said, "undermines the entire notion of national sovereignty as the basis for the U.N. Charter. It was on this basis that Secretary General Annan referred specifically to the vantage point of the U.N. Charter in his September 2004 finding that the war was illegal."

In an essay published in the spring 2004 newsletter of the Center for Defense Information General Zinni singled out what he called the "Ten Mistakes History Will Recall About the War in Iraq."[21] The first mistake, he wrote, was the Bush Administration's insistence that *containment of a potential threat* does not "work" as policy. But, alas, it did work, Zinni claimed, as during the prolonged Cold War against the ever-threatening Soviet Union. Admittedly, he added, "it's not a pleasant thing" to have to conduct containment. It requires troops full-time as well as the exertion of infinite patience. (By "containment" Zinni evidently meant keeping a constant inspection watch on Iraq, as supported by U.S. allies, while using U.N. sanctions when the Hussein regime in Baghdad defied international law.) True, Zinni added, there might be violence despite containment, yet in the long run containment is a lot cheaper than its alternative—making war.

The second mistake was to think that the Middle East would be "awed" by the U.S. intervention there. *The United States as "liberator" would unleash a wave of change throughout the region.* Zinni claims that the war was motivated by the notion that "the road to Jerusalem" led through Baghdad. But just the opposite was true: the road to Baghdad leads through Jerusalem. In other words, in the General's view the Israeli-Palestinian standoff had to be solved before other Middle East tensions could be dampened. Solving the crisis on the West Bank, Zinni argued, would have helped work out other problems throughout the region. Bush's war against Iraq headed the peace process in the wrong direction.

Another part of this mistake, according to Zinni, relates to the ill-informed notion that we can walk into the region and "be met with open arms." Zinni disputed the idea that people in the Middle East would latch onto democracy overnight. "The idea that strategically we will reform, reshape, and change the Middle East by this action" is mistaken. Then he added ironically "[Yes, by the war] we've changed it, all right!"

The third mistake was the way in which the Iraq War appeared to be a *rerun of the Vietnam War.* As with that war, Zinni said, "we had to create a false rationale for going in order to get public support. The books were cooked, in my mind. The intelligence was not there. I testified before the Senate Foreign Relations Committee one month before the war, and Senator [Richard] Lugar asked me: 'General Zinni, do you feel the threat from Saddam Hussein is imminent?' I said: 'No, not at all.' It was not an imminent threat. Not even close. [It was] not grave, gathering, imminent, serious, severe, mildly upsetting, none of those."

The fourth mistake was seen in the *failure to internationalize the effort.* "To the credit of President Bush 41," claimed Zinni, "he set a standard that held up throughout the post-Cold War period up until the Iraq war very well. He went to the United Nations before we undertook the operation to expel Saddam from Kuwait. Tremendous diplomatic effort to get a resolution from the United Nations to authorize the use of force and then a tremendous diplomatic effort on his part to create what I think is one of the most remarkable coalitions, the coalition we had in the Gulf War, where we had Arab countries, Islamic countries, European countries, contributions from the Far East all over the world."

Indeed, 54 countries eventually joined in the Persian Gulf War's coalition of 1990–1991. Many of the coalition partners made large financial and troop contributions. "That model was extremely successful," General Zinni wrote. "And if you think about it, every intervention we had since we used the model . . . worked. We did it in Somalia, in Haiti, in Bosnia, in Kosovo, (and) East Timor, there were variations on it, but it always started with that U.N. resolution. Why would we believe that we would not get it this time? Why would we believe that this time for some reason, unlike before, the inspectors would not call the shots honestly?"

Zinni faults the Administration for having repudiated U.N. inspections. "The inspectors don't make judgments; they just make reports of facts. We have Americans on inspection teams. Rolf Ekeus, Richard Butler [an Australian], they always came across with an honest assessment of what was happening. Why, suddenly, [were] Mohamed Elbaradei and Hans Blix suspect? And what was the rush to war?" Indeed, Butler, Elbaradei, and Blix all condemned the U.S. invasion.

It was especially revealing that the stern Australian Butler took this position. He was considered to be one of the "hardest" of all hard-line inspectors. He was not alone. Other hardworking inspectors harboring suspicions of Hussein's concealment of weapons likewise deplored Operation Iraqi Freedom.

According to General Zinni, the fifth mistake was that the Administration *underestimated the enormity of the task in occupying Iraq*. "Former combat commanders of U.S. Central Command, beginning with General Norman Schwarzkopf, have said you don't understand what you're getting into. You are not going to go through Edelman's 'cakewalk;' you are not going to go through Chalabi's dancing in the streets to receive you. You are about to go into a problem that you don't know the dimensions and the depth of, and are going to cause you a great deal of pain, time, expenditure of resources, and casualties down the road."

The sixth mistake, perhaps the biggest, he said, was "*propping up and trusting the exiles*, the infamous 'Gucci Guerrillas' from London." These Iraqi exiles had submitted various alarming intelligence reports. To the credit of the CIA, some of the reports were found not to be bona fide, which prompted Zinni to remark, "So, I guess the Defense Department created its own boutique intelligence agency to vet them." As a result, he continued, "we ended up with a lot of bad information that led the war planners to assume that U.S. invasion and occupation forces "would be welcomed with flowers in the streets . . . that this would be a cakewalk. When I testified before Congress in 1998 . . . I told them that these guys are not credible and they are going to lead us into something they we will regret. At that time, they were pushing a plan that Central Command would supply air support and Special Forces, and we would put it into Iraq, and they would Pied Piper their way up to Baghdad and the whole place would fall apart. This plan was created by two Senate staffers and a retired general. I happened to be the commander of Central Command, nobody bothered to ask me about how my troops would be used. And they were a little bit upset about me being upset about this."

The seventh mistake on General Zinni's list was the *lack of planning that went into the decision to invade and occupy Iraq*, a country the size of

California with a population of over 25 million. "I testified again during that period with the Senate Foreign Relations Committee," notes Zinni, "[seated] right behind the panel of planners from the State Department and the Department of Defense . . . I listened to them describe a 'plan.' I understood and knew that General [Tommy] Franks and CENTCOM would do their part. I knew damn right well the security piece would be taken care of, and I knew we had a good plan [But] I didn't hear anything that told me that they had the scope of planning for the political reconstruction, the economic reconstruction, social reconstruction, the development of building of infrastructure for that country. And I think that lack of planning, that idea that you can do this by the seat of the pants, reconstruct a country, to make decisions on the fly, to beam in on the side that has to that political, economic, social other parts, just a handful of people at the last minute to be able to do it was patently ridiculous. In my time at CENTCOM, we actually looked at a plan for reconstruction, and actually developed one at CENTCOM because I thought that we, the military, would get stuck with it. In my mind, we needed formidable teams at every provincial level. Eighteen teams. The size of the [entire occupation force] was about the size we felt we needed for one province."

The eighth mistake consisted in *not providing sufficient forces on the ground*, said General Zinni. "There were a lot more troops in my military plan for operations in Iraq. I know when that plan was presented, the Secretary of Defense [Rumsfeld] said it was old and stale. It sounded pretty. [Yet] those extra divisions we had in there were not to defeat the Republican Guard,," he said. "They were in there to freeze the security situation because we knew the chaos that would result once we uprooted an authoritarian regime like Saddam's."

Mistake number nine, Zinni claimed, concerned the *"ad hoc organization" we threw into Iraq.* "No one can tell me the Coalition Provisional Authority (CPA) had any planning for its structure," he said. "One hundred and forty-four bodies scraped from embassies around the world, people that I know, for fact, walked in and were selected and picked and put in the positions. Never quite fully manned-up until well into the operation. Never the kinds of qualifications or the breadth and scope and depth it needed to work the problems down to the grassroots level."

The tenth mistake, according to General Zinni, stemmed from the series of miscalculations that were made during the occupation. These included the failure to utilize former Baathist elements in Hussein's former regime. "De-Baathification" was overdone to the point where few native Iraqi security forces were available to the CPA in order to restore and keep order or carry out police and other public-administrative functions. Disbanding the Iraqi Army was a colossal blunder, the General insisted. The CPA had needed the cooperation of the Iraqi Army, and it would have duly won this if the Army had not been disbanded. Then, said Zinni, there were the problems of failing to identify with the various religious leadership ruling in areas throughout Iraq's Shiite- and Sunni-dominated provinces. CPA leaders up to and including Paul Bremer never bothered to have exchanges with these factions, Zinni claimed. In fact, Bremer "never met" any of these leaders.

7

Are the Laws of War Observed?

The Iraq War is no exception in applying the second group of principles for just war that are traditionally called *jus in bello*; that is, justness in the way a war is fought. Before weighing how and to what degree these principles are or are not applied by the combatants in that war, some background needs to be canvassed. Under the rubric of *jus in bello* fall several sacrosanct principles. Combatants on all sides are expected—at least since the seventeenth century— to observe these rules when fighting wars.

Known today as international humanitarian law as embodied in the Geneva Conventions of the nineteenth and twentieth centuries and in other documents, *jus in bello* along with *jus ad bellum* lie "at the heart of all that is most problematic in the moral reality of war," writes one authority on just and unjust war theory.[1] In his classic work, *The Conduct of Just and Limited War*, William V. O'Brien observes that *jus in bello* "emerged rather late in the development of just-war doctrine."[2] This author describes at length the influence of Christian teaching on the rules that should obtain in war. He notes that the origin of some of the "fair play," or "sportsmanship," reflected in these rules derives in part from medieval chivalry. Norms for *jus in bello* relate to the following:

- Prohibitions against deliberate targeting of noncombatant civilians;
- Proportionality in the way wars are fought so that "war aims are proportionate to the evil resulting from the war."

The latter principle could be interpreted as calling on combatants to adjust the means used in war to optimally match, but not exceed, the means used by the opposing side *so as not to bring on needless mayhem and suffering*. Also pertinent is measuring the goals of war against the lethal or unwanted costs that war exacts.

The establishment of principles of *jus in bello* go back to the early development of international law in the seventeenth century, by which time nation-states had become the principal combatants. The influence in this direction became known as the "Rousseau-Portalis Doctrine."[3] At the time these principles were being laid out and recognized, war was likened to a sport. Armies were viewed as if they were athletic teams. In this conception, noncombatants, or as we call them today, civilians, were viewed as virtual "spectators." Attacks on noncombatants as well as against nonmilitary targets were thus regarded as "unfair" and illegal. Such targets would include, for example, hospital installations, churches, and other strictly civilian installations.

The rules about making exceptions of noncombatants began, if slowly, to be incorporated in positive international law. The delay in formulating these rules stemmed in part from the complexities of defining exactly what a nonmilitary installation was. For instance, suppose an enemy ensconced itself in a church or monastery. In World War II there was the case of the monastery atop Mount Cassino in Italy that was occupied by German troops. The Germans used the building as an ideal fortress from which to target the enemy. Was exempting this holy site from retaliatory bombing warranted under such conditions? Indeed, the Mount Cassino monastery was decimated by Allied bombers and mortars.

The Geneva Conventions of the nineteenth century marked the beginning of the actual *codification* as a treaty document of the rules that should be observed in warfare.[4] By the middle of that century, public consciousness of the inhumanity of war and of the rampant violence characteristic of that time in general was on the increase. Although that century as a whole is widely, if mistakenly, regarded as a relatively peaceful one, the period nevertheless experienced an abundance of wars, which occurred almost annually.[5] This fact seemed to whet humanitarian awareness. One of the most ferocious nineteenth-century conflicts was the three-year Crimean War (1853–1856). Perhaps the senselessness and obvious immorality of this war, which was fought for narrow, imperial goals, made war's inhumanity seem particularly stark and intolerable. So were the casualties. Out of the 1,481,132 forces in combat, 615,378 soldiers were killed in action—that is, almost half of all those engaged in combat.

Fallout from this war and other wars preceding it, such as the Napoleonic Wars, fueled public demands to subject war to humanitarian rules. The heroine nurse Florence Nightingale became a one-person inspiration for such *jus in bello* literature during and after that war. The ensuing conventions were the results of efforts made in part by the humanitarian Henri Dunant. He was motivated by the horrors of war that he had personally witnessed in the Battle of Solferino of 1859, a bloody local conflict fought between the Sardinians and Austrians just four years following the Crimean War.

As public discussion accelerated in mid-century, the first Geneva Convention in 1864 was aimed at ameliorating the condition of the sick and wounded in battle.[6] These factors increased public awareness and consciousness of the inhumane aspects of war and played a major role in the further development of international law on the conduct of war under *jus in bello*.

The next developmental stage in humanitarian international law came with the Second Geneva Convention of 1907 (revised in 1949). It extended the same kinds of aid and amelioration to sailors that had previously been accorded ground troops. This convention was aimed at relieving the suffering of seamen who fell victim to naval engagements. (Steamships were then replacing the old sailing dreadnoughts.)

The Third Geneva Convention, signed by an increased number of states (12) as compared to some of the foregoing conventions, came into force in 1929 (also revised in 1949 and signed by 192 countries). It was aimed at assuring humanitarian treatment of prisoners of war (POWs). The convention was prompted by the much larger number of troops now engaged in modern warfare. This, in turn, was the result of the use of mass armies, conscription, and universal military training as seen in World War I. This meant that more persons were becoming involved in warfare and who thus might become POWs.

The Fourth Geneva Convention of 1949 (based in part on provisions of the Fourth Hague Convention of 1907) was specifically aimed at protecting noncombatant civilians victimized in war. This convention, too, was prompted by the times. By the mid-twentieth century, the danger of a nuclear war was widely feared. Nuclear weapons borne by bombers would, of course, be capable of killing an inordinate number of civilians. Associated in people's minds with nuclear war was the destruction wrought on civilians that was seen in the United States Air Force A-bomb raids on Hiroshima and Nagasaki in August 1945 that took the lives of around 214,000 Japanese.

To these conventions were subsequently added three Protocols in 1977 to 2005. Among other provisions, the Protocols extended humanitarian protection to victims in non-international armed conflicts, so-called "revolutionary" and/or local wars (including guerrilla or insurgency wars). The latter category included persons who were captured in the Iraq War or who were suspects following the terrorist attacks of 9/11 and who were imprisoned at Guantanamo as well as in Iraq and elsewhere. The status of these captives became the subject of heated controversy.

Besides the Geneva Conventions, a number of international agreements relating to war were signed at The Hague in the late nineteenth century and into the twentieth century. In the beginning these agreements mostly related to settling international disputes, such as characterized the first Hague "Settlement of Disputes" in 1899, whose principal signers were the German Emperor and the King of Prussia. Subsequent Hague conventions affected the means used in fighting on land and sea. The Hague Conference of 1907, for instance, resulted in the signing of various treaties prohibiting the use of sea mines while also updating earlier humanitarian provisions.

A novel feature of one of the 13 separate Hague rules emanating from the 1907 conference related to the concept of limited war. As updated and reiterated in the 1949 Geneva Conventions, this rule stated that the "right of belligerents to adopt means of injuring the enemy is not unlimited."[7]

THE CONVENTIONS AND THE IRAQ WAR

As we examine how the United States has or has not observed Geneva rules in the Iraq War, it must be noted that the conventions have been flouted often in past wars—by the United States as well as by other powers. For instance, not only in World War II but in the Korean War (1950–1953) there were instances in which the U.S. armed forces broke Geneva rules. North Korean POWs were abused in that war. [8] In the U.S. Panama intervention in 1990 during the presidency of George H. W. Bush, there was evidence that the United States had made indiscriminate attacks on civilians and had used methods of war that were unjustified by military necessity.[9] In applying Geneva and Hague convention principles to the Iraq War, the unique nature of that conflict needs to be taken into account and with it the Bush Doctrine that unfolded following the Al Qaeda attacks of September 11, 2001.

If the post-9/11 campaign to eradicate terrorism can be legitimately described in a general way as a "war," then it would seem that the rules of war must apply to it. Yet the question arises: would the rules apply if a given nation-state were not a proven sponsor of terrorism and if the terrorists were nonstate, rogue gangs? At the same time, an air, ground, and naval war against a sovereign country, Iraq, is obviously a conventional war even if it is rhetorically classified as a purely "counterterrorism action."

Moreover, none of the more than 100 major and minor local armed conflicts since World War II saw declarations of war before hostilities began. Thus, it does not clarify matters to apologize, as it were, that the war against Iraq was undeclared. Indeed, the mixture of elements of counterterrorism and conventional war might cloud the application of the rules of war in the way the Bush Administration claims to be waging its "global war against terrorism" as well as the Iraq War.

At the same time attempts have been made to spin a legalistic web so as to develop clearer criteria for applying international law (as affects, say, POWs in the Iraq War). For example, in 2005 the U.S. Supreme Court itself entered the picture by defining legally the rules that should apply to both types of war—those involving nation-states versus those involving bands of terrorists. Violations of humanitarian principles dating back to the nineteenth century were seen to be abused in both types of combat by the U.S. armed forces and ultimately by those U.S. Defense Department civilians overseeing the military. Through its judicial process, the U.S. Army sought to prosecute soldiers who abused Iraqi POWs. Some observers objected that those held responsible were noncommissioned officers who, it was claimed, were merely following the orders of their superiors. Yet the latter were not indicted.

On several occasions following 9/11, President George W. Bush described the U.S. mission to fight terrorism as, formally, a "war." This was a significant term. It raised the question whether the struggle could be considered a war as opposed to, say, a police action—that is, by viewing Al Qaeda (in Arabic, "the base") as a gang of criminals scattered about world. If it were a war in the conventional sense—that is, between states, as the President suggested—then the combat would be subject to the same moral and humanitarian principles and rules as any conventional conflict or war.

Indeed, in a monumental speech at the Air Force Academy on June 2, 2004, Bush compared this struggle "between tyranny and freedom" to World War II and the Cold War.[10] "Our goal of this generation is the same [as the World War II generation]," he said. "We will secure our nation and defend the peace through the forward march of freedom." In other speeches, the President compared the war in Iraq to the fight against terror in general. For instance, at a White House news conference held just before his trip to Boulder in June 2004, Bush said that "part of winning the war on terror is spreading freedom and democracy in the Middle East."[11]

How do the war in Iraq and the other aspects of the "war against terror" measure up to the requirements of international law with regard to humanitarian rules? How does that war fit the criterion of just proportionality of the means used against the enemy as well as the humanitarian laws and principles of justly fought war (according to *jus in bello*) as embodied in international conventions and traditions?

The picture is decidedly mixed. As we pointed out in the discussion of *jus ad bellum* in Part One, the justness of war is bound up with the way it is fought, and the way it is fought is likewise reflected upon *jus ad bellum*. In other words, if the very launching of war and its rationalization are flawed, then the combat subsequently unleashed by the attacker must also be viewed as unjust no matter what form is assumes.

Yet if we separate the two concepts and concentrate only on justness *in* war, we can still measure the degree of humanity or inhumanity used by the two contending sides. Regarding the principle of proportionality in the means used in the war, we see immediately that the enemies inside Iraq, known as the "insurgents" or internal "terrorists," do not at all recognize traditional principles of humanitarianism. They willfully attack civilians in brutal ways that have no relation to fighting war by the rules. The civilians can be described as unarmed, innocent bystanders. What we see instead is a type of latter-day guerrilla warfare. As explained by O'Brien in *The Conduct of Just and Limited War*, this type of insurgency could be best described as the "Marxist–Ho Chi Minh approach" as seen in the Vietnam War. [12] This type of warfare severely challenges an opponent who seeks to play by Geneva rules. The latter must develop a counterinsurgency strategy, which is lacking in U.S. theory and practice, to not only defeat such updated guerrilla-war tactics but to also remain true to humanitarian principles. In attempting to root out nests of insurgents in the remote, western parts of Iraq in 2004, for instance, U.S. forces took the lives of hundreds of civilians who appeared to be innocent of any known ties to the terrorists there.

Can it then be alleged that given the situation in the ground in Iraq, the United States has done about all it could in the choice of methods it has made to root out the terrorists? Has it done this so as not to violate the principle of proportionality and corresponding restraint in fighting against indiscriminate insurgency? The United States and the coalition were not widely accused of violating such principles in the invasion phase of the Iraq War. Instead of carpet bombing or mounting wanton attacks on civilians, the United States for the most part used precision-guided munitions (PGMs). These were used either in the air or on the ground to defeat the enemy. Such weaponry is regarded as more humane than former "unwired" types because of the way they can zero in on military targets with a high degree of accuracy. Yet, obviously these PGMs are not flawless.

This, in turn, raises the overriding issue of the morality of engaging in war if the cost in human life is high and when war is not necessary and can be avoided. Modern conventional and unconventional warfare, indeed, are costly in this way. Its ordnance is more powerful, even if precision-guided, than the ordnance used in any preceding conflict.

U.S. violation of established humanitarian principles in the Iraq War is found in other respects, namely in the matter of the holding and treatment of prisoners. The abuse of prisoners under U.S. supervision at Abu Ghraib Prison was inexcusable. It was a clear violation of Geneva conventions relating to treatment of POWs. Nor did the mistreatment inform U.S. intelligence in any substantial way. Willie J. Rowell, a veteran detention officer attached to the U.S. Army's Criminal Investigation Division informed *New Yorker* writer Seymour Hersh that humiliation of prisoners is "invariably counterproductive."[13] Hersh noted that under the fourth Geneva convention, an occupying power can legitimately jail civilians if they pose an "imperative" security threat, but the captor must establish a regular procedure for insuring that only civilians "who remain a genuine security threat be kept imprisoned." Meanwhile, prisoners have the right to appeal any internment decision and can have their cases reviewed. Human Rights Watch complained to Secretary of Defense Donald Rumsfeld that civilians in Iraq remained in custody month after month with no charges brought against them. Abu Ghraib became, in effect, another Guantanamo, notes Hersh.

The Administration is accused of violating a number of conventions. As noted earlier, the U.S. Supreme Court denounced such practices in a 2005 ruling bearing on treatment of prisoners and their right to due process of law. In its 5–3 decision in the Hamdan v. Rumsfeld case in 2006, the Supreme Court ruled in favor of Salim Ahmed Hamdan, a young Yemeni national who had worked as a driver and bodyguard for Osama bin Laden. During the U.S. invasion of Afghanistan in 2001, U.S. military forces captured Hamdan, who was then held without trial until July 2004. At that time he was charged with "conspiracy to commit terrorism," an indictment that was based primarily on his association with bin Laden.[14] He had not been accused of directly participating in or coordinating any terrorist acts. The Court's complex 73-page opinion, written by Justice John Paul Stevens and joined by justices Stephen Breyer, Ruth Bader Ginsburg, and David Souter, held that:

- "Enemy combatants" are protected by the Geneva Conventions.
- President Bush did not have the authority to create new tribunals without congressional mandate.
- Conspiracy is not a war crime under the Uniform Code of Military Justice.

Various experts concurred that this Supreme Court decision was monumental, perhaps "the most significant Supreme Court ruling to date dealing with the war on terror."[15] The ruling's main point was that all noncitizen prisoners are protected by the Geneva Conventions, which essentially renders illegal the Bush Administration's program of indefinite detention, mild torture, and extraordinary rendition. The decision, in effect, called on the Administration to treat all detainees in a manner consistent with international human rights standards. This, of course, implicitly includes the POWs held in Guantanamo, Cuba, or in secret prisons located in Eastern Europe.

Other judgments in these matters was expected in the coming years. The violations have inspired additional anti-U.S. public opinion around the world.

ABU GHRAIB POW VIOLATIONS

One of the first instances of violations of POWs came with the allegations of the torture of Iraqi captives perpetrated against Iraqi detainees at

Abu Ghraib Prison in Baghdad as well as alleged secret, U.S.-run prisons in other parts of the world. This inhumanity (e.g., "water-boarding" and humiliating forms of mistreatment) escalated into a major scandal that reflected on U.S. soldiers' behavior toward alleged terrorists and Iraqi POWs and on their commanders' failure to oversee abusive actions at the prisons. The evidence, much of it photographic as it was aired internationally on television, lent credence to condemnations of the United States for violating Geneva Convention norms on the treatment of prisoners. Beyond that it became a *cause célèbre* that gave further impetus to the wave of anti-U.S. feeling worldwide. As of 2006, investigation was still underway amid confusion as to where to place the accountability for the torture of some of the prisoners, although it fell mostly on lower-ranking soldiers.

The reaction by Bush Administration officials and spokespersons tended to be elusive, equivocal, and defensive, almost to the point of being in a "state of denial" rather than apologetic. "We do not torture," President Bush has stated from time to time.[16] Yet the President approved techniques that are defined as torture under the Geneva Conventions. In fact, he abrogated U.S. compliance with Article 3 of the Conventions that specifically prohibits torture. Indeed, his White House counsel at the time, now Attorney General Alberto Gonzales, contemptuously referred to the Conventions as "quaint."[17] In a memo dated August 1, 2002, written by the Justice Department's Office of Legal Counsel, the so-called "Bybee memo," after Jay Bybee, its director (since appointed by Bush to a federal judgeship), the Conventions seemed to be dismissed. In their place a new definition of torture was offered. Rather than the Conventions' stipulations against "cruel, inhumane, and degrading" treatment of prisoners and "outrages upon personal dignity, in particular, humiliating and degrading treatment," the Administration adopted new standards: "Physical pain amounting to torture must be equivalent to intensity to the pain accompanying serious physical injury, such as organ failure, impairment of bodily function, or even death." The Bush Administration's new torture policy seemed to have prompted the export of torture technique from Guantanamo to Abu Ghraib.

The Geneva Conventions make it incumbent upon the belligerent nations to avoid abuses inflicted on persons under their custody in wartime. Torture and other unwarranted treatment of POWs is strictly forbidden under international law. The alleged abuses perpetrated at Abu Ghraib—mindless torture, inhumane treatment to extract information from POWs, and the like—were a shocking case of the violation of "*jus in bello*," or rightful conduct in war. The U.S. Code of Military Justice makes it a punishable offense to disobey lawful orders, including those pertaining to guarding POWs.

In the fallout of discussion over the Abu Ghraib abuses came proposals for a number of preventive "therapies" that should have been previously undertaken in soldiers' combat training in order to prevent such occurrences.

Questions likewise arose over whether American political culture and public education had fulfilled their responsibilities in imparting sufficient knowledge and understanding of the humanitarian ideals of the Geneva Convention, especially as they apply in wartime. Many insisted that more attention needed to be paid to the dignity of the human person under any conditions.

Some Conclusions

It was a shameful thing to ask men to suffer and die, to persevere through god-awful afflictions and heartache, to endure the dehumanizing experiences that are unavoidable in combat, for a cause that the country wouldn't support over time and that our leaders so wrongly believed could be achieved at a smaller cost than our enemy was prepared to make us pay.

—John McCain[1]

MILITARY PRELUDE TO WAR

In the months preceding the U.S.-led invasion of Iraq in March 2003, the United States, together with some of the other coalition forces that took part in the 1991 Persian Gulf War, were enforcing Iraqi no-fly zones. Led by U.S. an U.K. air forces, they attacked Iraqi air-defense installations. This was, in effect, "low-level" combat in which the two allies were employing a form of military intrusion.[2]

By mid-2002, the administration broadened the no-fly zone attacks by selectively targeting the main Iraqi military command structure in southern parts of the country. Notably, this change in enforcement tactics, known as Operation Southern Focus, was not made public until months later. Yet the tonnage of bombs dropped in this campaign increased from zero in March 2002 and 0.3 ton in April 2002 to between 7 *and 14 tons per month* by May through August. By September 2002, as debates about Iraq were underway in the U.N. Security Council, this explosive tonnage had reached a pre-Iraq War peak of 54.6 tons (that is, prior to Congress's October 11 authorization of the invasion).

Finally, the big September 5, 100-aircraft attack on Iraq's main air defense site in western Iraq marked a further, dramatic escalation of the new, undeclared war against Iraq. This site was located at the furthest extreme of the southern no-fly zone and was destroyed, observed the U.K. journal *New Statesman*, "not because it was a threat to the patrols, but to allow allied Special Forces operating from Jordan to enter Iraq undetected."[3]

GRIM REALITIES OF PREVENTIVE WAR AND OCCUPATION

As we saw in preceding chapters, the Bush Administration decided early on in the fall of 2001 to go to war with Iraq. It appears that at Camp David on the weekend after the September 11 attacks, Deputy Defense Secretary Paul Wolfowitz floated the idea that Iraq, with more than 20 years of inclusion on the State Department's terror-sponsor list, be held immediately accountable. In his memoir, speechwriter David Frum recounts that, in December 2002, after the Afghanistan campaign against bin Laden and his Taliban sponsors, he was told to come up with a justification for war with Iraq. It was tasked to include material from Bush's emblematic "axis-of-evil" State of the Union address of January 2002.

The full-fledged war, which had been secretly anticipated, discussed, and planned among the top Bush officials since 2001 (e.g., as per the Downing Street Memoranda), and more intense warfare than what was perpetrated in the no-fly zones and against Iraqi command posts was about to be unleashed. After weeks of eluding U.N. Security consideration of putting increased pressure on Iraq to tighten the inspection regimen, the Bush Administration put into action its long-held plan of attacking Iraq in a full-scale invasion. On March 20, 2003, at approximately 02:30 UTC (about 90 minutes after the lapse of the 48-hour deadline at 05:30 local time), explosions were heard in Baghdad. These coincided with Australian Special Air Service Regiment personnel crossing the border into southern Iraq. At 03:15 UTC, or 10:15 pm EST, President George W. Bush announced that he had ordered the coalition to launch an "attack of opportunity" against targets in Iraq.

Before the invasion, many observers had expected a lengthy campaign of aerial bombing in advance of any ground action. This was traditional in conventional, large-scale, or "industrialized" war.[4] The assumption was that superior U.S. mobility and coordination would allow the United States to attack the heart of the Iraqi command structure and destroy it in a short time. This, in turn, would presumably minimize civilian deaths and damage to the Iraqi infrastructure. It was expected that the elimination of the Baathist leadership throughout Iraq would lead to total collapse of the rule in the country, thus easing the way to a smooth occupation. It was further assumed by the Pentagon and White House that once the Baathist government had been fatally weakened, the bulk of the Iraqi population would wholeheartedly support the invaders and occupiers.

Much of this turned out to be a rash assumption. Moreover, the military actions did not meet the criteria for *jus ad bellum* (see Part Two, Chapters 3 through 5). Indeed, early on a number of observers expressed the view that the United States erred by deploying insufficient troops to the invasion, the consummation of which lasted some three weeks. Critics alleged that this shortcoming, combined with the failure to occupy principal Iraq cities, put the coalition at a major disadvantage in achieving security and order throughout the country when local support for the occupation failed to meet the war planners' expectations.[5] They warned that this miscalculation would have a telling effect upon the war effort, pacifying the population and preparing the way for peaceful, postwar democratic rule in Iraq.

As we saw, numerous, experienced military senior officers, including members of the Joint Chiefs of Staff, voiced similar alarm. They even resigned or were dismissed because of their opposition to the tactics being used by the civilian-led Pentagon under the hands-on leadership of Secretary of Defense Donald Rumsfeld and the Bush White House.

In the meantime, during the invasion phase the oil-production infrastructure of Iraq was rapidly secured and suffered limited damage. Safeguarding Iraq's oil facilities had been deemed vital since revenue from Iraq's oil exports were to help defray the (mainly U.S.) costs of the war. As it turned out, however, insurgents interfered with that security. Amid chaos in the country, the decimation of the Baathist infrastructure at the grassroots, and the exodus of trained Iraqi personnel in the form of a whole "brain drain," Iraq's oil exports have not only declined during the war and occupation but have, in some cases, remained even below prewar levels. Moreover, the revenue from exported oil was reported in 2006 to be in the several billions of dollars, yet only 15 percent of these profits were spent to rebuild Iraq's war-torn roads, buildings, schools, and power stations. That such profits "would pay for the war" in terms of U.S. expenditures became, of course, a baseless assumption.[6]

In retrospect, the war proved, moreover, that the Hussein-built army had been severely weakened years before the opening of hostilities in March 2003; that is, since the Gulf War of 10 years before. The fact was that the Iraqis had no weapons that could stand up against coalition forces. If the hi-tech, U.S.-led coalition invaders were fighting a 1990s or a twenty-first century war, the Iraqis were fighting one that dated back to the 1970s. They managed only to stage a few ambushes, which gained media attention. Yet these Iraqi assets did nothing to slow the coalition advance. Above all, this Iraqi military weakness, which incidentally was known to many specialists before the invasion, suggested in turn that the description of Iraq as an "imminent threat"—even as to its conventional war-making capability— had been grossly exaggerated by the administration in Washington.

(We considered in Chapter 3 whether this constituted "lying" on the part of the U.S. administration.)

To cite a cardinal example of Iraqi feebleness, the Iraqis' Soviet-built T-72 tanks, the "main battle tank" together with the heaviest armored vehicles in the Iraqi Army, were antiquated and poorly maintained. When coalition forces encountered these so-called "principal assets" of the enemy, the tanks were easily destroyed, thanks in part to the coalition's domination of the air. In fact, the U.S. Air Force, Marine Corps, and Naval Aviation, together with the British Royal Air Force, had all operated in the invasion with virtual impunity throughout Iraq. Moreover, the Iraqi Army suffered from poor combat morale, even amongst the supposedly elite Republican Guard. Entire units simply melted away into the crowds upon the approach of coalition troops, a situation that resembled the route at the end of the Persian Gulf War in 1991.

As swift as the invasion subdued the enemy, a cardinal error was committed by the United States during the invasion phase: *the United States failed to guard and/or recover stolen Iraqi ammunition supplies.* This was one of the most crucial initial mistakes made by the civilian leadership in Washington. It reflected the failure to meet one of the traditional criteria for achieving a clear victory—one of the demands of *jus ad bellum*— given the elusive nature of the situation that confronted the occupiers in Iraq and the inadequate means applied to cope with it (see Chapter 3).

A second crucial error consisted in not reacting promptly and intelligently to the insurgent warfare waged against the occupation by a variety of Iraqi and foreign combatants. These guerrilla-type actions ensued soon after the invasion phase. Prior to the coalition invasion, Saddam Hussein had indicated publicly that he had intended to unleash a guerrilla war should Iraq be invaded. This turned out not to be a case of typical Saddam bluffing. Insurgency materialized in great force by 2005 and 2006. Its catastrophic consequences were overwhelming for the occupiers as well as the new government that was taking shape in Baghdad—and still are today.

LACK OF CONSENSUS

We have examined the other ways in which the war against Iraq raised serious questions (under *jus ad bellum*) about the justness of the application the new U.S. strategy of preemptive, or, better, preventive war. As we saw earlier, a major violation under *jus ad bellum* could be viewed as having been committed by the Administration of the principle of *legitimate authority*. This political process, in turn, as practiced in a democracy should express itself in an informed, firmly-established consensus among policymakers, the professional military, and the legislative branch of government, together with outside civilian consultants based on open access to all relevant, war-related information. In a democracy, the public at large also must be kept

informed. Yet, there was no such many-sided consensus that was based on a
fully informed legislative branch and broad public. This omission became
both obvious and ominous as the war dragged on. Failure to find WMD
was coupled with grim news from the war fronts. The body bags arriving on
U.S. shores began to haunt the Administration's war policy. By 2005–2006,
dire events in Iraq unleashed waves of public opinion that were in sharp
opposition to the war and that questioned the leadership of President George
W. Bush.

By autumn 2006, the nonpartisan, 10-member Baker-Hamilton
commission was established to take up the problem of "what to do next?"[7]
This, in itself, was an admission of failure. Predictably, the report noted in
particular the sharp increase in casualties of American forces as well as
among Iraqi civilians as it had mounted by autumn 2006. "Attacks against
U.S., coalition, and Iraqi security forces," the commission report warned,
"are persistent and growing." In fact, October 2006 had been the deadliest
month for U.S. forces since January 2005. In that period alone, 102
Americans were killed; that is, more than three years following the alleged
end of hostilities proclaimed triumphantly by Bush in spring 2003. Total
attacks in October 2006 averaged 180 per day, up from 70 per day in
January 2006. Daily attacks against Iraqi security forces in October were
more than double the level of the preceding January. Attacks against civilians in October likewise were four times higher than in January. Some
3,000 Iraqi civilians are killed every month.

INTELLIGENCE FAILURES

Instead of a cobbling together a firm consensus as to how to win in Iraq or,
if not, how to achieve a modicum of success, in less than a year into the occupation serious doubts about the wisdom of the invasion and the Administration's errant occupation policies began to be aired. This was heard in
committees in Congress, in the media, and among outside specialists. Public
opinion polls soon reflected the general dismay.

Some background is helpful in canvassing the relevance of openness and
unimpeded intelligence within the intelligence community.[8] The experience
should be enlightening as future war-threatening circumstances challenge
the United States. Absent openness and objective intelligence, the conduct
of war and occupation as a result will be seriously impaired and the justifiability of war severely questioned.

Recall that the Tower Commission was established in November 1987 to
investigate the Iran-Contra scandal, which had arisen because of secret,
illegal activities perpetrated at the highest levels of government behind the
backs of legislators and the public. The episode cast a shadow over the
Reagan Administration. On the positive side, it was hoped at the time
that a precedent of openness and unmanipulated intelligence would be

reinvigorated as a result of the commission's investigation. At the wind-up of its deliberations, the committee issued this caveat: "The democratic processes ... are subverted when intelligence is manipulated to affect decisions by elected officials and the public."[9]

Since then and since September 11, 2001, the two famous subsequent legislative resolutions that so empowered the White House to wage its "war against terrorism" illustrate the problem addressed back in 1987. With respect to Iraq in particular, the principle of openness has grown even more important during the ensuing seven years since the invasion. The Iraq war presented the U.S. administration with the challenge to devise a new strategy of preemptive or preventive war which, as it was assumed, was to be waged only in response to a clear and present danger or a prediction of a forthcoming attack against the United States or its allies (see Appendix A).

This potentially dangerous, offensive preventive or preemptive type of security policy, which was new in the American annals of military strategy,[10] made it all that more urgent to assure that the public and its representatives in Congress were able to base their support for war, or on the contrary oppose it, on the mass of intelligence to which it had in many cases no direct access. Any president and his closest aides are predetermined that their policies—in this case, the Bush Administration's war against Iraq—will see the light of day. It is nevertheless incumbent on the executive branch of government to show honesty and complete openness about the intelligence data that they have in hand and with which they seek to justify their war policy. As Historian John Lewis Gaddis has stated, "If an administration represents the intelligence unfairly, it effectively forecloses an informed choice about the most important question a nation faces: whether or not to go to war."[11] This violates the *jus ad bellum* principle of a full legitimacy of authority in waging a war. This breach, in turn, forecloses the efficacy of the principle in a democracy of legitimate authority for effectuating a war policy that has been assessed by unimpeded access to information and avoidance of misinformation, dishonesty, or tendentious manipulation. Yet this is exactly what the Bush administration did when it sought to convince the public and Congress that the United States should go to war with Iraq. (See discussion of the shibboleth of "imminence.")

From late August 2002 to mid-March of 2003, the Administration argued the case for war by singling out the threat allegedly posed to the United States by Saddam Hussein's nuclear, chemical, and biological weapons. An added threat, so the Administration alleged, was the Iraqi regime's links to Al Qaeda. In a speech in Nashville given on August 26, 2002, to a gathering of the Veterans of Foreign Wars, Vice President Cheney warned of a Saddam who was "armed with an arsenal of these weapons of terror [who can] directly threaten America's friends throughout the region and subject the United States or any other nation to nuclear blackmail ... What we must not do in the face of a mortal threat is give in to wishful thinking or willful blindness." For his part, Secretary of Defense Donald Rumsfeld claimed in Washington on September 26 that he had what he called "bulletproof" evidence of ties between Saddam and Al Qaeda. In Cincinnati on October 7, President Bush warned, "The Iraqi dictator must not be permitted to threaten America and the world with horrible poisons and diseases and gases and atomic weapons," adding that this "alliance with terrorists could allow the Iraqi regime to attack America without leaving any fingerprints."[12]

All this turned out to have been a chimera.

INTERNATIONAL LAW AGAINST THE BUSH POLICY

Even before the war, criticism of the war and the occupation had revolved around the question of such a war's legality, which in turn is a concomitant of just-war principles. The legality issue had been broached, among other authorities on international law, by Professor Thomas Franck, director of the Center for International Studies at NYU Law School. Franck did so as early as summer 2002.[13] As the future occupation became frustrated with growing violence and bloody sectarian, virtual civil war, the issue of the legality of the whole enterprise often reared its head. It was asked again and again whether an internationally-recognized government, however tyrannical its leadership, could be overthrown by another state without any legal authorization—e.g., by the United Nations Security Council. After all, in March 2003 the United States had not responded to any overt hostile act of aggression by Saddam Hussein's government (albeit that the first Persian Gulf War had not ended in a formal peace treaty).

As noted early on by Franck (in 2002), it was alleged by Administration spokespersons that Iraq had refused to allow weapons inspections to continue unimpeded according to Security Council Resolution 687, which established a cease-fire based on Baghdad's cooperation with the inspection regime. Yet this resolution in 1991 did not make the cease-fire conditional on Iraq's future cooperation with inspections.[14] The resolution merely stated that the Security Council "decides to remain seized of the matter and to take such further steps as may be required for the implementation of the present resolution and to secure peace and security in the area." This wording implied that another Security Council resolution would be needed to authorize further military action. This became the position taken by most of the European governments that are—or were—considered U.S. allies and which was included in the famous Resolution 1441 passed by a majority of the U.N. Security Council in autumn 2002. For instance, French President Jacques Chirac had said on July 30, 2002, that an attack "could only be justified if it were decided on by the Security Council." German Chancellor Gerhard Schroeder concurred by adding that there would be no support in Germany for a strike "without approval of the United Nations." Yet the Bush Administration was prepared to defy the Council, and as a result world public opinion. Whereas European and world press headlines after 9/11 read, "We Are All Americans!" those same foreign media later began to run quite different, anti-U.S. headlines.

Blocked in autumn and winter 2002–2003 by a majority of the U.N. Security Council that opposed military action against Iraq, the Bush Administration developed its own rationale for a wholesale military attack on a sovereign state. Namely, the United States claimed that Iraq's "imminent" threat necessitated an act of "self-defence."

Washington insisted that a correct understanding of the right of self-defence should now extend to authorizing preemptive/preventive attacks against potential aggressors. That is, Iraq should be stymied before it would be able to launch strikes against the United States. Such passive defensiveness, it was alleged, would prove devastating in their effect since WMD, it was claimed, would be involved. As we saw, this principle was tailored into U.S. strategy as a central tenet of the country's strategic posture and was sometimes dubbed the "Bush Doctrine." The first full venting of it came in Bush's speech at West Point in June 2002. The new strategy of preemptive or preventive war was further elaborated on by the White House in September (see Appendix A).

In these documents it was claimed that the United States faced "a threat with no precedent" from the proliferation of weapons of mass destruction and the emergence of global terrorism. In his West Point speech, Bush alleged that the traditional strategies of deterrence and containment were no longer sufficient. Deterrence, the president said, meant nothing "against shadowy terrorist networks with no nation or citizens to defend." Containment, the mantra of the Cold War threat represented by the USSR, could not work under present conditions, continued Bush, "when unbalanced dictators with weapons of mass destruction can deliver those weapons on missiles or secretly provide them to terrorist allies." Under these circumstances, he concluded, "if we wait for threats to fully materialize, we will have waited too long."[15]

Was this offencist doctrine intended to have wider application beyond Iraq? It certainly appeared to be. In his inaugural address of January 2001, the president had spoken in rueful terms of the "axis of evil" as a tangible threat to world peace. It was bandied about that a hypothetical case could arise in which Islamic militants in Pakistan might gain control of a nuclear weapon. Or if Iran went ahead with its own putative nuclear weapons program, a preemptive strike against the Bushehr nuclear power plant in that country might become necessary in coming years. Rogue states or terrorist groups might acquire miniaturized nukes and place them in targeted countries or cities in the West.

In 2002, the Crimes of War Project asked five prominent international experts for their views on the legality of the Iraq War.[16] Although their opinions were divided, they all recognized that the Bush Administration's proposals raised fundamental questions about the nature and scope of international law. As noted by these scholars, the starting point for any discussion of the subject should be international law as embodied in Article 51, Chapter VII, of the United Nations Charter. This article states that "nothing in the present Charter shall impair the inherent right of individual or collective self-defence if an armed attack occurs against a Member of the United Nations, until the Security Council has taken measures necessary to maintain international peace and security" (See Appendix B). The wording of the article seemingly is clear: the right of self-defence is generated when an attack *occurs*; that is, the attack must be occurring before the use of force in self-defense is legitimate.

Yet the experts pointed out a number of possible ways in which the picture may in fact be more complicated. Some observed that if the attack is not actually materializing, the threat of it nonetheless *must be clear and present in a way that gives the threatened state little time to prepare to defend itself*. The targeted state must be tangibly threatened, meaning above all that its sovereignty and independence were on the line. Dr. Eyal Benvenisti, director of the Minerva Center for Human Rights at the Hebrew University of Jerusalem, urged that the legitimacy of an act of preemptive self-defense or all-out preventive war depended on whether there were "means other than actual fighting to prevent the threatened attack." He compared the situation of a country under threat to that of a threatened individual under domestic law. In both cases, if one acted in self-defense, he then faced the burden of persuading the relevant authorities, or jury, that he had acted reasonably. "You have to convince the international community that you acted in self-defence, that you had no other choice, and that is similar to the situation of an individual within a society," said Dr. Benvenisti. "I mean, everyone has a right of private self-defence, when you are being attacked personally and you cannot call the police ... and then the question of whether you acted in self-defence will be judged ex post facto."

THE NEW TYPE OF WAR

At this point, it might well be asked, "What if a country makes its own decision?" British General Rupert Smith, veteran army commander in several modern wars, noted that modern counterinsurgency war—that is, as he put it, "war *amongst the people*", requires attention to the legitimacy of war, its justifiability, and its acceptance by the widest elements of the population for whose safety the war is waged. This applies to the population of the country waging the war as well as the population of the occupied country in war. Smith points out that it is no longer "irrelevant" to write off war's legality as a purely intellectual question fit merely for Academe or that such issues have no relation to public morale, to war's legitimacy, and to the wishes of the population directly involved in combat (of the guerrilla type).

As Smith writes of insurgent combat of the type fought in Algeria in the 1950s, in Vietnam in the 1960s and 1970s, or in Iraq today, it is:[17]

> no longer industrial war; the enemies are no longer the Third Reich or Japan, who posed absolute and clear threat in recognizable groupings, and therefore provided stable political contexts for operations; as we have seen, our opponents are formless, and their leaders and operatives are outside the structures in which we order the world and society. They are 'insurgents' in Iraq, the terrorists in the Philippines or the Israeli-occupied territories, or the armies of the 'war lords' in Afghanistan and Africa. In comparison to Western hi-tech forces they are ill-equipped, and adapt readily available civil technology to their own military ends, as with cell phones used for initiating an improvised explosive device—an event now so common it has the military acronym IED. The threats they pose are not directly to our states or territories but to the security of our people, of other peoples, our assets and way of life, so as to change our intentions and have their way. They are *of* and *amongst*—in the flesh and in the media—and it is there that the fight takes place. But this fight must be *won so as to achieve the ultimate objective of capturing the will of the people*; in other words, one can escalate with massive destruction—but beyond bringing great collateral damage, this will play into the hands of the opponent. Israel's attacks on Lebanese civilian infrastructure in the conflict in 2006 gives a good example of these consequences. Apart from raising serious legal and moral issues, *it is this way of thinking that leads to the phenomenon of winning every battle and losing the war.*

DOES AMERICA HAVE A "HABIT" OF MAKING WAR?

Until after 9/11 when the Bush administration declared a global "war on terrorism," the American habit of making war was confined, at least in the twentieth century, to responding to attack. Its postwar posture was traditionally passive. The World War I slogan, "The War to End All Wars," has been repeated, if not in those very words, before and after any number of past wars in which the United States has participated. Immediately after a bloody conflict, the sentiment for lasting peace is in the air in America at those times, whether in 1918 or 1945. This sentiment is accompanied by the hope that springs eternal that humanity has finally learned that war is futile.

Today with the brinkmanship of the Cold War a memory and as America's fourth and fifth major conflicts since World War II have reached a climax with an uncertain conclusion in both Afghanistan and Iraq, the specter of still another war "breaking out" somewhere haunts people's minds— meaning elsewhere in the Middle East or in East Asia. This dire fear of a war erupting in this or that region of the world seems to be unprecedented in our traditional psychic experience during a transition from war to peace. However, present conditions worldwide have brought about the change toward a more or less permanent condition of *angst* among Americans about the several ongoing threats to peace and, given nuclear proliferation, about the apocalyptic destruction a nuclear war would bring. The anxiety felt during the U.S.-Soviet bipolar Cold War when the Damoclean threat of thermonu-clear war hung over the world was different from today's multipolar threats. In the case of the bipolar standoff, there always seemed to be the chance that Moscow and Washington could control their relationship, even admit a certain degree of "détente" in their relationship (e.g., with the "hot line," summits, support of nonproliferation of nuclear weapons, test-ban agree-ments, and so on). Of course, an entirely new, anxiety-free era in the relations of the two countries opened with the demise of the USSR in December 1991.

Today, ongoing proliferation of nuclear weapons and the means to deliver them haunt today's quite different *multi*polar, post-Cold War era. Concern over WMD-carrying terrorists, such as Al Qaeda is also prevalent. (Docu-ments for obtaining such weapons were uncovered at Qaeda hideouts in Afghanistan.)

In his State of the Union speech in 2002, President Bush had listed three potential war makers worldwide, calling them the "axis of evil." So far only one of these, Iraq, has been targeted with military force. However, there are two more to go—Iran and North Korea. This situation raised a number of nagging questions in terms of just versus unjust war: Is preventive or pre-emptive war, as waged by the United States, including whatever allies it may acquire, the wave of the future? Are we headed for a period of one-war-to-end-all-future-wars after the other? If so, are such possible wars confined to the other pair of states of the "axis" or might other states be tar-geted? Moreover, what kinds of future wars might we be talking about—conventional, nuclear, low-level conflicts, or interventions? Or will they be in the nature of counterinsurgency, or what Colonel Thomas X. Hammes calls "fourth-generation warfare"?[18]

Finally, will or should the 2002 preemption strategy, assuming it was written back into U.S. war policy (it has since apparently been dropped in U.S. declaratory doctrine), remain in place as the most suitable way to meet all such contingencies?

With the prolonged Iraq War, the United States began to act as though it no longer believed that war as a human habit could ever retreat into the past. Current pessimism about this seems endemic. It was clearly expressed by both candidates, Bush and John Kerry, in the presidential election campaign of 2004. Kerry, in fact, acknowledged that he expected that the war in Iraq would not be able to be terminated before 2008. Other politicians speak of the likelihood of armed conflicts continuing into the indefinite future.

AMERICA'S FORMER WARS AND PEACE-MINDEDNESS

Having equipped itself with a preemption doctrine, America's present we-are-engaged-in-a-war-against-terrorism posture remains unique in terms of its own history. The fallout from 9/11, of course, has been the key impetus behind this new attitude, as is the policy announced by the Bush Administration since that fatal day and the war-enabling legislation passed by Congress in 2001–2002 that has enhanced presidential war making. In the context of *jus ad bellum*, the run-up and our fighting in the Iraq War are unique to the American experience in the several ways that were discussed in Chapter 7.

Consider our past experience as a wartime, noncombatant supplier of armaments to an allied side engaged in war. During all preceding major wars, America at first helped allies before actually entering into war itself. When it finally did enter the given war, it did so side-by-side with allies as it helped terminate hostilities, signed truce and/or peace treaties, and brought the troops home with as much dispatch as possible. Victory was clearly won—with the exception, of course, of the Vietnam War.

After a major war, America then scaled back on defense expenditures and development and virtually disarmed itself. War was soon put out of sight, out of mind. The record suggests a number of alternative policies that have present interest.

Recall in the twentieth century that in the period before World War I, America had no military-industrial potential to speak of. The nation was unprepared, both physically and psychologically, for a future war of any kind. Nowhere in American industry at that time were there blueprints to produce weapons and other equipment on a large scale. Yet by that war's start in 1914, 3 million men were enrolled in military service, most as volunteers.

As the war started in Europe, we watched passively at first as foreign tanks and airplanes appeared in the field of combat, models and technological specs that could not be found in any significant numbers in the tiny U.S. arsenal or in its skimpy research and development of weaponry. By 1915, with two more years to go before we entered the war, President Woodrow Wilson called on manufacturers throughout the 48 states to draw up a list of factories and plants located in their locales. In this way, the government in Washington could at least begin the process of assigning war production tasks in case the need arose.

America prepared for possible war while also deciding to aid allies already engaged in hostilities. In Massachusetts, then as now a state with a strong military-industrial potential, 1,500 industrial companies responded to Wilson's call, the makers of the Springfield rifle being one of the first respondents. Yet seven months passed with nothing really being done by the Bay State to gear up for defense production. When Americans finally entered the war in 1917, America learned firsthand how complex was the process of tooling up. Unlike the German wartime government under Chancellor Ludendorff, America had no ready-made, war-related administration or table of organization assigned to managing war production. Nevertheless, under the industrial management of the talented industrialist Bernard Baruch, the United States managed to start the job of producing weapons as the war in Europe progressed. Conversion of factories into defense production took place with remarkable speed. American industry was able to manage this surge of demand despite shortages here and there across the country in electric power and coal.

As to the weaponry itself, the standard infantry weapon was the old bolt-operated Springfield rifle. The U.S. Army had only about 225,000 copies of this rifle. Even during the war, the Army was chronically short of this basic weapon. In their basic training, the recruits had to use wooden rifle mock-ups. The best and only mobile military vehicles at that time were passenger cars and trucks. The Model T Ford truck saw a lot of service in the field of battle in France. So did the old Dodge touring car, which had been used to pursue Pancho Villa across the Mexican border in 1916. Later, a few American tanks showed up in combat.

In those times American-made aircraft were in critically short supply. Billy Mitchell, commanding some 1,500 military aircraft in the American sector on the front, had to use mostly French Spuds and British de Havillands on missions (consisting mainly of "dogfights") against the German Luftwaffe. In short, America's "air arm" was woefully lacking in machines, the result of inattention to defense before the war as well as the inability to catch up in the short term once Americans were fighting in the war. Similar shortages were seen in artillery, tanks, and ships. With regard to food and clothing, on the other hand, the Americans not only managed to keep themselves relatively well fed and clothed, but they also supplied these and other types of aid to their allies. In fact, an early form of U.S. multimillion-dollar "Lend-Lease" aid was one of the crucial aspects of America's participation in World War I.

Perhaps the most important assistance of all, however, was the factor of U.S. manpower that took the form of the quarter-million-strong American Expeditionary Force. These men and women, recruits and volunteers, fought and died alongside the Allied soldiers under the extreme conditions of trench warfare. According to some reports on the war, it was American participation in World War I that had turned the tide against the Central Powers at the crucial juncture in 1917–1918 in the terminal fighting on the Western Front. This was the summer and fall and the winter when the Russian war effort was collapsing on the Eastern Front following Lenin's coup d'etat against the Russian Provisional Government, and Soviet Russia's subsequent withdrawal from the war altogether.

The next period of America's loss of the habit of preparing and making war together with its usual unpreparedness set in during the 21-year inter-war period before World War II. By the time of Pearl Harbor, December 7, 1941, America was lagging behind all the other combatants in the conflict that had begun on September 1, 1939. Yet it is true that under President Franklin D. Roosevelt's Administration, America had already begun to tool up for war. Research and development of state-of-the-art weaponry were well underway by 1939–1940, so much so that defense plants were penetrated by Soviet spies, who also penetrated key offices of the federal government. America eventually (by spring 1941) devoted a good deal of its precious defense output to Lend-Lease shipments to England. Then by autumn 1941 the aid was extended to Soviet Russia following the German attack in June. The feeling was that America could act as the "arsenal of democracy" without itself having to enter the fray as a combatant. Both candidates in the presidential campaigns of 1940—Republican Wendell Willkie and Democrat FDR—had pledged to keep America out of "foreign wars." When the Japanese attack on Pearl Harbor changed all that, American industry had to make a radical shift-into-second, as it had done in World War I, to meet the rising demand for weapons of all types. The conversion to defense production was truly stunning, so striking, in fact, that Hitler found it unbelievable that the United States could become such an "arsenal." There is no doubt that the early start it got by 1940 was crucial.[19]

What is the "message" here as learned from America's historical experience in the last century? It is perhaps twofold. First, the United States needs to carefully assess the impending or ongoing military conflict in terms of its national interests and those of its traditional, democratic allies as it considers how best to aid the friendly side in the conflict. Second, the United States needs to carefully choose the correct strategy for its own possible (or likely) participation in war as well as do the research and development to equip itself so as to participate in the conflict in the most effective way and/or, as the "arsenal of democracy," to best assist its allies.

As we examine the pre-World War II period of the late 1930s and early 1940s, we see how radical, as well as swift and profound, was the makeover of the American psyche in the direction of war making. The death of American service personnel and the staggering loss of capital ships and aircraft at Pearl Harbor on that fateful Sunday morning in December 1941 had inflicted an enormous shock to the population. Yet in the months just prior to Pearl Harbor, public opinion had expressed an almost unanimous opposition to American participation in the war. West Coast and East Coast states tended to be the only ones that showed an awareness of American defense vulnerability. Some opinion expressed in those regions of the nation showed the public's acknowledgement that one day the United States would likely join the Allies in the war against the Axis. However, that America would eventually face a two-theater war—one in Europe, the other in the Far East—was very far from the minds of most Americans. This experience was radically different from the "shock" inflicted on America on 9/11. Yet there are some parallels, among them the United State's swift response to the attacks that day.

There are also lessons to be learned from our typical, postwar flaccidity and lack of attention to our defense needs. After World War II, America, true to its tradition of all but disarming itself after a war, tried to put any future war making out of its collective mind. Industry returned happily to the production of consumer goods, the public's mental state turned to peaceful postwar life, to raising families and building homes and pursuing entertainment. The inattention to defense needs—despite the looming Cold War with a militant USSR that rose threateningly over that hoped-for peaceful world following four long years of intense warfare—became notorious. President Truman's defense "czar," James Forrestal, even committed suicide in 1947 out of apparent frustration over American failure to keep its powder dry as trouble loomed on the horizon.

Then, just five short years after the capitulations of Germany and Japan, North Korean troops in great force crossed the 38th Parallel on the Korean Peninsula, thus triggering the Korean War (1950–1953). Once again, Uncle Sam had been caught unawares. The shock was so great and the casualties piled up so tragically that within two years of the fighting public opinion began to turn against America's continued participation in the remote war on the Korean Peninsula, despite the obviousness of the justness of that war as an allied, U.N.-supported defense against aggression.

What is the message from this prewar and postwar history? It is that during the post-World War II period as well as during the Korean and Vietnam Wars, the prevalent feeling in America was that large-scale war, if at all preventable, should be avoided. American participation in war, as it was in the past and should be in the future, should be an extremely rare phenomena. There was no feeling in the United States of a necessary state of perpetual fear of war or any military expression of Trotsky's slogan of "permanent revolution." Above all, in the case of these past wars, public patience began to wear thin in the midst of war, as was revealed in polls taken near the end of both conflicts, in Korea and in Vietnam. These wars were terminated as the impatience took the form of congressional reticence to appropriate the necessary funds to keep the wars going. *But the outstanding difference between these later two wars and World War II was the fact that the latter was a clear-cut case of America responding to an attack against its territory (i.e., Hawaii) launched in force by an enemy.*

What about during the Cold War? The reigning principles then were *containment* of the Soviets and *deterrence of Soviet military offensive strength* in the form of America's imposing nuclear arsenal. These were the means, *short of war*, that U.S. policymakers adopted, with the intent of keeping America safe without actually using the "ultimate" weapons of mass destruction in war. Hence, the term "cold" as in "cold war." Bluff, on both sides of the standoff, accompanied their looming arsenals. By the time of Mikhail Gorbachev's ascent to power in the Kremlin in 1985, the Soviet leadership was prepared generally to accept the principle of *mutual deterrence*, or "cold peace." This was followed by modest reductions in their nuclear arsenals and the realization of tangible détente, together with a warmer peace than had ever prevailed between Russia and the United States since World War I.

Up to 9/11, the idea widely held in America that wars, once terminated, meant extended peace and the avoidance of future wars at almost any cost—short of America being attacked as it was at Pearl Harbor—was an attitude that dominated this country's mentality. There was no popular notion of a perennial need for *permanent preparedness*, least of all the threat of recurring war, or seemingly "permanent war" of the type that has characterized much public thinking, and official statements, since September 11, 2001.

What is significant is that after 9/11, a sea change in the focus of U.S. policy was made by the Bush Administration. Bush and his team of advisers began to characterize America as a virtual world gendarme committed by its power to proactively enforce international law, as construed in Washington, throughout the world. In this manner America, under the George W. Bush Administration, acquired a new proclivity for making war in the name of peace. While Americans may not, as before, "want" war, the administration seemed to allege, nevertheless, America would be ready to make war in ways that strike an ominous contrast with most of this country's preceding history. (But could the White House legitimately mean the *American people*? With the Iraq War, based on an offensive strategy of preventive war, America found itself mired in a lengthy conflict of protracted duration, with no victory in sight and whose duration extended beyond any previous war in which the United States had participated, including World War II. This "quagmire" of our occupation of Iraq was further complicated by the fact that the country had descended into a widespread civil war by 2005–2006.

What the United States and its leaders—in Congress, in the White House, and amongst the public—must now determine is under what *clearly-stated conditions* this nation will choose to wage war in the future. Above all, the procedures for initiating and continuing war must be clarified beyond even the rules in the 1973 War Powers Act, which, in any case under present conditions, has become outdated. The government must make sure that a procedure is explicitly laid out to make war only when it is absolutely unavoidable. It must follow the letter and spirit of the "Founders" as well as precedents in declaring war after a broad firm consensus has been formed.

Can a war sanctioned by the War Powers Act and by enabling legislation of the U.S. Congress that empowered the president to initiate hostilities be, as it were, "undeclared" by updated legislation replacing the former? As pointed out by New York University legal scholar Noah Feldmann[20], U.S. constitutional tradition "does not clearly resolve this question. Once Congress has authorized war, as it did the war in Iraq, the president's power as commander-in-chief surely allows him to conduct the war without being micromanaged from Capitol Hill." During the Civil Wear, Congress had agreed to create the Joint Committee on the Conduct of the War. This body supervised with a vengeance, as Feldmann pointed out, by debriefing Union generals on the way they conducted certain missions and their use of tactics. All this greatly embarrassed President Lincoln. Ever since then, Congress has declined to interfere this way during wartime.

According to Feldmann, then, any congressional "quarterbacking," as he put it, is what the "Constitution prohibits." Yet perhaps this is debatable. To begin with, there is no such prohibition stated in the Constitution. Moreover, Congress not only holds the purse strings (meaning the funding of wars) as a crucial sanction against executive authority, but it is also entitled to pass legislation affecting wars, such as their very declaration; a power— incidentally, even if neglected today (at least since December 8, 1941)—that was strongly recommended by the Founding Fathers. Furthermore, in modern times, Congress has passed enabling legislation affecting the president's war-making authority—specifically as to time, place, and duration of hostilities. That being true, it seems clear that Congress could, constitutionally and by precedent, update any past enabling legislation it had passed without seeming to "micromanage" the commander-in-chief during actual hostilities. Article I, which specifies powers belonging to Congress, was, after all, placed at the beginning of the Constitution precisely because of its transcendent importance within tripartite separation of powers (which pride of place by Congress was also noted by commentators on the Constitution going back to time of *The Federalist Papers*).

In early 2007, the process of reexamining the way this country involves itself in war, and in the Iraq War in particular, appeared to be under serious review in Congress. The results of these discussions, which today are ongoing in relevant Senate and House committees, may eventually have an enormous bearing on recognizing *jus ad bellum* principles concerning the justifiability and the authority that warrant going to war (as discussed in Part One) as well as the way war is conducted (as discussed in Part Two). In this reexamination, any Washington administration's war planning must remain true to the principles of *jus ad bellum*. Moreover, when a war—that is, of necessity—is fought, it must honor the rules of *jus in bello*. In his acceptance speech at the Democratic National Convention in 2004, candidate John Kerry stated that America never seeks or wants war. It fights only when absolutely necessary. This statement, however, skirts the question as to *how* the necessity of making war should be concretely determined in a given situation, *how* it is to be waged according to what basic military doctrine, be it a defensive one or an offencist, preemptive one, and *how* certain just principles should be observed.

AFGHANISTAN AND IRAQ AND THE "WAR ON TERRORISM"

In the post-9/11 environment as viewed by the Bush Administration, the four brutal and dramatic attacks on that day by Al Qaeda produced a "Pearl Harbor" trauma. That is, these attacks on States-side targets were cast by the administration, as were the events of December 7, 1941, as an *act of war*. Yet on that day in 2001, a "war" against the United States was not initiated by a *nation-state*, as Japan had done with its attacks in Hawaii. The 9/11 attacks were perpetrated by a group of terrorists. Added to this depiction of the events of that day as a war, as with the subsequent terrorist acts in Spain, Britain, and so forth, was the Administration's insistence that Al Qaeda's 9/11 attacks represented an assault not only against America but against "world civilization". As late in the Iraq War as September 2006, President Bush called that war a "struggle for civilization" and that the war against it was required in order to "maintain the way of life enjoyed by free nations."[21]

Was this an apt description not only of the war in Iraq but of the situation worldwide as far as acts of terrorism are concerned (as with terrorist acts in Afghanistan, Iraq, or against civilians in Israel)? Is the Administration guilty, as some allege, of a misconception of the global struggle against terrorism by casting it as a "war," and by so epitomizing it in the "preventive" war against Iraq initiated in March 2003? If so, what are the consequences of this putative misconception?

In the U.S.-led invasion and occupation of *Afghanistan* in 2002, much of just war philosophy and law is supportive of that war, as it was fought with troops from several West European states as prescribed by policies adopted by NATO. The Taliban Government in Kabul was openly harboring Al Qaeda. Its regime openly supported Al Qaeda-initiated terrorist attacks against "infidels" throughout the world. In an effort to root out the nests of Al Qaeda operatives hiding in Afghanistan, and which included their top leader, Osama bin Laden, U.S. defense policy was obviously justified. That NATO and West European powers eventually joined in this effort was a reflection of the all but universal acknowledgement that the Afghan base for Al Qaeda had to be eliminated through war. In that sense, the "war against terrorism" was aptly centered on Al Qaeda in Afghanistan and the regime there that helped these terrorist cells flourish.

However, when the "war on terrorism" was extended to include Saddam Hussein's regime in Baghdad, a vastly different "target" was singled out by the Bush Administration. The fact was that Al Qaeda was not established in Iraq until *after* the American-led invasion and occupation. The latter had so weakened and disunited Iraq that foreign "jihadists," not only including Al Qaeda elements (such as the late Abu Musab al-Zarqawi, who had previously been anathema to bin Laden and his group) could set up shop throughout that country, particularly in its vulnerable "soft" region in the western-most province of Anbar. It is not uncommon for multi-ethnic countries, when liberated of their dictators who suppressed nationalistic feelings within the population, to fall into internecine struggle. (In this respect, witness post-Tito Yugoslavia.) The American-led war, an application of the so-called "Bush Doctrine," had aggravated the situation and made things worse by "accentuating the negative."[22] Instead of declaring victory against terrorists after disabling much of their financial infrastructure, setting up defensive means States-side to detect future terrorist plots, and forcing bin Laden into deeper hiding or concentrating solely on finding and eliminating his base, the United States had decided to invade Iraq in defiance of its own allies on the Security Council and world public opinion. It thus was detracted from its intended liquidation of Al Qaeda in Afghanistan and neighboring Pakistan. Thereby, the administration had set the threshold against terrorism too high. It had done this by characterizing it as a "war" while presenting the invasion and occupation of Iraq as the criterion for "making America safe."

As one observer points out, "When you define victory that way, when you treat one attack from a disorganized band of fanatics as a menace to civilization, you've doomed yourself to defeat and caused more damage than they could."[23] Terrorism, as it has become scattered into a limited number of terrorist cells worldwide, cannot be "stopped" in this vast, "world-historical" way. It certainly cannot be halted by sending U.S. servicemen into a civil war situation in Iraq, expending huge amounts of treasure while losing more lives than would be lost even in any imaginable terrorist attack.

TERMINATING AN INSURGENT WAR

As we saw in the discussion in Parts One and Two on *jus ad bellum* and *jus in bello*, one of the criteria for war justifiability is that the termination of hostilities is both feasible and as short term as possible. As the criteria for just war dictate, any war must be entered into by the defending, counterinsurgency side, with a clear notion of victory that is attainable in as short a time as possible so that peace can be restored quickly. The administration failed to anticipate a *protracted* war (requiring a prolonged occupation of a large a country that was so obviously disunited by tribal, ethnic, and religious divisions). It did not carefully weigh and react to the warnings about these complexities that were forthcoming from civilian, military, and academic specialists. U.S. and coalition armed forces were thus put into a cauldron of potential and later actual insurgency warfare. The Iraqi dictator himself had openly declared that an invasion and occupation would be met with armed, insurgent opposition, which Saddam actively began to organize before March 2003. The war planners in Washington should have taken precautions against the outbreak of this type of struggle. One of the first such countermeasures should have been, above all, to deploy adequate numbers of troops with adequate *protective* gear for the troops as well as sufficiently armored vehicles (e.g., Humvees). Such protective measures were sorely lacking to cope with the likely insurgency. Secretary of Defense Rumsfeld dismissed such warnings with his virtual brushoff that forces must enter war with the equipment they have, not necessarily with the equipment they wish they had.

It is not a matter of second-guessing to point out that insurgency-type warfare possesses certain well-known characteristics. Besides innovative weapons that are fired or planted and exploded unexpectedly in unconventional ways (e.g., bombs with remote or installed timing devices or explosives attached to individual suicide bombers), such wars are commonly seen by military specialists to be of *long duration*. Professor Ronald Stoker of the U.S. Naval War College, for example, points out in his January 2007 analysis that although insurgency warfare is sometimes depicted as "invincible," it can be defeated by a well-rounded and well-buttressed counterinsurgency strategy.[24] He warns, however, that any such struggle against well-armed insurgents will likely be of long duration. Counterinsurgent victory can be lost if the methods of fighting the elusive guerrillas do not measure up to the task, and if that "irregular" (unconventional) struggle is not recognized as likely being a protracted one in which the patience of counterinsurgency forces will be severely tried. As Professor Stoker writes:

Myths about invincible guerrillas and insurgents are a direct result of America's collective misunderstanding of its defeat in South Vietnam. This loss is generally credited to the brilliance and military virtues of the pajama-clad Vietcong. The Vietnamese may have been tough and persistent, but they were not brilliant. Rather, they were lucky—they faced an opponent with leaders unwilling to learn from their failures: the United States...It was North Vietnam's will and American failure, not skillful use of an insurgency, that were the keys to Hanoi's victory. Of course, history is not without genuine insurgent successes. Fidel Castro's victory in Cuba is probably the best known, and there was the IRA's partial triumph in 1922, as well as Algeria's defeat of the French between 1954 and 1962. But the list of failed insurgencies is longer: Malayan Communists, Greek Communists, Filipino Huks, Nicaraguan Contras, Communists in El Salvador, Che Guevara in Bolivia, the Boers in South Africa (twice), Savimbi in Angola, and Sindero Luminoso in Peru, to name just a few. *If the current U.S. administration maintains its will, establishes security in Baghdad, and succeeds in building a functioning government and army, there is no reason that the Iraqi insurgency cannot be similarly destroyed, or at least reduced to the level of terrorist thugs.*

Stoker has made a number of critical assumptions:

1. That the insurgency in Iraq will not be further complicated and abetted by outside forces that the U.S.-led effort would not or could not block;
2. That "surge" efforts to increase the numbers of U.S.-led counterinsurgency forces and to enhance their strategy by making important changes in the earlier, unsuccessful methods does not become a case of "too little, too late";

3. That the new methods are continually buttressed and maintained, perhaps
   even by additional deployments of troops, and that surges are not allowed to
   wither on the vine because of nonsupport on the U.S. domestic front.[25]

••••

Given these imponderables, the focus again reverts to the very conception
of waging war against and occupying the particular country, Iraq. This
war's peculiar hazards were simply not taken into account. It was as though
the Pentagon's war planners regarded the whole enterprise as "slam dunk."
By making the initial error of underestimating the numbers and types of
forces that would be necessary to occupy a country the size of California,
then confounding that fatal mistake with a series of other errors (most of
which were in violation of the principles and traditions of just war), the
administration got American forces into a virtual quagmire—*moral as well
as military*—that involved an intolerable loss of life and treasure.

"Those who forget the past are doomed to repeat it"—along with its past
mistakes. In the case of the Iraq War, Santayana's famous truism is two-
pronged. First, the lessons of the Vietnam War and other insurgency struggles, such as those in Algeria in the 1960s, had not sunk in and were not
taken into account when mounting a hi-tech war against Iraq in March
2003. Among these lessons should have been the awareness by the war planners, civilian and military, that fighting a counterinsurgent war in Iraq
meant deploying more than adequate forces to win victory.

Moreover, the cause in fighting such a war had to be such as to be able
without reservations to rally the American population to lend unwavering
support to such a struggle in the long term since this type of war is more than
likely to be protracted. The Administration had failed not only to make
these anticipations, but it showed a dismal inability or unwillingness to com-
municate in candid ways to the population the difficulties that soon arose in
mounting the counterinsurgency. This criticism is not a case of "Monday
morning quarterbacking." Plenty of historical experience was there for the
Administration to ponder, and with these deliberations to urge reluctance
to enter such a war given the circumstances. Among these were not only
the misinformation about Iraqi WMD, the major reason for entering into
war, but also the American population's well-known impatience about
wars that drag on interminably, as victory fades out of view like a retreating
horizon.

These factors again prompt the caveat: When it is not absolutely necessary
to wage a war, it is necessary not to wage it. We must bear this in mind in the
future. Any war in which America may engage from now on must be a just
war, as perceived widely throughout the world and as measured by deep-
seated tradition. An isolated, "pariah" America is more than just unpleasant
or "bad for business." It becomes a critical *security* issue. Even the world's
number-one superpower cannot fight major wars alone, virtually

unilaterally. When and if it individually ever lies in clear and present danger of an imminent attack on itself, the United States nevertheless will need allies. This is especially true when and if it chose under extremely dire conditions to wage a preventive or preemptive war against such a tangible enemy threat. Any such war must be seen as a defensive one, be warranted by principle, and be fought in just ways for justifiable reasons.

Epilogue

Unfortunately, U.S. leadership in recent years unintentionally, but most unwisely, contributed to the currently threatening state of affairs [in the Middle East and elsewhere]. The combination of Washington's arrogant unilateralism in Iraq and its demagogic Islamophobic sloganeering weakened the unity of NATO and focused aroused Muslim resentments on the United States and the West more generally.

> —Zbigniew Brzezinski ("An Agenda for NATO," *Foreign Affairs*, September/October 2009, p. 12)

This study has examined the issue of whether the choice of waging war against Saddam Hussein's Iraq in March 2003 met the criteria of *jus ad bellum* and *jus in bello*. Also critiqued was the "Bush Doctrine" of war-making rationales based on a putative *imminence of a tangible danger of attack* that would justify planning and waging *preventive* or *preemptive* war against Iraq in 2002–2003.

Readers might have agreed that the factor of imminence as a rationale for choosing war against a weakened, all but dysfunctional Iraq was grossly overstated by the Bush administration. No weapons of mass destruction (WMD) were found in Iraq by U.N. inspectors shortly before the invasion or after it when U.S. forces began occupying Iraq.

Furthermore, the absence of WMD had been anticipated well before the war by a number of informed persons, including U.N. inspectors and others. When the Bush Administration's line on the rationale for war thereafter shifted to one of nation building and the democratization of Iraq, the principal motivation for undertaking the bloody, expensive military enterprise was thereupon "revised" and undercut. As the occupation of Iraq ensued for more than six years, countless additional violations of the principles for waging war followed amid declining U.S. public support for the war as U.S. military casualties mounted.

The conclusion on the part of the larger portion of the American population implied that the war had been a costly mistake. Also implied was the notion that the United States should avoid making such a choice of war in the future. Indeed, by 2007 the former NSS 2002 strategy of preemption itself was formally removed from this country's declarative military strategy. (By contrast, some other nation-states left the preemption option within their declared strategy after 9/11. The Russian Federation was one such state. So is Japan.)[1]

Nevertheless, a question lingering in people's minds: Could a dire, threatening situation, implying the imminence of aggressive war, nevertheless arise in the foreseeable future? Would that threat legitimize preemptive war as waged by a country or by one of its allies?

This is no "academic question." For instance, Israel today faces such a mounting danger, a potentially imminent threat. The leadership of Iran appears not only to be developing the capacity to build nuclear weapons, but is also actively testing the rocket platforms for delivering warheads at respectable "medium" ranges. Tehran's government, as presumably authorized by the Supreme Leader, Ayatollah Khamenei, has several times stated publicly that it favors the "destruction" of Israel. Once before, a neighboring state, Iraq, had similarly threatened Israel as Saddam Hussein in 1981 was constructing a nuclear reactor at Osirak on the outskirts of Baghdad. That regime, too, was making threatening statements against Israel. The result was that the Israeli air force made a preemptive surgical strike on the reactor structure and destroyed it. It apparently did the same in 2008 against a reactor structure being built in Syria.

A large volume of professional literature developed by legal scholars followed this dramatic action by Israel against Osirak a generation ago. At that time, experts on international law were divided on the question as to whether the Israeli action was justifiable. Some found Israel's preemptive—perhaps, better, *preventive*—strike to have been warranted on the grounds that the attack had been *defensive* in the face of a tangible threat emanating from an overly hostile Iraq. Other law specialists argued that the building of an atomic reactor by a hostile country was not grounds enough for a preemptive attack. If it were, couldn't the United States have taken preventive action against the USSR during the most threatening days of the Cold War? After all, Soviet civilian and military literature had explicitly described the United States as the "main enemy."

Moreover, open and closed Soviet military literature had even suggested, threateningly, that preemption might prove necessary as an American "imperialist threat" took shape. Interviews with its senior strategic command military officers revealed that Soviet long-range missiles (ICBM) were, indeed, targeted on the United States, just as the American counterparts were targeted on the Soviets. But the Soviet strategy appeared to be one of "launch-on-warning" (LOW) while the U.S. strategy was one of "launch-on-attack" (LOA).

Threats aside, it seemed that both sides had decided to live with these mutual threats, regarding them as mutual deterrents. This was true even when, in 1983, one side, the Soviet Union, under the leadership of General Secretary and President Yuri V. Andropov, was reportedly preparing to launch a disarming, preemptive (or "counterforce") strike against U.S. missile bases. The Soviets imagined the danger at that time as the threat of an "imminent" U.S. missile attack, which appeared to Soviet strategists to be mounting.[2]

As mentioned above, Israel faces a potentially tangible danger to its external security from a nuclear-armed Iran. The rationale for its taking preemptive action against an overtly threatening state is at least arguable on the grounds of international law. Iran's government (to date) has explicitly deemed Israel to be an enemy deserving of destruction. The same rationale for "active defense" might one day be applicable by the United States and its allies to North Korea (DPRK).

This state is led by a regime that is openly hostile and threatening to the United States and its nearest neighbors, the Republic of Korea and Japan. The DPRK under dictator Kim Jong Il is accumulating nuclear weapons while testing missiles that could carry such warheads at medium and strategic distances that would include the Japanese islands as well as Alaska.

Most international law specialists agree that determining the degree of threat and therefore the "proven" legitimacy for taking preemptive military action are in some cases controversial. They deem it essential that all other nonmilitary means, such as diplomacy, be used and exhausted (as they were not prior to the U.S. choice of war against Iraq in 2003) before a resort to arms is made. When that margin may be crossed and when war appears to be warranted is for statesmen on the defending side to determine. They must weigh the wisdom of their ultimate decision to adopt forceful means, which are fraught with unpredictable consequences and casualties, only after careful thought. Above all, the decisions must be reached in consultation and cooperation with allies who are willing to take up arms together against the common enemy.

The adoption of such extreme measures must be based on the honored principles of *jus ad bellum* and *jus in bello*.

Appendices

Appendix A

President's Introduction to NSS 2002

The great struggles of the twentieth century between liberty and totalitarianism ended with a decisive victory for the forces of freedom—and a single sustainable model for national success: freedom, democracy, and free enterprise. In the twenty-first century, only nations that share a commitment to protecting basic human rights and guaranteeing political and economic freedom will be able to unleash the potential of their people and assure their future prosperity. People everywhere want to be able to speak freely; choose who will govern them; worship as they please; educate their children—male and female; own property; and enjoy the benefits of their labor. These values of freedom are right and true for every person, in every society—and the duty of protecting these values against their enemies is the common calling of freedom-loving people across the globe and across the ages.

Today, the United States enjoys a position of unparalleled military strength and great economic and political influence. In keeping with our heritage and principles, we do not use our strength to press for unilateral advantage. We seek instead to create a balance of power that favors human freedom: conditions in which all nations and all societies can choose for themselves the rewards and challenges of political and economic liberty. In a world that is safe, people will be able to make their own lives better. We will defend the peace by fighting terrorists and tyrants. We will preserve the peace by building good relations among the great powers. We will extend the peace by encouraging free and open societies on every continent.

Defending our Nation against its enemies is the first and fundamental commitment of the Federal Government. Today, that task has changed dramatically. Enemies in the past needed great armies and great industrial capabilities to endanger America. Now, shadowy networks of individuals can bring great chaos and suffering to our shores for less than it costs to purchase a single tank. Terrorists are organized to penetrate open societies and to turn the power of modern technologies against us.

To defeat this threat we must make use of every tool in our arsenal—military power, better homeland defenses, law enforcement, intelligence, and vigorous efforts to cut off terrorist financing. The war against terrorists of global reach is a global enterprise of uncertain duration. America will help nations that need our assistance in combating terror. And America will hold to account nations that are compromised by terror, including those who harbor terrorists— because the allies of terror are the enemies of civilization. The United States and countries cooperating with us must not allow the terrorists to develop new home bases. Together, we will seek to deny them sanctuary at every turn.

The gravest danger our Nation faces lies at the crossroads of radicalism and technology. Our enemies have openly declared that they are seeking weapons of mass destruction, and evidence indicates that they are doing so with determination. The United States will not allow these efforts to succeed. We will build defenses against ballistic missiles and other means of delivery. We will cooperate with other nations to deny, contain, and curtail our enemies' efforts to acquire dangerous technologies. And, as a matter of common sense and self-defense, America will act against such emerging threats before they are fully formed. We cannot defend America and our friends by hoping for the best. So we must be prepared to defeat our enemies' plans, using the best intelligence and proceeding with deliberation. History will judge harshly those who saw this coming danger but failed to act. In the new world we have entered, the only path to peace and security is the path of action.

As we defend the peace, we will also take advantage of an historic opportunity to preserve the peace. Today, the international community has the best chance since the rise of the nation-state in the seventeenth century to build a world where great powers compete in peace instead of continually prepare for war. Today, the world's great powers find ourselves on the same side—united by common dangers of terrorist violence and chaos. The United States will build on these common interests to promote global security. We are also increasingly united by common values. Russia is in the midst of a hopeful transition, reaching for its democratic future and a partner in the war on terror. Chinese leaders are discovering that economic freedom is the only source of national wealth. In time, they will find that social and political freedom is the only source of national greatness. America will encourage the advancement of democracy and economic openness in both nations, because these are the best foundations for domestic stability and international order. We will strongly resist aggression from other great powers—even as we welcome their peaceful pursuit of prosperity, trade, and cultural advancement.

Finally, the United States will use this moment of opportunity to extend the benefits of freedom across the globe. We will actively work to bring the hope of democracy, development, free markets, and free trade to every corner of the world. The events of September 11, 2001, taught us that weak states, like Afghanistan, can pose as great a danger to our national interests as strong states. Poverty does not make poor people into terrorists and murderers. Yet poverty, weak institutions, and corruption can make weak states vulnerable to terrorist networks and drug cartels within their borders.

The United States will stand beside any nation determined to build a better future by seeking the rewards of liberty for its people. Free trade and free markets have proven their ability to lift whole societies out of poverty—so the United States will work with individual nations, entire regions, and the entire global trading community to build a world that trades in freedom and therefore grows in prosperity. The United States will deliver greater development assistance through the New Millennium Challenge Account to nations that govern justly, invest in their people, and encourage economic freedom. We will also continue to lead the world in efforts to reduce the terrible toll of HIV/AIDS and other infectious diseases.

In building a balance of power that favors freedom, the United States is guided by the conviction that all nations have important responsibilities. Nations that enjoy freedom must actively fight terror. Nations that depend on international stability must help prevent the spread of weapons of mass destruction. Nations that seek international aid must govern themselves wisely, so that aid is well spent. For freedom to thrive, accountability must be expected and required.

We are also guided by the conviction that no nation can build a safer, better world alone. Alliances and multilateral institutions can multiply the strength of freedom-loving nations. The United States is committed to lasting institutions like the United Nations, the World Trade Organization, the Organization of American States, and NATO as well as other long-standing alliances. Coalitions of the willing can augment these permanent institutions. In all cases, international obligations are to be taken seriously. They are not to be undertaken symbolically to rally support for an ideal without furthering its attainment.

Freedom is the non-negotiable demand of human dignity; the birthright of every person—in every civilization. Throughout history, freedom has been threatened by war and terror; it has been challenged by the clashing wills of powerful states and the evil designs of tyrants; and it has been tested by widespread poverty and disease. Today, humanity holds in its hands the opportunity to further freedom's triumph over all these foes. The United States welcomes our responsibility to lead in this great mission.

George W. Bush
THE WHITE HOUSE,
September 17, 2002

Appendix B

Text of Chapter VII of U.N. Charter

ACTION WITH RESPECT TO THREATS TO THE PEACE, BREACHES
OF THE PEACE, AND ACTS OF AGGRESSION

Article 39
The Security Council shall determine the existence of any threat to the
peace, breach of the peace, or act of aggression and shall make recommendations, or decide what measures shall be taken in accordance with
Articles 41 and 42, to maintain or restore international peace and
security.

Article 40
In order to prevent an aggravation of the situation, the Security Council
may, before making the recommendations or deciding upon the measures
provided for in Article 39, call upon the parties concerned to comply with
such provisional measures as it deems necessary or desirable. Such
provisional measures shall be without prejudice to the rights, claims, or
position of the parties concerned. The Security Council shall duly take
account of failure to comply with such provisional measures.

Article 41
The Security Council may decide what measures not involving the use of
armed force are to be employed to give effect to its decisions, and it may call
upon the Members of the United Nations to apply such measures. These may
include complete or partial interruption of economic relations and of rail,

sea, air, postal, telegraphic, radio, and other means of communication, and the severance of diplomatic relations.

Article 42
Should the Security Council consider that measures provided for in Article 41 would be inadequate or have proved to be inadequate, it may take such action by air, sea, or land forces as may be necessary to maintain or restore international peace and security. Such action may include demonstrations, blockade, and other operations by air, sea, or land forces of Members of the United Nations.

Article 43
All Members of the United Nations, in order to contribute to the maintenance of international peace and security, undertake to make available to the Security Council, on its call and in accordance with a special agreement or agreements, armed forces, assistance, and facilities, including rights of passage, necessary for the purpose of maintaining international peace and security.
Such agreement or agreements shall govern the numbers and types of forces, their degree of readiness and general location, and the nature of the facilities and assistance to be provided.
The agreement or agreements shall be negotiated as soon as possible on the initiative of the Security Council. They shall be concluded between the Security Council and Members or between the Security Council and groups of Members and shall be subject to ratification by the signatory states in accordance with their respective constitutional processes.

Article 44
When the Security Council has decided to use force it shall, before calling upon a Member not represented on it to provide armed forces in fulfilment of the obligations assumed under Article 43, invite that Member, if the Member so desires, to participate in the decisions of the Security Council concerning the employment of contingents of that Member's armed forces.

Article 45
In order to enable the United Nations to take urgent military measures, Members shall hold immediately available national air-force contingents for combined international enforcement action. The strength and degree of readiness of these contingents and plans for their combined action shall be determined within the limits laid down in the special agreement or agreements referred to in Article 43, by the Security Council with the assistance of the Military Staff Committee.

Article 46
Plans for the application of armed force shall be made by the Security Council with the assistance of the Military Staff Committee.

Article 47

There shall be established a Military Staff Committee to advise and assist the Security Council on all questions relating to the Security Council's military requirements for the maintenance of international peace and security, the employment and command of forces placed at its disposal, the regulation of armaments, and possible disarmament.

The Military Staff Committee shall consist of the Chiefs of Staff of the permanent members of the Security Council or their representatives. Any Member of the United Nations not permanently represented on the Committee shall be invited by the Committee to be associated with it when the efficient discharge of the Committee's responsibilities requires the participation of that Member in its work.

The Military Staff Committee shall be responsible under the Security Council for the strategic direction of any armed forces placed at the disposal of the Security Council. Questions relating to the command of such forces shall be worked out subsequently.

The Military Staff Committee, with the authorization of the Security Council and after consultation with appropriate regional agencies, may establish regional sub-committees.

Article 48

The action required to carry out the decisions of the Security Council for the maintenance of international peace and security shall be taken by all the Members of the United Nations or by some of them, as the Security Council may determine. Such decisions shall be carried out by the Members of the United Nations directly and through their action in the appropriate international agencies of which they remembers.

Article 49

The Members of the United Nations shall join in affording mutual assistance in carrying out the measures decided upon by the Security Council.

Article 50

If preventive or enforcement measures against any state are taken by the Security Council, any other state, whether a Member of the United Nations or not, which finds itself confronted with special economic problems arising from the carrying out of those measures shall have the right to consult the Security Council with regard to a solution of those problems.

Article 51

Nothing in the present Charter shall impair the inherent right of individual or collective self-defence if an armed attack occurs against a Member of the United Nations, until the Security Council has taken measures necessary to maintain international peace and security. Measures taken by Members in the exercise of this right of self-defence shall be immediately reported to the Security Council and shall not in any way affect the authority and responsibility of the Security Council under the present Charter to take at any time such action as it deems necessary in order to maintain or restore international peace and security.

Appendix C

This statement, issued June 16, 2004, was signed by 27 retired U.S. military officers and former State Department officials. A similar statement was published in the United Kingdom around the same time and was signed by over 50 British officials.

•••

The undersigned have held positions of responsibility for the planning and execution of American foreign and defense policy. Collectively, we have served every president since Harry S. Truman. Some of us are Democrats, some are Republicans or Independents, many voted for George W. Bush. But we all believe that current Administration policies have failed in the primary responsibilities of preserving national security and providing world leadership. Serious issues are at stake. We need a change.

From the outset, President George W. Bush adopted an overbearing approach to America's role in the world, relying upon military might and righteousness, insensitive to the concerns of traditional friends and allies, and disdainful of the United Nations. Instead of building upon America's great economic and moral strength to lead other nations in a coordinated campaign to address the causes of terrorism and to stifle its resources, the Administration, motivated more by ideology than by reasoned analysis, struck out on its own. It led the United States into an ill-planned and costly war from which exit is uncertain. It justified the invasion of Iraq by manipulation of uncertain intelligence about weapons of mass destruction, and by a cynical campaign to persuade the public that Saddam Hussein was linked to Al Qaeda and the attacks of September 11. The evidence did not support this argument.

Our security has been weakened. While American airmen and women, marines, soldiers and sailors have performed gallantly, our armed forces were not prepared for military occupation and nation building. Public opinion polls throughout the world report hostility toward us. Muslim youth are turning to anti-American terrorism. Never in the two and a quarter centuries of our history has the United States been so isolated among the nations, so broadly feared and distrusted. No loyal American would question our ultimate right to act alone in our national interest; but responsible leadership would not turn to unilateral military action before diplomacy had been thoroughly explored.

The United States suffers from close identification with autocratic regimes in the Muslim world, and from the perception of unquestioning support for the policies and actions of the present Israeli Government. To enhance credibility with Islamic peoples we must pursue courageous, energetic and balanced efforts to establish peace between Israelis and Palestinians, and policies that encourage responsible democratic reforms.

We face profound challenges in the 21st Century: proliferation of weapons of mass destruction, unequal distribution of wealth and the fruits of globalization, terrorism, environmental degradation, population growth in the developing world, HIV/AIDS, ethnic and religious confrontations. Such problems can not be resolved by military force, nor by the sole remaining superpower alone; they demand patient, coordinated global effort under the leadership of the United States.

The Bush Administration has shown that it does not grasp these circumstances of the new era, and is not able to rise to the responsibilities of world leadership in either style or substance. It is time for a change.

Avis T. Bohlen—assistant secretary of State for arms control, 1999–2002; deputy assistant secretary of State for European affairs 1989–1991.
Retired Adm. William J. Crowe Jr.—chairman, President's Foreign Intelligence Advisory Committee, 1993–94; ambassador to Britain, 1993–97; chairman of the Joint Chiefs of Staff, 1985–89.
Jeffrey S. Davidow—ambassador to Mexico, 1998–2002; assistant secretary of State for Inter-American Affairs, 1996
William A. DePree—ambassador to Bangladesh, 1987–1990.
Donald B. Easum—ambassador to Nigeria, 1975–79.
Charles W. Freeman Jr. — assistant secretary of Defense, International Security Affairs, 1993–94; ambassador to Saudi Arabia, 1989–1992.

William C. Harrop — ambassador to Israel, 1991–93; ambassador to Zaire, 1987–1991.

Arthur A. Hartman — ambassador to the Soviet Union, 1981–87; ambassador to France, 1977–1981.

Retired Marine Gen. Joseph P. Hoar — commander in chief of U.S. Central Command, overseeing forces in the Middle East, 1991–94; deputy chief of staff, Marine Corps, 1990–94.

H. Allen Holmes — assistant secretary of Defense for special operations, 1993–99; assistant secretary of State for politico-military affairs, 1986–89.

Robert V. Keeley — ambassador to Greece, 1985–89; ambassador to Zimbabwe, 1980–84.

Samuel W. Lewis — director of State Department policy and planning, 1993–94; ambassador to Israel, 1977–1985.

Princeton N. Lyman — assistant secretary of State for International Organization Affairs, 1995–98; ambassador to South Africa, 1992–95.

Jack F. Matlock Jr. — ambassador to the Soviet Union, 1987–1991; director for European and Soviet Affairs, National Security Council, 1983–86; ambassador to Czechoslovakia, 1981–83.

Donald F. McHenry — ambassador to the United Nations, 1979–1981.

Retired Air Force Gen. Merrill A. McPeak — chief of staff, U.S. Air Force, 1990–94.

George E. Moose — assistant secretary of State for African affairs, 1993–97; ambassador to Senegal, 1988–91.

David D. Newsom — acting secretary of State, 1980; undersecretary of State for political affairs, 1978–1981; ambassador to Indonesia, 1973–77

Phyllis E. Oakley — assistant secretary of State for intelligence and research, 1997–99.

James Daniel Phillips — ambassador to the Republic of Congo, 1990–93; ambassador to Burundi, 1986–1990.

John E. Reinhardt — professor of political science, University of Vermont, 1987–91; ambassador to Nigeria, 1971–75.

Retired Air Force Gen. William Y. Smith — deputy commander in chief, U.S. European Command, 1981–83.

Ronald I. Spiers — undersecretary-general of the United Nations for Political Affairs, 1989–1992; ambassador to Pakistan, 1981–83.

Michael Sterner — deputy assistant secretary of State for Near East affairs, 1977–1981; ambassador to the United Arab Emirates, 1974–76.

Retired Adm. Stansfield Turner — director of the Central Intelligence Agency, 1977–1981.

Alexander F. Watson — assistant secretary of State for Inter-American affairs, 1993–96; deputy permanent representative to the U.N., 1989–1993.

Source: Official statement of Diplomats and Military Commanders for Change, June 16, 2004.

Appendix D

Joint Resolution of Congress: October 2, 2002

To authorize the use of United States Armed Forces against Iraq.

Whereas in 1990 in response to Iraq's war of aggression against and illegal occupation of Kuwait, the United States forged a coalition of nations to liberate Kuwait and its people in order to defend the national security of the United States and enforce United Nations Security Council resolutions relating to Iraq;

Whereas after the liberation of Kuwait in 1991, Iraq entered into a United Nations sponsored cease-fire agreement pursuant to which Iraq unequivocally agreed, among other things, to eliminate its nuclear, biological, and chemical weapons programs and the means to deliver and develop them, and to end its support for international terrorism;

Whereas the efforts of international weapons inspectors, United States intelligence agencies, and Iraqi defectors led to the discovery that Iraq had large stockpiles of chemical weapons and a large scale biological weapons program, and that Iraq had an advanced nuclear weapons development program that was much closer to producing a nuclear weapon than intelligence reporting had previously indicated;

Whereas Iraq, in direct and flagrant violation of the cease-fire, attempted to thwart the efforts of weapons inspectors to identify and destroy Iraq's weapons of mass destruction stockpiles and development capabilities, which finally resulted in the withdrawal of inspectors from Iraq on October 31, 1998;

Whereas in Public Law 105–235 (August 14, 1998), Congress concluded that Iraq's continuing weapons of mass destruction programs threatened vital United States interests and international peace and security, declared Iraq to be in 'material and unacceptable breach of its international obligations' and urged the President 'to take appropriate action, in accordance with the Constitution and relevant laws of the United States, to bring Iraq into compliance with its international obligations';

Whereas Iraq both poses a continuing threat to the national security of the United States and international peace and security in the Persian Gulf region and remains in material and unacceptable breach of its international obligations by, among other things, continuing to possess and develop a significant chemical and biological weapons capability, actively seeking a nuclear weapons capability, and supporting and harboring terrorist organizations;

Whereas Iraq persists in violating resolution of the United Nations Security Council by continuing to engage in brutal repression of its civilian population thereby threatening international peace and security in the region, by refusing to release, repatriate, or account for non-Iraqi citizens wrongfully detained by Iraq, including an American serviceman, and by failing to return property wrongfully seized by Iraq from Kuwait;

Whereas the current Iraqi regime has demonstrated its capability and willingness to use weapons of mass destruction against other nations and its own people;

Whereas the current Iraqi regime has demonstrated its continuing hostility toward, and willingness to attack, the United States, including by attempting in 1993 to assassinate former President Bush and by firing on many thousands of occasions on United States and Coalition Armed Forces engaged in enforcing the resolutions of the United Nations Security Council;

Whereas members of al Qaida, an organization bearing responsibility for attacks on the United States, its citizens, and interests, including the attacks that occurred on September 11, 2001, are known to be in Iraq;

Whereas Iraq continues to aid and harbor other international terrorist organizations, including organizations that threaten the lives and safety of United States citizens;

Whereas the attacks on the United States of September 11, 2001, underscored the gravity of the threat posed by the acquisition of weapons of mass destruction by international terrorist organizations;

Whereas Iraq's demonstrated capability and willingness to use weapons of mass destruction, the risk that the current Iraqi regime will either employ those weapons to launch a surprise attack against the United States or its Armed Forces or provide them to international terrorists who would do so, and the extreme magnitude of harm that would result to the United States and its citizens from such an attack, combine to justify action by the United States to defend itself;

Whereas United Nations Security Council Resolution 678 (1990) authorizes the use of all necessary means to enforce United Nations Security Council Resolution 660 (1990) and subsequent relevant resolutions and to compel Iraq to cease certain activities that threaten international peace and security, including the development of weapons of mass destruction and refusal or obstruction of United Nations weapons inspections in violation of United Nations Security Council Resolution 687 (1991), repression of its civilian population in violation of United Nations Security Council Resolution 688 (1991), and threatening its neighbors or United Nations operations in Iraq in violation of United Nations Security Council Resolution 949 (1994);

Whereas in the Authorization for Use of Military Force Against Iraq Resolution (Public Law 102–1), Congress has authorized the President 'to use United States Armed Forces pursuant to United Nations Security Council Resolution 678 (1990) in order to achieve implementation of Security Council Resolution 660, 661, 662, 664, 665, 666, 667, 669, 670, 674, and 677';

Whereas in December 1991, Congress expressed its sense that it 'supports the use of all necessary means to achieve the goals of United Nations Security Council Resolution 687 as being consistent with the Authorization of Use of Military Force Against Iraq Resolution (Public Law 102–1),' that Iraq's repression of its civilian population violates United Nations Security Council Resolution 688 and 'constitutes a continuing threat to the peace, security, and stability of the Persian Gulf region,' and that Congress, 'supports the use of all necessary means to achieve the goals of United Nations Security Council Resolution 688';

Whereas the Iraq Liberation Act of 1998 (Public Law 105–338) expressed the sense of Congress that it should be the policy of the United States to support efforts to remove from power the current Iraqi regime and promote the emergence of a democratic government to replace that regime;

Whereas on ... September 12, 2002, President Bush committed the United States to 'work with the United Nations Security Council to meet our common challenge' posed by Iraq and to 'work for the necessary resolutions,' while also making clear that 'the Security Council resolutions will be enforced, and the just demands of peace and security will be met, or action will be unavoidable';

Whereas the United States is determined to prosecute the war on terrorism and Iraq's ongoing support for international terrorist groups combined with its development of weapons of mass destruction in direct violation of its obligations under the 1991 cease-fire and other United Nations Security Council resolutions make clear that it is in the national security interests of the United States and in furtherance of the war on terrorism that all relevant United Nations Security Council resolutions be enforced, including through the use of force if necessary;

Whereas Congress has taken steps to pursue vigorously the war on terrorism through the provision of authorities and funding requested by the

President to take the necessary actions against international terrorists and terrorist organizations, including those nations, organizations, or persons who planned, authorized, committed, or aided the terrorist attacks that occurred on September 11, 2001, or harbored such persons or organizations;

Whereas the President and Congress are determined to continue to take all appropriate actions against international terrorists and terrorist organizations, including those nations, organizations, or persons who planned, authorized, committed, or aided the terrorist attacks that occurred on September 11, 2001, or harbored such persons or organizations;

Whereas the President has authority under the Constitution to take action in order to deter and prevent acts of international terrorism against the United States, as Congress recognized in the joint resolution on Authorization for Use of Military Force (Public Law 107–40); and

Whereas it is in the national security interests of the United States to restore international peace and security to the Persian Gulf region: Now, therefore, be it

Resolved by the Senate and House of Representatives of the United States of America in Congress assembled,

SECTION 1. SHORT TITLE.

This joint resolution may be cited as the 'Authorization for Use of Military Force Against Iraq Resolution of 2002'.

SEC. 2. SUPPORT FOR UNITED STATES DIPLOMATIC EFFORTS.

The Congress of the United States supports the efforts by the President to—

(1) strictly enforce through the United Nations Security Council all relevant Security Council resolutions regarding Iraq and encourages him in those efforts; and

(2) obtain prompt and decisive action by the Security Council to ensure that Iraq abandons its strategy of delay, evasion and noncompliance and promptly and strictly complies with all relevant Security Council resolutions regarding Iraq.

SEC. 3. AUTHORIZATION FOR USE OF UNITED STATES ARMED FORCES.

(a) AUTHORIZATION.—The President is authorized to use the Armed Forces of the United States as he determines to be necessary and appropriate in order to—

(1) defend the national security of the United States against the continuing threat posed by Iraq; and

(2) enforce all relevant United Nations Security Council resolutions regarding Iraq.

(b) PRESIDENTIAL DETERMINATION.—In connection with the exercise of the authority granted in subsection (a) to use force the President shall, prior to such exercise or as soon thereafter as may be feasible, but no later than 48 hours after exercising such authority, make available to the Speaker of the House of Representatives and the President pro tempore of the Senate his determination that—

(1) reliance by the United States on further diplomatic or other peaceful means alone either will not adequately protect the national security of the United States against the continuing threat posed by Iraq or is not likely to lead to enforcement of all relevant United Nations Security Council resolutions regarding Iraq; and

(2) acting pursuant to this joint resolution is consistent with the United States and other countries continuing to take the necessary actions against international terrorist and terrorist organizations, including those nations, organizations, or persons who planned, authorized, committed or aided the terrorist attacks that occurred on September 11, 2001.

(c) WAR POWERS RESOLUTION REQUIREMENTS.—

(1) Specific Statutory Authorization.—Consistent with section 8(a)(1) of the War Powers Resolution, the Congress declares that this section is intended to constitute specific statutory authorization within the meaning of section 5 (b) of the War Powers Resolution.

(2) Applicability of Other Requirements.—Nothing in this joint resolution supersedes any requirement of the War Powers Resolution.

SEC. 4. REPORTS TO CONGRESS.

(a) REPORTS.—The President shall, at least once every 60 days, submit to the Congress a report on matters relevant to this joint resolution, including actions taken pursuant to the exercise of authority granted in section 3 and the status of planning for efforts that are expected to be required after such actions are completed, including those actions described in section 7 of the Iraq Liberation Act of 1998 (Public Law 105–338).

(b) SINGLE CONSOLIDATED REPORT.—To the extent that the submission of any report described in subsection (a) coincides with the submission of any other report on matters relevant to this joint resolution otherwise required to be submitted to Congress pursuant to the reporting requirements of the War Powers Resolution (Public Law 93–148), all such reports may be submitted as a single consolidated report to the Congress.

(c) RULE OF CONSTRUCTION.—To the extent that the information required by section 3 of the Authorization for Use of Military Force Against Iraq Resolution (Public Law 102–1) is included in the report required by this section, such report shall be considered as meeting the requirements of section 3 of such resolution. Union Calendar No. 451

107th CONGRESS
2d Session
H. J. RES. 114
[Report No. 107–721]

Notes

PREFACE

1. *The New York Times*, August 26, 2004. Three months before the Bush interview, Richard Perle, former aide to Defense Secretary Donald Rumsfeld, described the war as a "grave error." Speaking in London in late May 2004, Perle, who had initially supported the invasion of Iraq, criticized the Administration for having failed immediately to turn the occupation over to the Iraqis. Instead, he complained that the United States became an unwelcome "occupier." Later in 2008 and in 2009, this type of criticism surfaced in many quarters in the United States, among civilians as well as the military and in the media. It was a grave error, many said, to have destroyed the former ruling Iraqi Baath establishment and the Iraqi Army command that left the country rudderless. Many of these ex-Saddam officials, after all, had welcomed the invasion, yet the Bush occupation policy had treated them as irreconcilable enemies. Iraq was thus left in a virtually chaotic state and "at the mercy" of the U.S. military occupation, which steadily alienated the Iraqi population. By 2007, some polls within Iraq showed that two-thirds of the Iraqi population wanted the United States to withdraw.

2. http://en.wikipedia.org/wiki/Colin_Powell. Powell aide Wilkerson described the U.N. presentation as a "hoax." In Karen DeYoung's, *Soldier: The Life of Colin Powell* (Knopf, NY, 2006), p. 459, we learn that Powell had assigned Near Eastern Affairs (NEA) Assistant Secretary of State William Burns with his deputy, Ryan Crocker (later appointed ambassador to Iraq), to prepare a memorandum "on every-thing that could go wrong" in the Iraq War and occupation. Burns's department worked on this task and produced a dozen single-spaced pages, which they titled "Perfect Storm." The report itemized the following serious issues, which were ignored by higher-ups in the White House: Iraq's complex ethnic and religious divisions as well as how the majority Shiites, once free of the Sunni-dominated dictatorship of Saddam Hussein, would "settle accounts and vie . . . violently for dominance over the minority Sunnis." Other elements of the "storm" were catalogued. The invasion, the report concluded, had left "Iraq's infrastructure in tatters." Similar predictions had been made before the invasion by American, British, and other scholars on the Middle. East. Their input was ignored.

3. *The New York Times*, "Investigation Is Ordered into CIA Abuse Charges," August 25, 2009, p. 1. Such abuse by the CIA and its contractors included water-boarding, threatening a prisoner with a pistol, posing threats against his family, and the like. The purpose of such torture, in violation of Geneva Conventions and domestic laws (as discussed in this book), was to attempt to force a tortured prisoner to provide information in the "war against terrorism." The federal investigators were also looking into whether the CIA had willfully destroyed some of the evidence of such abuse.

4. Not surprisingly, there is ongoing disagreement among American historians and foreign policy specialists as to just what is the "default," or mainstream tradition in U.S. defense planning and war fighting. One school contends that the U.S. tendency in defense and foreign policy has been largely defensive and reactive, even at times simply isolationist. Others counter that in world affairs America has not always lived up to its own principles. In the past it has displayed elements of expansionist idealism and the waging of preemptive and/or interventionist war. On this point, see Mackubin Thomas Owens, "The Bush Doctrine: The Foreign Policy of Republican Empire" *Orbis*, Winter 2009, p. 25–40. See Chapter 8 for a discussion of realist philosophy in U.S. foreign policy.

INTRODUCTION

1. According to *New York Times* polls taken May 4–8, 2006, 67 percent of all adults nationwide disapproved of the way President Bush "was handling the situation with Iraq." By late January 2007, public support of the President, which seemingly means especially his performance in relation to the war, stood at the lowest approval rate for any president in modern times. (A CBS News poll taken in the last quarter of January 2007 revealed that 28 percent of the sample approved of the way the President "is handling his job." http://query.nytimes.com/gst/fullpage.html? sec=health&res=9406E4D71F30F930A15752C0A9619C8B63). As early as December 2005, a *Time* magazine poll showed that 51 percent of the sample thought the war had made the United States "more vulnerable" to terrorist attacks. In the same poll, another 50 percent thought the U.S. decision to go to war in Iraq was "wrong." The public's estimate of President Bush also sharply declined in 2005, with a disapproval rating of 60 percent for Bush's handling of the war alone. Forty-eight percent said that the President had "deliberately misled" the public about the need to go to war (*Time,* December 13, 2005, p. 38). Polls taken by other sources earlier in 2005–2006 showed the same negativity within the American population about the war and its rationale. In a CBS News poll taken in January 2007 only 23 percent of the sample approved of the handling of the war" by the Bush Administration while 72 percent disapproved. (http://en.wikipedia.org/wiki/American_popular_opinion _of_invasion_of_Iraq).

2. Cf. Chris Tomlinson, "Morale Reportedly Flagging as US Soldiers Who Invaded Iraq Just Want to Go Home," Associated Press report, May 28, 2006.

3. *The New York Times*, December 15, 2005, p. A18. The latest U.N. estimate of Iraqi noncombatant deaths in the single year of 2006 was put at 34,000. Since February 2006, 470,094 Iraqis have abandoned their home country by fleeing fled abroad (*The New York Times*, January 17, 2007, p. A8).

4. Carl von Clausewitz, *On War*, Princeton, Princeton University Press, 1976, Book One, Chapter 2, p. 92; Book Two, Chapter 2, p. 137 This edition mistranslates the German word, *Zweck*, which means "purpose" or "aim," as in the phrase "*politische Zweck*." In reading Clausewitz's writings, it is clear that by "political purpose" he also meant moral purpose. In his extensive correspondence and in *On War*, he frequently addressed the importance of soldiers' morale, their motivation, their patriotic spirit, and the overall moral purpose for waging war as well as the motives of the leaders who send the soldiers into battle, which he in turn described as a brutal "last resort" in resolving differences between states. Clausewitz, moreover, was a follower of the moral philosophy of Immanuel Kant (1724–1804), author of *Perpetual Peace: A Philosophical Sketch* (1795).

5. Sun Tzu, *The Art of War*, New York, Oxford University Press, 1963, respectively, pp. 40; 77; 83.

6. From a speech by President Barack Obama in Phoenix, Arizona, on August 17, 2009. "Obama Defends Afghanistan as a "War of Necessity." *The New York Times*, August 18, 2009, p. 6.

7. This last rationalization, the only one arguable intact a trip to Iraq, put this figure at 80 percent. In a meeting in Cairo in autumn 2005, representing over 100 Shiite, Sunni, and Kurdish leaders, members of the Arab League called unanimously for a timetable for the withdrawal of all foreign troops from Iraq (*The Christian Science Monitor*, December 15, 2005, p. 9). In May and June 2006, the Iraqi Government itself protested the killings of dozens of Iraqi civilians in several locales by rampaging U.S. servicemen in Iraq (*The New York Times*, June 3, 2006, p. 1). The United States has not used its armies on a large scale specifically to depose a genocidal regime. If so, it would have targeted over one-third of the world's "unfree" populations (by Freedom House, Inc. calculus) for liberation since World War II. Indeed, since President Bush's classification of the three "axis of evil" countries," all three of these regimes would have been targeted for invasion if this rationalization were applied consistently. So would many other polities worldwide.

8. *Time*, December 19, 2005, p. 52. Sixty-five percent of the Iraqi sample said that they opposed the "presence of coalition troops in Iraq." By contrast, Rep. John Murtha, addressing Congress on November 17, 2005, stated: "A poll recently conducted shows that over 80% of Iraqis are strongly opposed to the presence of coalition troops, and about 45% of the Iraqi population believe attacks against American troops are justified. I believe we need to turn Iraq over to the Iraqis." (Full text at http://usliberals.about.com/od/homelandsecurit1/a/MurthaSpeech_2.htm.

9. Throughout 2006, the U.S. administration has complained of Iranian intrusions into Iraq's territory neighboring Iran in the southeast. The Shiite leadership of Iran appeared to be encouraging militant Shiite militias to oppose the Iraqi government. In 2006, the bipartisan Iraq Study Group (ISG) proposed that the United States engage in new diplomatic relations with such countries and Iran and Syria. As indicated in the National Intelligence Estimate report of February 2007 (*The New York Times*, February 5, 2007, p. 1), these two countries have been involved in destabilizing Iraqi society either by allowing foreign jihadists to enter Iraq from the west (from Syria) or abetting Shiite militias by providing them with arms (from Iran in southeast Iraq). The ISG position in recommending America's reopening diplomatic relations with these two countries is based on the assumption that diplomatic intercourse not only encourages laying the cards on the table (i.e., Syrian and

Iranian meddling in Iraq) and airing those activities that are referenced in the 2007 NIE report. Diplomacy could possibly lead to a regional conference in which a number of Middle Eastern countries would be included in a joint, multi-state effort to allow Iraq peacefully to solve its internal problems without outside interference. So far, the Bush Administration has indicated that it has no interest in this ISG proposal.

10. Wesley K. Clark, "The New Iraq Offensive," *The New York Times*, December 6, 2005, p. A31.

11. *Commentary*, Nieman Watchdog (http://www.niemanwatchdog.org), November 11, 2005.

12. The distinction between "preventive" war and "preemptive" war will be made throughout this book in the context of the Iraq War. For now, the distinction can be briefly defined as follows: *Preventive* war is rationalized as necessary in order to preclude or disrupt allegedly clear and present, palpable, and proven aggressive military preparations and hostile intentions by another state. Such preparations are seen as having been actively undertaken over an extended period by the threatening state that harbors aggressive designs against another state. The latter state deems it crucial in terms of its own security to liquidate this proven danger by military means. By contrast, *preemptive* war—or as it sometimes called, "preemptive attack" or "strike"—is one that is directed at a state that is tangibly on the *very brink* of launching aggressive war against the another state in the near future. This type of military engagement is contrasted with preventive war because of the *immediacy* of its tangible threat presented by the putatively aggressive state, whose forces are actually poised and ready to attack. As will be perceived, the Iraq War was deemed by many observers, including spokespersons for the Bush Administration, to be "preemptive" in nature (i.e., foreclosing impending, or "imminent," hostilities from the Iraqi side in the long or short term). However, it is possible to view the U.S.-led war and the military strategy (NSS 2002) upon which it was purportedly based as a unique *combination of both preventive and preemptive war rationalization*. As we will see, this type of offensive war, whether seen as strictly preventive or preemptive, invites numerous hazards together with the distinct possibility of its provoking the taint of immorality and illegality. Robert Jervis of Columbia University has noted the contradiction in the Bush administration's use of the term "preemption" as follows: "Calling this aspect of the Bush Doctrine and our policy against Iraq 'preemptive,' as the Bush administration does, is to do violence to the English language. No one thought that Iraq was about to attack anyone; rather, the argument was that Iraq, and perhaps others, are terrible menaces that *eventually* [my emphases] would do the United States great harm, and had to be dealt with before they could do so and while prophylactic actions could be taken at reasonable cost" Robert Jervis, American Foreign Policy in a New Era, New York, Routledge, 2005, Footnote 20, p. 162. Neoconservative Francis Fukuyama has noted: "*If* a country is clearly faced with a catastrophic threat from a non-state actor or a rogue state, and *if* it is unable to get help from existing international institutions to meet the threat, it can legitimately take matters into its own hands and move preemptively to break up that threat. ... The problem with the NSS doctrine was that in order to justify stretching the definition of preemption to include preventive war against non-imminent threats, the administration needed to be right about the dangers facing the United States. As it turned out, it

overestimated the threat from Iraq specifically, and from terrorism more generally. Furthermore, the administration conflated the threat of nuclear terrorism with the rogue state/proliferation problem, and applied the preventive war remedy to the lesser of two dangers" (Francis Fukuyama, *America at the Crossroads: Democracy, Power, and the Neoconservative Legacy*, New Haven, Yale University Press, 2006, p. 84. Columbia University International Relations Professor Randall L. Schweller points out that preventive wars refer to "those wars that are motivated by the fear that one's military power and potential are declining relative to that of a rising adversary" (Randall L. Schweller, "Democratic Structure and Preventive War: Are Democracies More Pacific?" *World Politics*, 44 January 1992).

CHAPTER 1

1. Cf. James Turner Johnson, *Can Modern War Be Just?* Yale University Press, New Haven, 1984; William V. O'Brien, *The Conduct of Just and Limited War*, New York, Praeger Publishers, 1981; James Turner Johnson, *Morality and Contemporary Warfare*, New Haven, Yale University Press, 1999; Peter S. Temes, *The Just War: An American Reflection on the Morality of War in Our Time*, Chicago, Ivan R. Dee, 2003; Michael Walzer, op. cit. and Walzer, *Arguing About War*, New Haven, Yale University Press, 2004; Jean Bethke Elshtain, *Just War Against Terror The Burden of American Power in a Violent World*, New York, Basic Books, 2003.

2. Found online at http://www.brainyquote.com/quotes/quotes/s/stanleybal 108563.html.

3. Immanuel Kant, *Conjectures on the Beginning of Human History*, in H. S. Reiss (ed), *Kant Political Writings*, New York, Cambridge University Press, 2004, pp. 231–232.

4. Cf. Stephane Courtois, et al., *The Black Book of Communism: Crimes, Terror, Repression*, Cambridge, Harvard University Press, 1999, and Francois Furet, *The Passing of an Illusion: The Idea of Communism in the Twentieth Century*, Chicago, University of Chicago Press, 1999. These references tabulate merely Communist-perpetrated deaths. Adding the Fascist and Nazi toll during the prewar and World War II period would increase the total by at least another one-third. The statistics do not include deaths in international war, in which all such regimes also share the blame.

5. Thomas Jefferson, Letter to James Madison, 1787, *Writings*, Washington, The Library of America, 1984, p. 1039. It was a common belief in the eighteenth century that "nature" was rational being governed by divine law and reason. Whatever was common within mankind could be seen as having a divine purpose. Of course, this did not apply to willfully making war. The Old and New Testaments provided evidence enough to the faithful that killing was an abomination, even in the form of sacrifice to God, as the story of Abraham and Isaac shows. The Ten Commandments proscribe killing. In his own recapitulation of the Commandments, Jesus ranked the prohibition against killing higher than did the original formulation of the Ten Commandments in the Old Testament.

6. "Preventive War, Common Security and the State," Melbourne Independent Media Center http://www.melbourne.indymedia.org/print.php?id=59888.

7. Peter Myers, "Arthur Koestler on Psychology, Communism, Zionism, and being a Jew," January 8, 2002, found online at http://mailstar.net/koestler.html.

8. "The Next Target of Bioterrorism: Your Food," Environmental Health Perspectives, http://www.ehponline.org/docs/2000/108-3/spheres.html.

9. Full text of Einstein-Freud Correspondence is at http://www.idst.vt.edu/modernworld/d/Einstein.html. Considerable discussion still revolves about the issue of mankind's habit of making war and whether this trait is "inborn" or nurtured through societal and political institutions. A new study of habits of violence among primates and how they might be "conditioned" into more cooperative, nonviolent behavior is related in Robert M. Sapolsky, "A Natural History of Peace," *Foreign Affairs*, January/February 2006, pp. 104–120.

10. The mid-2002 Downing Street Memoranda virtually described Bush Administration rationalization of war against Iraq in this disingenuous, moralistic way.

11. Immanuel Kant, *Perpetual Peace: A Philosophical Sketch*, Indianapolis, Hackett Publishing Co., 1983, p. 123. "War is a bad bet," he added, "because it produces more evil people than it eliminates." Cf. Kant, *Ideas for a Universal History with a Cosmopolitan Intent*, in Kant, op. cit., pp. 37–38.

12. In my examination of Greek literature, I am mainly indebted to the analysis and the excerpts from that literature provided in the classic work by Gerardo Zampaglione, *The Idea of Peace in Antiquity*, Notre Dame, University of Notre Dame Press, 1973.

13. Ibid., p. 22.

14. Ibid., p. 20.

CHAPTER 2

1. Ernst Cassirer, *An Essay on Man*, New Haven, Yale University Press, 1972, p. 108. It may be objected that the Bible has not always been on the side of peace and nonviolence. Two passages in the New Testament are sometimes cited: "I come not to send peace but a sword" (*Matthew* 10:34); and, "But as for these enemies of mine who did not want me to be king over them—bring them here and slaughter them in my presence" (*Luke* 19:27). Interpreters of the first saying by Jesus insist that "sword" is a metaphor for God's word and is not to be taken literally.

2. "Exhortation to the Greeks," Book III, *Clement of Alexandria*, Cambridge, Loew Classical Library of Harvard University Press, 1982, p. 91.

3. Mumford, op.cit., pp. 58–59.

4. Ibid., pp. 54–55.

5. Zampaglione, op. cit., p. 306. Augustine could write in the *City of God*: "For so good is peace that even where earthly and mortal affairs are in question no other word is heard with more pleasure, nothing else is desired with greater longing, and finally nothing better can be found" (Ibid., p. 300).

6. Among these works are *Origen: Contra Celsum*; Porphyry, *Against the Christians*; Julian Apostate, *Against the Galileans*. The counterattack by pagans against the Christian writers is reviewed in Jeffrey W. Hargis, *Against the Christians The Rise of Early Anti-Christian Polemic*, New York, Peter Lang, 1999.

7. Charles Peirce, *Selected Writings*, New York, Dover Publications, 1966, "Architecture of Theories," p. 150.

8. Thomas addressed these questions in *Summa Theologica* and *Regimine Principum*.

9. In modern times, Immanuel Kant wrote that this government should be a constitutional republic representing the will of the people. Such a government, he thought, moreover, would be less likely to condone war than an authoritarian government.

10. St. Thomas Aquinas, *Summa Theologica*, Part II, Question 40, Of War, in St. Thomas Aquinas, *Summa Theologica*, Christian Classics, Westminster, MD, Benziger Bros., 148, vol. 3, pp. 1353–1356.

11. This tradition continued into modern times: During the Vietnam War, for instance, tyrannicide cropped up in the writings of the later imprisoned Catholic priests, the Berrigan Brothers, Daniel and Philip. In 1968–69, they were members of the "Catonsville Nine." Their inspiration for "eliminating" a perceived tyrant came from the sixteenth-century teachings of the Jesuit theologian, Francisco Mariana, of Toledo, Spain.

12. Not all such oath-swearing worldwide today embodies the principal of ultimate, transcendent legitimation. For instance, in his inauguration in January 2007, Venezuelan President Hugo Chavez simply penned his own oath upon which he solemnly laid his hand as he became president. There was no mention in his pledge of an hypostatized source—that is, God—that ultimately sanctioned his authority and which he was foresworn to acknowledge above his own temporal authority.

13. "Every man has a 'property' in his own 'person'" (John Locke, *The Second Treatise on Civil Government*, Roslyn, NY, Walter J. Black, Inc., 1947. p. 88. This key passage in Locke is frequently overlooked in discussions of his philosophy. Some editors and commentators single out Locke's emphasis on a person's right to own *physical* property while missing his more subtle assertion of an individual's right to "owning," so to speak, his own "person"—an implicit recognition of one's individual right to privacy and *survival*. This Lockean principle has enormous implications for such latter-day issues as a person's assertion of conscientious objection to participating in war, which in turn is related to Locke's assertion of religious toleration.

14. Ron Epstein, "Buddhist Ideas of Peace," Lectures for the Global Peace Studies Program, San Francisco, San Francisco State University, November 7–9, 1988 (http://online.sfsu.edu/~rone/Buddhism/Buddhism.htm).

15. James A. Beverley, "Islam a religion of peace?" *Christianity Today*, http://www.christianitytoday.com/ct/2002/001/1.32.html. My discussion here is also guided in part by Dr. Matthew (Lazar) Lemberger of the History Department of the University of Miami, *The Questions and Answer Guide to Judaism and Islam*, Hollywood, FL, Lazar Publications, 1998; by my reading of the Koran itself (see Note 18 in this chapter); William H. McNeill, *The Rise of the West A History of the Human Community*, Chicago, University of Chicago Press, 1991, Chapter XI, 'The Moslem World"; and Albert Houranim, *A History of the Arab Peoples*, New York, Warner Books, 1991, particularly pp. 62–65 on "The Power and Justice of God."

16. Ibid.

17. Ibid.

18. *Al-Qur'an, A Contemporary Translation*, Princeton, Princeton University Press, 1993. p. 45. For readiugs on war as construed by the world's religions, see Gregory A. Reichberg, et al., *The Ethics of War: Classic and Contemporary Readings*, Maiden, MA, Blackwell Publishing, 2006, and Joseph Fahey; Richard Armstrong, *A Peace Reade,: Essential Readings on War, Justice, Non-Violence and World Order*, New York, Paulist Press, 1987.

19. Ibid., p. 102.

20. Yahiya Emerick, *Understanding Islam*, New York, Alpha Pearson Education Company, 2002, p. 174.

21. *Christianity Today*. See Note 13 in this chapter.

22. Albert L. Weeks, "Samuel P. Huntington's The Clash of Civilizations: The Debate," *Foreign Affairs*, September-October 1993, New York, *Foreign Affairs*, 1996, pp. 53–54. In my essay here rebutting Huntington, I criticized the writer for failing to acknowledge (in his Summer 1993 article in the journal) the existence of factions, not only within Islamic civilization but between Islamic states and even between Islamic sects. Thus, no stereotypical model, as Huntington attempts to use, can be erected to describe an alleged monolithic "Islamic civilization" of the modern world any more than can an Arab state be so described. Such a depiction is complicated by the fact of the contrasting ways that their religion is interpreted by Muslims. Also relevant is the contrasting manner in which it is expressed, or not, in relations among the states with Muslim populations and between those states and non-Muslim states. This was exemplified by the multifaceted membership and war aims of the coalition of 54 states that opposed Iraq's invasion of Kuwait in 1990–91 and that included several Arab states. Failure to perceive the nuanced differences between Arab states and Islamic movements can in part disorient policymaking toward them by "lumping them together" and stigmatizing them without making meaningful distinctions between them.

23. Michael J. Nojeim, *Gandhi and King The Power of Nonviolent Resistance*, Westport, Praeger Publishers, 2004, p. 26.

24. Cf. Richard Dawkins, *The God Delusion*, Houghton Mifflin, NY, 2006, pp. 304–308. Dawkins quotes Voltaire, "Those who make you believe absurdities can make you commit atrocities." In *God Is Not Great: How Religion Poisons Everything*, Christopher Hitchens insists that "organized religion ought to have a great deal on its conscience," (Hitchens, op. cit. Warner Books, N.Y. 2007, p. 56). "[It is] violent, irrational, intolerant, allied with racism and tribalism and bigotry." Both writers ignore religious/moral condemnation of violence in human society.

CHAPTER 3

1. The writer here incorporates touchstones prompted by his research and reflection. Some of these criteria are discussed in the following works: Gary Rosen (ed.), *The Right War? The Conservative Debate on Iraq*, New York, Cambridge University Press, 2005; John Lewis Gaddis, *Surprise, Security, and the American Experience*, Cambridge, Harvard University Press, 2004; Simon Chesterman, *Just War or Just Peace? Humanitarian Intervention and International Law*, New York, Oxford University Press, 2003; Jack N. Barkenbus, *Ethics, Nuclear Deterrence, and War*, New York, Paragon House, 1992; John S. Bowman (ed.), *Facts About the American Wars, New York*, The H.W. Wilson Company, 1998; Walzer, op. cit. supra; Johnson, op. cit. supra; Temes, op. cit. supra.

2. The "Downing Street memo," also known as the "smoking gun memo," originated in the United Kingdom in the form of a précis of a top-secret meeting held on July 23, 2002 in London among officials of the government's defence and intelligence officers who were discussing the run-up to the expected war against Iraq. The memorandum made explicit reference to the classified United States policy concerning its

plans vis-à-vis Iraq. The memorandum contained these statements: "It seemed clear that Bush had made up his mind to take military action, even if the timing was not yet decided. But the case was thin. Saddam was not threatening his neighbors, and his WMD capability was less than that of Libya, North Korea or Iran." And: "Bush wanted to remove Saddam, through military action, justified by the conjunction of terrorism and WMD. But the intelligence and facts were being fixed around the policy. The NSC had no patience with the UN route, and no enthusiasm for publishing material on the Iraqi regime's record. There was little discussion in Washington of the aftermath after military action." (Texts of the memorandum and other relevant documents as to joint U.S.-U.K. war planning may be found in Mark Danner, *The Secret Way to War: The Downing Street Memo and the Iraq War's Buried History*, *New York Review of Books*, New York, 2006. Further discussion may be found at http://en.wikipedia.org/wiki/Downing_Street_memo.)

3. Alleged presidential deception, manipulation, and withholding of intelligence information proceeding the Japanese attack on Pearl Harbor, December 7, 1941, has engaged a number of researchers and authors. They have accused President Franklin D. Roosevelt of intentionally allowing the attack on the United States air and naval bases in Honolulu to occur in order to bring the United States into World War II. One of these authors, Robert Stinnett, in *Day of Deceit: The Truth About FDR and Pearl Harbor*, New York, Free Press, 2001, claims that FDR knew of Japan's intention to attack Hawaii but did nothing to abort Tokyo's plans.

4. The false Niger claim again came up in mid-2005. This was when Bush adviser Karl Rove was accused of leaking the identity of the wife of Joseph Wilson, she a CIA employee. Wilson had exposed the Niger claim as a fake in an op-ed published in *The New York Times* in 2003 after fulfilling his assignment by the Administration to go to Niger, where he had once served as U.S. Ambassador, to verify the yellowcake claim. Controversy swirled over whether Rove had retaliated against Wilson's exposure of fakery, and in the course of which Rove, it was alleged, illegally revealed the identity of Wilson's wife as a U.S. intelligence agent. The circumstances surrounding "Yellowcakegate" are related in Ambassador Joseph Wilson's book, *The Politics of Truth: Inside the Lies that Led to War and Betrayed My Wife's CIA Identity: A Diplomat's Memoir*. Wilson and several other informed sources testified that the contacts between Iraq and Niger did not include a deal for Niger to export uranium yellowcake to Iraq. In a follow-up interview broadcast on the Lehrer News Hour, July 27, 2004, the Ambassador repeated his testimony. He again accused the Administration of lying. Ironically, President George H. W. Bush had once described the Ambassador as "a true American hero."

5. Kant discusses the ethics of lying in, e.g., *The Metaphysics of Morals* 6:429–431. Kant scholar Allen W. Wood presents an analysis of Kant's views toward lying in *Kant's Ethical Thought*, New York, Cambridge University Press, 1999, pp. 140; 167; 200; 332, passim.

6. This writer canvassed all speeches and press interviews given by top Administration officials, who, of course, included President George W. Bush and their spokespeople,

7. Sissela Bok, *Lying Moral Choice in Public and Private Life*, New York, Vintage Books, 1978, p. 10. Writing in *Harper's* magazine, Lewis Lapham found 237 false or misleading statements concerning Iraq that had been made by the Bush administration and 55 specifically by the President in which he linked Saddam

Hussein and Al-Qaeda with quotes such as "you can't distinguish between Al-Qaeda and Saddam" in the war on terror. http://www.nthposition.com/ inthecrosshairsof.php/. Lapham's article, "The Case for Impeachment: Why We Can No Longer Afford George W. Bush," appeared in the March 2006 issue of *Harper's*.

8. Michael N. Schmitt, "Preemptive Strategies and International Law," *Michigan Journal of International Law*, Vol. 24, Winter 2001, pp. 513–549. University of California (Berkeley) Law Professor David D. Caron said of "preemptive self-defense" at a forum on that campus, April 1, 2003: "The preemptive self-defense argument obviously is more accommodating to the use of force but many if not all use of force have unknown destabilizing tendencies. The conventional wisdom has been that a stable international order requires a doctrine on use of force with bright lines. An armed attack is a bright line. The assertion that another country's possession or possible possession of weapons of mass destruction and that country's hostile intent, or possible hostile intent toward a target country, is not a bright line. Indeed, in my mind, the element of objective restraint in the proposed doctrine of preemptive self-defense is so minimal that it is more a statement of what I would call discretionary self-defense."   www.berkeley.edu/news/media/releases/2003/04/02_forum _caron.shtml. These are the prepared remarks delivered by David D. Caron at a forum of University of California (Berkeley) faculty experts convened at Zellerbach Hall on April 1, 2003, to discuss the war with Iraq. Caron is on the faculty of the Boalt Hall School of Law.

9. Brent Scowcroft, national security adviser to President George H. W. Bush, was an early critic of the war. Basic to his criticism was his often-stated concern that an invasion of Iraq would encourage radical Islamism throughout the Muslim world and "inflame old sectarian passions." (*Newsweek*, December 11, 2006, p. 35). He also expressed doubts about President George W. Bush's program of democratizing the Middle East and indicated that he thought the present regimes in the region, even if in some cases authoritarian, did manage to keep their societies stabilized. Scowcroft was also of the opinion that U.S. policy was too beholden to Israel. In an interview, he bluntly told *The Financial Times of London*, October 16, 2004, that Bush had been "mesmerized" by Israeli Prime Minister Ariel Sharon, who had, said Scowcroft, influenced the president to embark on the "failing venture" in Iraq. (–http://www.washingtonpost.com/wp-dyn/articles/A36644-2004Oct15.html)

10. Akhil Reed Amar provides an up-to-date analysis of the muscular power of the executive branch in *America's Constitution: A Biography*,Random House, New York, 2005, pp. 137–142.

11. Found online at –http://www.whitehouse.gov/news/releases/2003/03/iraq/ 20030317-7.html.

12. Cf. Thomas E. Ricks, *Fiasco The American Military Adventure in Iraq*, New York, Penguin Press, 2006, pp. 21, 23; Robert J. Lieber, *The American Era Power and Strategy for the 21st Century*, New York, Cambridge University Press, 2005, pp. 132–133; Gordon and Trainor, op. cit., pp. 58–61. General Anthony Zinni, former commander of U.S. Persian Gulf forces described Iraq in the late 1990s as "weak, fragmented, chaotic" (Ricks, op. cit., p. 23). These among other authors provide expert testimony of the weakness of Saddam Hussein's military, the fragility of his hold on power following the Persian Gulf War, and the rampant ethnic disunity existing within Iraq. To cope with all of this, in General Zinni's opinion, would

require an occupation force of upward to 300,000 troops (Ibid, p. 37). This is not to minimize the effectiveness of Saddam's organization of anti-occupation armed fedayeen in the form of militias and paramilitary forces that would conduct guerrilla-type insurgency against foreign occupiers. Saddam had evidently studied the use of Soviet "partisans" (guerrillas) in World War II who had fought effectively, by means of sabotage, killings, etc., against the Nazi occupiers of the western USSR.

13. Cf. James Mann, *Rise of the Vulcans: The History of Bush's War Cabinet*, New York, Viking, 2004; David D. Kirkpatrick, "War Heats Up in the Neoconservative Fold," *The New York Times*, Week in Review, August 25, 2004, p. 3. George Packer, *The Assassin's Gate America in Iraq*, New York, Farrar Straus and Giroux, 2005, provides a thoughtful analysis of neocon philosophy. One author, who defended the war and the arguments made for it by neoconservatives, disputes the claim that pro-Israeli, Jewish officials within the top echelons of the Administration were themselves instrumental in convincing the President and Vice President to go to war. Such claims, writes Lieber (op. cit., pp. 186–189), are "overtly conspiratorial" and evidently motivated by anti-Semitism. Lieber notes that Jews can be found in both the pro- and anti-war camps, that, in any case, the White House officials with the most power to make decisions about going to war were non-Jews. Among these were President Bush himself, Cheney, Rumsfeld, Powell, and Rice together with the Joint Chiefs of Staff and most of the other senior military.

14. The policy of excluding Israel paralleled President George H. W. Bush's policy in the Persian Gulf War. It kept Israel out of the 54-nation coalition, which included some Arab states that drove Iraq out of Kuwait. It was also in Israel's own interest in both cases not to be involved and stand aside as other powers assumed the task of eliminating the Iraqi threat to peace in the region. Speaking of the coalitions, the group of nations, numbering 31 with mostly noncombatant occupying forces totaling 24,000 who had joined in Operation Iraqi Freedom by 2004, consisted by half of former communist states of Eastern Europe. Of these, 11 were "new-born," ex-Soviet Republic sovereign states and such minor players on the world stage as Azerbaijan, Georgia, Kazakhstan, Ukraine, and the Baltic States (Ricks, op. cit., pp. 347–348). The number of coalition participants contrasted ironically with the much greater number of fighters in the so-called "coalition of the willing," that is, the armed international jihadists who swarmed into Iraq to fight an insurgent war against the American-led occupation.

15. That such regimes and guerrilla movements—whether in Chile, Nicaragua, El Salvador, Panama, Grenada, or elsewhere—should be viewed as tangible threats to Western Hemisphere security and democracy is described in the "Mitrokhin Archive" of secret documents in which Soviet planning to create client states throughout the region is evidenced. Cf. Christopher Andrew and Vasili Mitrokhin, *The World Was Going Our Way: The KGB and the Battle for the Third World*, New York, Basic Books, 2005. Notably, however, the means used by the administrations of Reagan and George H. W. Bush to liquidate these perceived threats did not include all-out military invasion (with the exception of the U.S. operation in Grenada in 1983). Other limited-scale, U.S.-initiated interventions under other administrations whether conducted in Haiti, Somalia, or Bosnia and Kosovo, which in some cases were called "humanitarian interventions," are discussed in Chapter 8.

16. http://www.iwar.org.uk/cyberterror/resources/gwot/bounding-ssi.htm—for text of Record's article, pp. 15–17. in the Spring 2001 issue of *Parameters*, journal of the U.S. Army War College.

17. Max Boot, *Foreign Policy*, January/February 2004 at http://www.foreignpolicy .com/story/cms.php?story_id=2426. The leadership style of Defense Secretary Donald Rumsfeld was such that the professional military became intimidated and unable to have their informed views aired or respected. A joke was made about this when Rumsfeld gave his "farewell" speech at the Pentagon, December 8, 2006. A questioner in the audience asked the retired Def/Sec what advice he might offer his successor in the Pentagon. Before Rumsfeld could respond, Chairman of the Joint Chiefs of Staff General Peter Pace chimed in with this ironic remark: "Listen to the Chairman" (*The New York Times*, December 9, 2006, p. A8)

18. *The New York Times*, December 15, 2005, p. 1.

19. In mid-2006 conservatives at the American Enterprise Institute and the Pentagon's Foreign Military Studies Office claimed that Al Qaeda had established pre-2003 links to Saddam's regime in Baghdad. Yet the CIA, NSA, and DIA intelligence community's view that there were no such operational links was confirmed by the 2004 9/11 Commission Report and the Senate Report of Pre-war Intelligence on Iraq. These reports maintained that there was not a cooperative effort between Qaeda and Saddam and that the Iraqi dictator did not lend tangible support to the 9/11 attacks. According to this view as held within the intelligence community, the significant differences in ideology between Saddam and al-Qaeda made cooperation between them in mounting terrorist attacks unlikely. The Senate report discussed the possibility of Saddam's offering Al-Qaeda training and safe-haven. Yet it confirmed the CIA's finding that there was no evidence of actual operational cooperation between the two. Not that Saddam Hussein let 9/11 pass without a comment. Ironically, less than two months before 9/11, the state-controlled Iraqi newspaper "Al-Nasiriya" carried a column headlined, "America, an Obsession Called Osama Bin Ladin." [July 21, 2001] In the piece, Baath Party writer Naeem Abd Muhalhal predicted that bin Laden would attack the United States "with the seriousness of the Bedouin of the desert about the way he will try to bomb the Pentagon after he destroys the White House." The same state-approved column also insisted that bin Laden "will strike America on the arm that is already hurting," and that the United States "will curse the memory of Frank Sinatra every time he hears his songs"—an apparent reference to the Sinatra classic, "New York, New York."

20. Detailed discussion of the exposure and correction of these intelligence errors, as cited in general by President Bush in December 2005, may be found in: Ricks, op. cit., pp. 56–57, 90–94, and 222–225; Dominick McGoldrick, *From 9–11 to the Iraq War of 2003*, Portland, Hart Publishing, 2004, 2004, pp. 152–153; Yossef Bodansky, *The Secret History of the Iraq War*, New York, Regan Books, 2004, pp. 495–501; James Bamford, *A Pretext for War*, New York, Doubleday, 2004, pp. 560–561. Additional information on intelligence failures may be found in the records of hearings held by the Senate Armed Forces and Intelligence Committees and their reports published in the *Congressional Record*, 2004–2005.

21. Greg Thielmann, an intelligence officer for 26 years and former Acting Director of the State Department's Office of Strategic Proliferation and Military Affairs, was the official in charge of conducting analysis in Powell's own intelligence office of an alleged Iraqi WMD threat. This aide to Power told CBS News, February 4, 2004 (http://www.cbsnews.com/stories/2003/10/14/60II/main577975.shtml): "I had a couple of initial reactions. Then I had a more mature reaction," he said, referring to Powell's presentation to the U.N. Security Council on February 5,

2003. "I think my conclusion now is that it's probably one of the low points in his long, distinguished service to the nation." Thielmann's staff had the highest security clearances. He reviewed virtually all intelligence data whether originating with the CIA or the Defense Department. When Powell delivered his report to the Security Council, showing the Council members incriminating pictures that putatively documented Saddam's WMD "threat," Thielmann maintains that at that time Iraq did not represent an "imminent threat" to the United States As he told newsmen: "I think [Iraq] didn't even constitute an imminent threat to its neighbors at the time we went to war." One of the most "disturbing" parts of Powell's report, according to Thielmann, concerned the charge that Iraq was importing aluminum tubes for use in a program to build nuclear weapons. Intelligence agents had intercepted the tubes in 2001. According to CIA reports, the tubes were parts for a "centrifuge to enrich uranium." However, Thielmann later admitted that he was not sure that this allegation was at all true. Experts at the Oak Ridge National Laboratory—that is, scientists who enriched uranium for American bombs—submitted their opinion about the tubes at the time, says Thielmann. They advised that the tubes were not at all suited for an A-bomb development program. At about the same time, Thielmann's staff was working on another explanation of the tubes. It turned out, they determined, the tubes' dimensions perfectly matched an Iraqi conventional rocket. "The aluminum was exactly, I think, what the Iraqis wanted for artillery," recalls Thielmann, who added that he had sent this estimate up to the Secretary of State months before. Former Secretary Powell told *The Washington Post* at the time of Thielmann's interview with CBS that he didn't know if he would have recommended the invasion of Iraq if he had known then that there were no stockpiles of weapons. He also described his performance before the U.N. Security Council as a low point in his career. "They were really blind and deaf to any kind of countervailing information the intelligence community would produce. I would assign some blame to the intelligence community and most of the blame to the senior administration officials." Other former intelligence officials have also disowned the faulty intelligence of the pre-invasion period while indicating that such doubts had been relayed to higher officials, but were ignored. Cf. Ricks, op. cit., pp. 90–94, for a detailed account of the false information emanating from an Iraqi defector, code-named "Curveball," and the doubts expressed by some informed officials.

22. As shown in several public opinion polls in 2003, when the public supported the war versus polls taken later in 2005–2006, when the public became skeptical as to the initial rationale for the war. During the first days of the war in March 2003, a Gallup poll showed that 75 percent of Americans felt that the U.S. military action was the right course. However, since October 2003, between 40 and 44 percent of those polled have said the U.S. military involvement was a mistake. By mid-2004, 54 percent in a Gallup poll taken at that time said that the U.S. military involvement in Iraq had been a mistake. In 2005–2006 opposition to the war continued to increase. A CBS News poll conducted April 28–30, 2006, showed that only 30 percent of those polled approved of the way Bush was "handling the Iraq situation" while 64 percent disapproved with 6 percent unsure. Fifty-one percent of those polled felt that America should have stayed out of Iraq; 44 percent said the invasion was the right thing to do, with 5 percent unsure. A CBS/*New York Times* poll, conducted July 21–25, 2006, showed that only 30 percent of those polled believed the invasion of Iraq to have been worth the American casualties and other costs of the war, while

63 percent said the war was not worth it, with 6 percent unsure. Only one-third said that they approved of the way President George W. Bush was handling the situation in Iraq while 62 percent disapproved, with 6 percent unsure. A *Washington Post-ABC* poll, taken December 11, 2006, found that seven out of ten Americans disapproved of the handling of Iraq War; six in ten said the war was not worth fighting. An Associated Press poll taken December 8, 2006, found that only 9 percent of the sample believed that a coalition victory was possible in Iraq. http://www.ap-ipsosresults.com/. http://en.wikipedia.org/wiki/American_popular_opinion_on_invasion_of_Iraq#July_2000; The Washington Post. December 12, 2006, p. A1. http://www.pbs.org/newshour/bb/politics/july-dec06/shieldslowry_12-08.html.

23. *The Iraq Study Group Report* of December 2006 made no reference to the Bush notion of democratizing the Middle East. Administration critics point out that the United States dealt with a totalitarian USSR after Washington recognized the regime in 1933 as well as during World War II and throughout the 45-year, postwar cold war. In recent years, even the Bush Administration has held talks and negotiations with representatives of Kim Jong Il's repressive regime in North Korea, which President Bush had called a member of the "axis of evil." Such critics add that Iran was of help to the United States and its allies in the invasion of Afghanistan. Cf. James A. Baker, III and Lee H. Hamilton, *The Iraq Study Group Report*, New York, Random House, 2006, p. 52. Instead, the 141-page report recommended that the Bush Administration engage Iran and Syria in diplomacy, which Bush initially rejected in the days following issuance of the report. If democratization remained part of the Bush approach to Middle East affairs, it is obvious that dealing diplomatically with an undemocratically-ruled state like Syria and a theocratically ruled one like Iran would appear to be counterproductive for an administration that is dedicated to prioritizing the promotion democracy among all states of the world while virtually quarantining anti- or non-democratic regimes.

CHAPTER 4

1. The term "legitimacy" in this context is not to be confused with the question of whether a war is just, that is, "legitimate." Legitimacy here refers to the governing authority. Peter R. Temes writes in *The Just War An American Reflection on the Morality of War in Our Time*, Chicago, Ivan R. Dee, 2003, that the "modern state centralizes, structures, and codifies power [and recognizes] the significance of the individual citizen. [A dramatic modernization of Just War thinking is] the shift from the question of legitimate authority . . . to the affirmation that legitimate government requires the consent of the governed, and that a Just War cannot be waged necessarily mean that a democratic state that does not hold its citizens "captive" might nevertheless succeed in hoodwinking the public and its governmental institutions or skirt popular consent when such an authority planned or initiated war. There are many examples, in fact, of democratic states that have indulged in such practices. Some historians maintain, for instance, that President Woodrow Wilson deliberately encouraged propaganda that led the American population to favor the Triple Entente over the Central Powers in the Great War when, in fact, the culpability for the unleashing of hostilities was shared by both sides. This interpretation is argued vehemently by Jim Powell, Senior Fellow at the conservative Cato Institute, in *Wilson's War: How Woodrow Wilson's Great Blunder Led to Hitler, Lenin, Stalin, World*

War II. The Case for Staying Out of Other's People's Wars, New York, Random House, Inc., 2005.

2. James Madison, *"Helvidius" No. 1*, in *Writings*, New York, The Library of America, 1999, pp. 543–544. Also *Letter to Thomas Jefferson*, June 13, 1793, op. cit. supra, pp. 535–536.

3. Saul K. Padover (ed) *Jefferson on Democracy*, New York, Penguin Books, Inc., 1948, in his *Notes on Virginia*, Query 14, p. 162, and Thomas Jefferson, *Writings*, New York, The Library of America, 1984, p. 274.

4. Neoconservative author Francis Fukuyama notes that in 2001 "proponents of the war in the Pentagon and vice president's office became excessively distrustful of anyone who did not share their views, a distrust that extended to Secretary of State Colin Powell and much of the intelligence community. Bureaucratic tribalism exists in all administrations, but it rose to poisonous levels in Bush's first term. Team loyalty trumped open-minded discussion, and was directly responsible for the administration's failure to plan adequately for the period after the end of active combat" (Francis Fukuyama, *America at the Crossroads: Democracy, Power, and the Neoconservative Legacy*, New Haven, Yale University Press, 2006, p. 61. Powell's wife, Alma, revealed that Powell was given the job of presenting the evidence for WMD in Iraq to the U.N. Security Council because, said his wife, Alma, "they knew people would believe *him*" (Mrs. Powell is quoted in *The New York Times Book Review* of Karen de Young's biography, *The Life of Colin Powell*, November 26, 2006, p. 17).

5. The following quotes are derived from various speeches and remarks by President George W. Bush before and during the war in Iraq may be found in Bob Woodward, *Plan of Attack*, New York, Simon & Schuster, 2004. For a roundup of Administration quotes, cf. *The New York Times*, June 20, 2004, Week in Review, p. 4

6. Woodward, op. cit., p. 248. Later Tenet lamented that "those were the two dumbest words I ever said" (*Newsweek,* December 19, 2005).

7. NBC "Meet the Press," July 11, 2004.

8. *The New York Times*, July 15, 2004, p. A6. The Downing Street memoranda of 2002 were not discussed in the report.

9. In his interview with ABC News, September 13, 2005, Powell described his U.N. speech as follows: "It's a blot. I'm the one who presented it on behalf of the United States to the world, and [it] will always be a part of my record. It was painful. It's painful now." http://www.opednews.com/articles/. De Young reports in her biography of Powell that his chief of staff at State had said of the consensus that supported the erroneous information about alleged WMD in Iraq: "What we were all involved in—group think isn't the right word—it was a process of putting data to points in the speech rather than challenging the data themselves" (*The New York Times Book Review*, November 26, 2006, p. 17).

10. As to renouncing a policy of nation-building, Bush had said in 2000: "I don't think our troops ought to be used for what's called nation-building. I think our troops ought to be used to fight and win war" (quoted In Francis Fukuyama, op. cit., p. 46).

11. Such polls showed sinking support for the war within the U.S. population throughout 2006. By the time of the mid-term elections on November 7, less than 25 percent of the U.S. population thought that the war against Iraq was justifiable. The issue of public support for war is linked to the *jus ad bellum* principle of the feasibility of success and victory in war, which is discussed in the next chapter.

12. *The New York Times*, September 8, 2005, p. A1. The Washington Institute's Policy/Peace Watch reported in Issue #1033 in fall of 2005 that the reelection of Mubarak was carried out amid restrictions on opposing political groups, that little could be expected by way of promised democratic top-down reform from the Mubarak regime despite application of U.S. pressure. Cf. http://www .washingtoninstitute.org for a list of the needed reforms in Egypt in a democratic direction. Egypt is no exception in the Middle East with respect to the dim prospects for authentic democratization throughout the region in the foreseeable future despite U.S. Secretary of State Condoleeza Rice's speech-making stops there during the year to encourage this process. The annual report by Freedom House, Inc. for 2006 found that out of 18 Middle Eastern countries only one, Israel, as the only electoral democracy in the region, was ranked as "free." According to the survey there are six "partly free" (33 percent) in the region while 11 countries (61 percent) are classed as "unfree." See http://freedomhouse.org. Neoconservative writer Robert Kagan has called the Bush Administration's democratization crusade a reflection of its "messianic impulse" (William Safire, "On Language: Realism," *The New York Times Magazine*, December 24, 2006, p. 20).

13. This was, in fact, the plaint made by Bush 43's former Secretary of the Treasury, Paul O'Neill. Cf. Ron Suskind, *The Price of Loyalty: George W. Bush, the White House, and the Education of Paul O'Neill*, New York, Simon & Schuster, 2004. O'Neill notes (pp. 78–79) that the thinking that underlay Bush's inner circle and that pointed in the direction of an America that would in future act like a world crusader was embodied in a classified Pentagon report, entitled *Defense Policy Guidance*, which emerged in 1992 but had for a time been tabled. Written at that time by the later Pentagon policy chief Paul Wolfowitz, who in the earlier years served as Defense Secretary Dick Cheney's undersecretary at the Pentagon, the report recommended that the United States be forceful in deterring the growth of hostile "competitors" in the region. Later, reports O'Neill, other neocons were brought into the Bush 43 Administration, such as Richard Perle and Donald Rumsfeld, whom George W. Bush appointed as his Secretary of Defense. As Bush Cabinet member O'Neill recalls (p. 86): "There was never any rigorous talk about this sweeping idea [of forcibly unseating Saddam Hussein] that seemed to be driving all the specific actions. From the start we were building the case against Hussein and looking at how we could take him out and change Iraq into a new country. And, if we did that, it would solve everything. It was all about *finding a way to do it*. That was the tone of it. The President saying, 'Fine. Go find me a way to do this.' " Author Christian Alfonsi notes that as early as September 2001 the President and close Pentagon aides, Rumsfeld and Wolfowitz, were discussing a U.S. attack against Iraq. Secretary of State Colin Powell and his deputy, Richard Armitage, were opposed to an invasion. On September 11, 2001, Rumsfeld confided to Gen. Richard Myers, vice chairman of the Joint Chiefs of Staff: "My instinct is to hit Saddam at the same time, not just bin Laden [in Afghanistan]" (Christian Alfonsi, *Circle in the Sand: Why We Went Back to Iraq*, New York, Doubleday, 2006, p. 385).

CHAPTER 5

1. *Summa Theologica*, Question 40, Of War, in the Christian Classics version, op. cit., p. 1354.

2. Michael Walzer, *Just and Unjust Wars A Moral Argument with Historical Illustrations*, New York, Basic Books, 3rd ed., 1977, p. 157.

3. This problem was surveyed in two articles in *Foreign Affairs*. John Mueller had argued in "The Iraq Syndrome" (in the November/December 2005 issue) that increasing casualties are the main depressors of the American public's support of war, as illustrated, he pointed out, during the Korean War. The same effect, he argued, was seen in sagging support of the Iraq War within the American public. Countering Mueller's argument was Christopher Geldi writing in "Misdiagnosis," *Foreign Affairs*, January-February 2006, pp. 139–142, that the public's declining support for war and the Iraq War in particular (in 2005), is not a function of mounting casualties as much as it is a growing popular perception that the war is not succeeding and going badly. The public, Geldi argued, must have "benchmarks by which [the public] can measure progress" in the war. Geldi also faulted Mueller for not linking declining public support for the war with the president's sinking popularity that was seen in poll results in summer 2005. The discussion tends to illustrate the point raised in the context of *jus ad bellum* as to perception of success, or the lack of success, in war. The difficulties encountered in the occupation and the indiscernibility of ultimate victory gave an ironic twist to President Bush's somewhat equivocal statement in an interview on the Today Show, August 20, 2003, on the "unwinnability" in of a war against terrorism. "I don't think you can win," he said, "but I think you can create conditions so that those who use terror as a tool are less acceptable in parts of the world."

4. "Trust Colin Powell?" consortiumnews.com, http://www.consortiumnews .com/2003/020603a.html.

5. Sen. John McCain (R-AZ), complained (CNN, September 18, 2004)) that it was "a serious mistake" not to have had enough troops in place "after the initial successes," that this error had led to "very, very significant" difficulties. McCain had voiced this warning ever since the March 2003 invasion. He was joined in this criticism by Senators Chuck Hagel (R-NE) and John Kyl (R-AZ), and many other senators and Congressmen of both political parties.

6. Colonel Douglas A. Macgregor, in his 2003 study, *Transformation Under Fire: Revolutionizing How America Fights*, New York, Praeger, 2003, which touts hi-tech warfare and strategy, omits any analysis of counterinsurgency. Instead, the author described Iraqi resort to suicide bombings as a "pathetic" weapon that insurgents thought—mistakenly, the author observes—would demoralize and intimidate their enemies, including implicitly the Iraqi population. In this premature book, Macgregor thus reflected the erroneous thinking that Influenced the Pentagon under Rumsfeld's leadership in making its decisions as to how to achieve victory in Iraq in the period of occupation—i.e., with a minimal number of occupation forces. Cf. Macgregor, op. cit., p. 215. Another author, Bruce Berkowitz, a RAND military specialist, in his book, *The New Face of War: How War Will be Fought in the 21st Century*, New York, The Free Press, 2003, shows the same oversight by omitting any discussion of insurgency and counterinsurgency warfare in the context of war in Afghanistan and Iraq.

7. Packer, op. cit., p. 265. Packer notes that "Saddam always kept a wary distance from Islamist terrorist groups; he co-opted conservative Sunni imams in Iraq only to use them as window dressing. But after the fall of the regime, the most potent ideological force behind the insurgency was Islam and its hostility to non-Islamic intruders" (ibid., p. 309).

8. *The New York Times*, February 26, 2003, p. A1.

9. Packer, op. cit., p. 114.

10. "The Army, Faced with Its Limits," *The New York Times*, January 1, 2006, Week in Review, p. 6.

11. Ibid. Korb added that by "long war" he meant one lasting two years or more. The fifth year of the war will open in March 2007. Complicating the picture was the fact that by end of 2006 attacks by militants on American and Iraqi targets by militants hit record levels. At the end of 2006, such assaults against Iraqi citizens and U.S. troops averaged 960 a week (*The New York Times*, December 19, 2006, p. 1). To cope with this problem, which some observers attribute to the initial administration underestimation of the number of needed coalition occupation troops, officials in Washington, including the new Defense Secretary Robert Gates, were considering the possibility of launching a "surge." That is, the administration seemed to be considering the deployment of an increased number of U.S. armed forces to quell the increased violence. This surge, in turn, could put a strain on available Army manpower. As it is, recruitment is not meeting demand despite recent lowering of standards, raising enlistment age from 35 up to an allowable 42, plus sweetening education and financial incentives in order to attract more recruits (*The New York Times,* December 24, 2006, p. 19).

12. Korb, ibid.

13. Ibid.

14. *The New York Times*, November 22, 2005, p. A1. When asked in late 2004 why U.S. soldiers were not adequately protected with body armor, Defense Secretary Rumsfeld replied: "As you know, you go to war with the Army you have. They're not the Army you might want or wish to have at a later time." This suggested that forces were unavoidably vulnerable, which in turn would imply that missions could not possibly be fully accomplished—a handicap that could adversely affect the outcome in battle and hobble the chance of success as per *jus in bello* (*The Washington Post*, December 14, 2004, p. A33).

15. Associated Press, September 13, 2004.

16. William H. McNeill, *The Rise of the West A History of the Human Community*, Chicago, University of Chicago Press, 1991, pp. 391–393.

CHAPTER 6

1. Peter S. Temes, *An American Reflection on the Morality of War in Our Time*, Chicago, Ivan R. Dee, 2003, pp. 28–29.

2. James Turner Johnson, *Morality and Contemporary Warfare*. New Haven, Yale University Press, 1999, pp. 36–8. In Allied bombing raids over Germany, Italy, and Japan and their allies in World War II, bomber commands sometimes intentionally targeted civilian urban centers The bombing strategy was based on the assumption that the civilian population would be come demoralized by the massive destruction that would thereby help unleash disunity and disaffection within enemy countries and those occupied by the Axis. The Allies' policy of targeting civilian populations is generally considered not to have worked as effectively in this way as was intended. It has since been widely criticized as inhumane.

3. Discussion of this criteria within *jus in bello* is based in part on the following book-length studies: Michael R. Gordon and General Bernard E. Trainor, *Cobra II*

The Inside Story of the Invasion and Occupation of Iraq, New York, 2006; General Tony Zinni, *The Battle for Peace A Frontline Vision of America's Power and Purpose*, New York, MacMillan, 2006; George Packer, *The Assassins' Gate America in Iraq*, Farrar, New York, Straus and Giroux, 2005; Gary Rosen (ed), *The Right War? The Conservative Debate on Iraq*, Cambridge, Cambridge University Press, 2005; Yossef Bodansky, *The Secret History of the Iraq War*, New York, Regan Books, 2004. As noted in Part One, intelligence failures also contributed to false estimates of the number of troops that would be necessary both to invade as well as occupy Iraq. For the latter controversy, see "Former CIA Official Says Intelligence Was Ignored," *The New York Times*, April 22, 2006. The official, Tyler Drumheller, former chief of CIA European operations, in an interview aired on CBS 60 Minutes, April 23, whose content was previewed in the *Times* the day before, disclosed that information about chaos that would likely ensue in Iraq following the invasion was ignored. This jived with the information that had appeared in an article in the March-April 2006 issue of *Foreign Affairs* by former supervisor of Middle East intelligence for the CIA, Paul R. Pillar.

4. Also relevant among the oversights was the inadequate protection provided the soldiers in the form of body armor as well as in the Humvee armored troop carrier vehicles, whose undersides were not sufficiently outfitted against land mines (IEDs). It seems that the Humvees, deployed for service in Iraq, were too small. Manufacture of a larger version is now in the works. Cf. http://usmilitary.about.com/b/a/216352 .htm?iam=momma_100_SKD&terms=%22humvee%22. The many errors are summarized in Thomas E. Ricks, *Fiasco: The American Military Adventure in Iraq*, New York, Penguin Press, 2006, pp. 164–172; 252–253; 352–356. On December 8, 2004, Secretary of Defense Rumsfeld described such shortcomings in the following apologetic way: "You go to war with the army that you have, not army you might want or wish to have at a later time."

5. Gordon and Trainor, op. cit., p. 353. These generals who spoke of the errors struck a contrast with other military officers who held the opposite view—such retired General Tommy Franks and Centcom CinC General John Abizaid, who insisted that the job could be done by a much smaller force—are known as members of the "small footprint" school. In February 2003 the U.S. Army War College released a study that criticized the lack of U.S. Interagency war planning in 2002–2003. It called for a multiyear commitment to develop a "real nation-building plan" for Iraq. Yet this was never done (*U.S. News & World Report*, November 27, 2006, p. 40).

6. Gordon and Trainor, op. cit., Epilogue, pp. 497–507. Cf. Zinni, op. cit., p. 112; Packer, op. cit., pp. 113–116.

7. Gordon and Trainor, op. cit., p. 499.

8. Ibid., p. 500.

9. Ibid., p. 501.

10. Douglas A. Macgregor, *Transformation Under Fire Revolutionizing How America Fights*, Westport, Praeger Publishers, 2003, p. 279. In January 2007, President Bush reconstructed his Iraq strategy and appointed General David Petraeus as CinC of Central Command. He was the authority behind the altered counterinsurgency tactics outlined in the Department of the Army's *Counterinsurgency Field Manual* of December 2006. Eventually the General supported a new "surge" in Iraq, which was begun in early 2008 together with the addition of more troops. Petraeus stated that the security

of the population, especially in Baghdad, and in partnership with the Iraqi Security Forces, including the Sunni minority and pacified remnants of Saddam's regime, would become the focus of the military effort. Much else in Petraeus's program, including elements of civilian-oriented nation-building, contrasted to the largely military strategy pursued by the Bush administration in Iraq from 2003 to 2008. "Counterinsurgency" under Petraeus thus appeared to take on new meaning. The same, modified strategy later began to be applied to the war in Afghanistan.

11. It is difficult to agree with those on the neoconservative right, such as Johns Hopkins Professor Eliot A. Cohen, who maintain that senior U.S. military officers should keep a "respectful" silence about military matters—whether in peace or during war. Cohen's, et al., advice amounts to a recasting of Clemenceau's much-quoted advice against leaving wars up to generals. Yet it has been the outspokenness of some of our most experienced senior military officers, most of whom are retired men and women, former commanders with invaluable combat experience, who have spearheaded recent, useful criticism expressed against unnecessary preemptive war. The idea that such voices should be silenced has very little to do with the indispensable premium placed by democracy on the expression of expert opinion. As Jefferson wrote, "If a nation expects to be ignorant and free, in a state of civilization, it expects what never was and never will be." The "spread of information" he insisted, supports "free and good government."

12. Gordon and Trainor, op. cit., p. 502.

13. Ibid. This policymaking breakdown in terms of preventing a full airing of decision-making relates as well to principles under *jus ad bellum*. See discussion above in Section One, Chapter 4, The War in Iraq and Legitimate Authority. Powell is said to have told his State Department chief of staff, Lawrence Wilkerson: "I wonder what we'll do when we put half a million troops on the ground in Iraq and search it from one end and the other—and find nothing" (Wilkerson, quoted in*The New York Times Book Review*, November 26, 2006, p. 17).

14. Ibid., p. 503. Cf. Packer, op. cit., pp. 241–242. Cf. Naomi Klein, "Baghdad Year Zero—Pillaging Iraq in Search of a Neocon Utopia," *Harper's* Magazine, September 2004.

15. Quoted in Francis Fukuyama, op. cit., p. 46.

16. Gordon and Trainor, op. cit., pp. 503–4.

17. The seven were General Merrill "Tony" McPeak, Air Force chief of staff, 1990–94; Admiral Stansfield Turner, NATO Allied commander for Southern Europe, 1975–77; CIA director, 1977–81; Lieutenant General William Odom, Director of the National Security Agency, 1985–88; Gen. Anthony Zinni, Commander in Chief of the United States Central Command, 1997–2000; Lieutenant General Claudia Kennedy, Army deputy chief of staff for intelligence, 1997–2000; Gen. Wesley Clark, NATO supreme Allied commander for Europe, 1997–2000; Admiral William Crowe, Chairman of the Joint Chiefs of Staff, 1985–89. http://www.rolling stone.com/politics/story/6593163/the_generals_speak/.

18. Phyllis Bennis and Erik Leaver, "The Iraq Quagmire," Institute for Policy Studies. http://www.fpif.org/fpiftxt/467.

19. http://www.antiwar.com/casualties/; *The New York Times*, November 23, 2006, p. 1, quoting the report of the United Nations Assistance Mission in Iraq, November 22, 2006.

20. *The Washington Post*, April 27, 2006, p. A16. Adding the cost of the war in Afghanistan raises the projected cost for both wars to about $500 billion (*The Christian Science Monitor*, November 21, 2006, p. 1).

21. http://www.cdi.org/news/defense-monitor/DM-june04.pdf and Anthony Zinni, "The 10 Mistakes that Bush Made," http://artsci.wustl.edu/~canfrobt/zinni10 mistakesweb.htm.

CHAPTER 7

1. Michael Walzer, *Just and Unjust Wars A Moral Argument with Historical Illustrations*, Basic Books, New York, NY, 1977, p. 128. Walzer observes that the "crucial point is that there are rules of war, though there are no rules of robbery (or of rape or murder). The moral equality of the battlefield distinguishes combat from domestic crime."

2. William V. O'Brien, *The Conduct of Just and Limited War*, New York, Praeger Publishers, 1981, p. 37. Cf. Walzer, op. cit., pp. 21 and 128.

3. O'Brien, op. cit., pp. 43–44.

4. Joseph Modeste Sweeney, *The International Legal System*, University Casebook Series, 2nd ed., The Foundation Press, Inc., Mineola, NY, 1981, Chapters 14–15, pp. 886–1021; O'Brien, op.cit., pp. 64–70.

5. Statistics from the Crimean War, found online at Statistics of Wars, Oppressions and Atrocities of the Nineteenth Century (the 1800s), http://users.erols.com /mwhite28/wars19c.htm#Crim.

6. This convention was revised in 1949, a year that saw several revisions of the earlier three conventions. They highlighted the consciousness of the brutality of war that followed World War II and that arose during the heightened tensions during the U.S.-Soviet cold war. For a complete list of the conventions and other documents related to humanitarianism in war, see http://www.icrc.org/ihl.nsf/INTRO ?OpenView.

7. O'Brien, op. cit., p. 38.

8. John S. Bowman (ed), *Facts About American Wars*, New York, H.W. Wilson Company, 1998, p. 588.

9. Ibid., p. 598.

10. From the White House briefing room, http://www.whitehouse.gov/news/ releases/2004/06/20040602.html.

11. For the text, see http://www.whitehouse.gov/news/releases/2004/06/ 20040602.html.

12. O'Brien, op. cit., p. 155.

13. *The New Yorker*, May 10, 2005. Posted at http://www.newyorker.com/fact/ content/articles/040510fa_fact?040510fa_fact.

14. Full Text of the Supreme Court's Decision in Hamdan v. Rumsfeld (2006), with Concurrence and Dissents: http://civilliberty.about.com/od/waronterror/p/ hamdan.htm.

15. Ibid.

16. For the Bush administration's negative reactions to the accusations of torture, see http://thinkprogress.org/?tag=Administration&paged=3.

17. For a review of the accusations and evidence of the torture of detainees at Guantanamo and elsewhere, see http://www.whatreallyhappened.com/archives/week_2006_03_05.html.

CHAPTER 8

1. Quoted from David Halberstam's *The Best and the Brightest, The New York Times*, December 11, 2006, p. A29.

2. Cf. Christian Alfonsi, *Circle in the Sand: Why We Went Back to Iraq*, New York, Doubleday, 2006, pp. 381–382. The author attributes the stepped-up military activity against Iraq in the pre-9/11 period of early 2001 in part to "growing disillusionment within the ranks of neoconservatives at the foreign policy direction the new administration was taking. This disillusionment had begun even before President Bush was inaugurated." By the time of 9/11, Defense Secretary Donald Rumsfeld had confided to Gen. Richard Myers, vice chairman of the JCS, "My instinct is to hit Saddam at the same time, not just bin Laden." On September 12, a sharp discussion had taken place at the White House over whether to attack Iraq, with Rumsfeld and his deputy Paul Wolfowitz arguing for such an attack, and Colin Powell and his deputy Rich Armitage arguing against. Later that same evening, in a famous exchange, President Bush himself ordered his NSC [National Security Council] counterterrorism chief, Richard Clarke, "See if Saddam did this. See if he's linked in any way" (op. cit., p. 385). Then came unproved administration allegations that Saddam was collaborating or sought to collaborate with Al Qaeda. Yet the latter organization was extremely hostile to Hussein's strictly *secular*-oriented Baathist regime as, indeed, the Baathists were toward that group of Salafist Muslims. On the theocratic ideology of Salafism and its contrast with Baathist ideology, see John Keegan, *The Iraq War*, New York, Alfred A. Knopf, 2004, p. 95.

3. Arthur Schlesinger, Jr., "Unilateral Preventive War: Illegitimate And Immoral," *Ratville Times*, http://www.ratical.org/ratville/CAH/UPWIaI.html.

4. British Army General Rupert Smith defines this type of American-style war as having originated in U.S. war-fighting tradition during the Civil War. The American Civil War, the author writes, "was an important milestone in the evolution of interstate industrial war, not the least because of its subsequent influence on the American way of war, and because of the many European observers dispatched from across the Atlantic. The conclusions they took back from their strong impressions of the battlefields may not always have been correct, but nonetheless had enormous impact on the evolution of total war in Europe" (Rupert Smith, *The Utility of Force: The Art of War in the Modern World*, New York, Alfred A. Knopf, 2007, p. 84).

5. Ibid.

6. *The New York Times*, December 11, 2006, p. A1.

7. *The Iraq Study Group Report*, New York, Vintage Books, 2006. In early 2007, some leading voices in Congress began calling for new war-empowering legislation that would limit the presidential authority that had been granted President Bush immediately after 9/11 (resolutions in 2001 and 2002). If such new legislation ever saw the light of day, an important precedent would be established in the relationship between the two branches of government in the United States, the executive and the Congress, affecting the waging of war. Meantime, the White House responded

critically to such congressional gambits calling them attempts by legislators, as Vice President Cheney described them, January 14, 2007, to "wage war by committee" (http://www.thenation.com/blogs/thebeat/161542).

8. "The Iran-Contra Affair 1983–1988," Southern Nazerene University, http://home.snu.edu/~dwilliam/s98/usarab/icscandal.htm.

9. John B. Judis, Spencer Ackerman, "The Selling of the Iraq War: The First Casualty," *New Republic*, June 30, 2003. Text at http://www.globalpolicy.org/security/issues/iraq/unmovic/2003/0630selling.htm.

10. John Lewis Gaddis, *Surprise, Security, and the American Experience,* Cambridge, Harvard University Press, 2004, pp. 21–22. In his volume Gaddis argued that preemptive war is not new to American military history. He cited examples of this by way of our various enforcements of the Monroe Doctrine in the 19th and 20th centuries that accompanied America's continental expansion (e.g., the Mexican War, or, as it is known in Mexico, "The War of American Aggression," of 1846 and 1848). But such American-initiated conflict was extending geographically after the frontier was closed, the Spanish-American War being an exception. As Gaddis wrote of contemporary times: "So when President George W. Bush warned, at West Point in June 2003, that America must 'be ready for preemptive action when necessary to defend our liberty and defend our lives,' he was echoing an old tradition rather than establishing a new one." In his book, *Power, Terror, Peace, and War: America's Grand Strategy in a World at Risk,* New York, Alfred A. Knopf, 2004, Walter Russell Mead tends to agree with Gaddis, adding that the United States currently has even attempted to extend the Monroe Doctrine to include Europe (p. 122). It should be noted, as Gaddis did not at any length, that there is a difference between all-out preventive or preemptive war versus limited, in time and scope, intervention of the type conducted by the United States in the 1980s in the cases of Grenada (1983) and Panama (1989). However, that both of these interventions had a "preventive" as well as "preemptive" edge cannot be denied. Moreover, that they both raised serious issues in international law is also undeniable. In the case of Grenada, the U.S. Government attempted to justify its actions in invading the island state by the fact that the Soviets and Cubans, as indicated in captured documents of Soviet and Cuban origin, sought to convert Grenada into a communist satellite. It appeared not only to the United States but to several governments in the southeast Caribbean that Grenada was to serve as base for exporting Soviet-Cuban ideology and the communist system to neighboring states and beyond (cf. Washington, D.C., *Grenada Documents: An Overview and Selection*, U.S. Department of State and Department of Defense, September 1984).

11. Ibid. According to Judis and Spencer, it appears that In October 2001, Wolfowitz, Rumsfeld, and Undersecretary of Defense for Policy Douglas Feith set up a special intelligence operation in the Pentagon to "think through how the various terrorist organizations relate to each other and . . . state sponsors," in Feith's description. "Their approach echoed the "Team B" strategy that conservatives had used in the past by establishing a separate entity to offer alternative intelligence analyses to the CIA. Conservatives had done this in 1976, criticizing and intimidating the agency over its estimates of Soviet military strength, and again in 1998, arguing for the necessity of missile defense. (Wolfowitz had participated in both projects; the latter was run by Rumsfeld.) This time, the new entity—headed by Perle protégé, Abram Shulsky—reassessed intelligence already collected by the CIA along with information from Iraqi defectors and, as Feith remarked coyly at a press conference, "came up with some

interesting observations about the linkages between Iraq and Al Qaeda." In August 2002, Feith brought the unit to Langley to brief the CIA about its findings. If the separate intelligence unit wasn't enough to challenge the CIA, Rumsfeld also began publicly discussing the creation of a new Pentagon post, an undersecretary for intelligence, "who would rival the CIA director and diminish the authority of the agency."Wolfowitz, speaking in London, said of the need to supplant diplomacy with force (ironically, after the Bush Administration had already decided on unleashing war to unseat Saddam Hussein) on December 2, 2002: "Just stop and think for a moment. Just when were the attacks of September 11th imminent? Certainly they were imminent on September 10th, although we didn't know it. In fact, the September 11th terrorists had established themselves in the United States long before that date. Anyone who believes that we can wait until we have certain knowledge that attacks are imminent, has failed to connect the dots that led to September 11th. As we seek a peaceful outcome to the Iraq situation, we recognize that we would never have succeeded in the U.N. without the support of our coalition partners. And we would have no chance of getting Saddam Hussein to take the U.N.'s seventeenth and latest resolution seriously were it not backed up by the resolve of the brave men and women in the armed forces of our two nations and many others. In fact, a growing number of countries have indicated that they would participate in a coalition if Iraq refuses to give up its weapons of mass destruction. They see, as we do, that our hope for peace rests with the credible threat of force. Winston Churchill expressed a similar truth about the will and means to use force when he observed in 1949 that 'we arm to parley.' As that great statesman and leader knew so well, in some cases, only a credible threat of force opens the way to diplomacy" (http://www.iiss.org/recent-key-addresses/wolfowitz-address/).

12. Ibid.

13. Crimes of War Project, "Iraq and the 'Bush Doctrine' of Pre-emptive Self-Defense, August 20, 2002. Thomas Franck is Director of the Center for International Studies at NYU Law School http://www.crimesofwar.org/expert/bush-franck.html.

14. Ibid.

15. http://www.whitehouse.gov/news/releases/2002/06/20020601-3.html.

16. Crimes of War Project, op. cit. supra.

17. Thomas X. Hammes, *The Sling and the Stone: On War in the 21st Century*, St. Paul, Zenith Press, 2004. Colonel Hammes, who was among the first to mount a detailed critique of U.S. flawed tactics and strategy in Iraq, defined "fourth generation war" as a revised type of guerrilla warfare. It was first employed on a large scale in modern times by Mao Tsetung's armed communist forces in seizing power in Mainland China in the late 1940s. The U.S. military, alleges the colonel, is still ill-equipped in tactics and weaponry in order to defend against this form of warfare as seen in Iraq. General Smith calls guerrilla or insurgency combat "war amongst the people" (op. cit., pp. 154–182).

18. Smith, op. cit., pp. 375–6.

19. Ernst Nolte, *Yevropeiskaya grazhdanskaya voina (1917–1945): Natsional-sotsializm i bol'shevizm* (The European Civil War [1917–194]: National- Socialism and Bolshevism), Moscow, Logos, 2003, p. 384. Nolte points out that Stalin, unlike Hitler, counted on eventual U.S. aid against the Axis and had the greatest respect for America's inherent capability to tool up rapidly for war. Soviet intelligence operating in America, unlike the less efficient Nazi effort at espionage, was evidently better

informed on American defense capability than that of the Germans. The Soviet NKVD, in fact, had stolen a number of U.S. military secrets that in turn informed and impressed Moscow of American defense capability. U.S. Lend-Lease had already gotten underway by 1941, that is, before the German invasion of the USSR in June. Stalin was also aware of American and Allied willingness, often more than hinted at by President Franklin D. Roosevelt and British Prime Minister Winston Churchill before June 1941, to come to the aid of the Soviets if events led to their involvement in war with the Axis.

20. Noah Feldmann, "Whose War Powers Can Congress Tell the President How to Fight in Iraq. Should It?" The New York Times Magazine, February 4, 2007, pp. 21–22.

21. John Tierney, "Osama's Spin Lessons," *The New York Times*, September 12, 2006, p. A25. Tierney's op-ed summarized a widely shared view among specialists on international affairs. Cf., e.g., Robert Jervis, *American Foreign Policy in a New Era*, New York, Routledge, 2005, pp. 13–14 and 46–51. As the author writes (pp. 46–47): "In his speech to a joint session of Congress nine days after the 9/11 attack, President Bush declared that the United States would wage war against terrorism, accepting the formulation used by Secretary of Defense Rumsfeld just hours after the planes struck. [But] the very label is contentious and questionable.... The label 'war' implies the primacy of military force. Other instruments, such as diplomacy and intelligence, may be used.... This conceptual frame is unfortunate when it comes to dealing with terrorism. Here diplomacy, the international criminal justice system, and especially intelligence are primary. With good information terrorism is easy to attack; without it very little is possible.... If they are sacrificed in order to gain military advantage, the policy will suffer. Conceiving of military action aimed at terrorists as war, then, gets us thinking in the wrong terms."

22. Tierney, Ibid.

23. Ibid. On this point, cf. Louise Richardson, *What the Terrorists Want: Understanding the Enemy, Containing the Threat*, New York, Random House, 2007 (as reviewed by Martin Walker in *The New York Times Book Review*, September 10, 2006, p. 30).

24. Donald Stoker, "Insurgencies Rarely Win—And Iraq Won't Be Any Different (Maybe)," *Foreign Policy*, January 2007. Stoker teaches military strategy at the U.S. Naval War College in Monterey, CA.

25. ABC News at http://abcnews.go.com/Politics/PollVault/story?id=1968029. As of late January 2007, the President's approval rating stood at only 33 percent, or the lowest measured for any president in modern times. A weakened, lame-duck president may also encounter serious opposition in the Congress. It could take the form of cutting off funding for the war in Iraq.

EPILOGUE

1. Russian Minister of Defense Sergei Ivanov made this statement on October 5, 2003: "It is necessary to develop measures to preempt any attempts to use force against Russia, to disrupt any armed provocations, and to preempt any terrorists' actions." Cf. *Wall Street Journal*, January 11, 2006, an op-ed by Ivanov. For the Soviet background on justifying preemptive war, see Mark E. Miller, *Soviet Strategic Power and Doctrine: The Quest for Superiority*, Advanced International Studies Institute, The University of Miami, 1982; Albert L. Weeks, "The Garthoff-Pipes

Debate on Soviet Doctrine: Another Perspective," *Strategic Review*, Winter 1983, pp. 57–64. News of Japan's adoption of a preemptive posture appeared in *Jane's Defense Weekly*, June 3, 2009, p. 5. The magazine's Tokyo correspondent noted that a government "defence policy panel [of the ruling LDP Party] is set to argue for the country's right to launch preemptive strikes in the face of an imminent attack by another state." Japan has been alarmed by North Korea's firing of missiles over its territory and the detonations by the DPRK of two nuclear devices in 2009.

   2. Christopher Andrew and Oleg Gordievsky, *KGB: The Inside Story*, pp. 583–585.

Bibliography

BOOKS

Adragna, Steven P. *On Guard for Victory: Military Doctrine and Ballistic Missile Defense in the USSR.* Washington, D.C.: Pergamon-Brassey's, 1987.

Anonymous. *Imperial Hubris: Why the West Is Losing the War on Terror.* Washington, D.C.:Brassey's, Inc., 2004.

Barnett, Thomas P. *The Pentagon's New Map War and Peace in the Twenty-First Century.* New York: G. P. Putnam's Sons, 2004.

Blainey, Geoffrey. *The Causes of War.* New York: The Free Press, 1988.

Blix, Hans. *Disarming Iraq.* New York: Pantheon Books, 2004.

Bok, Sissela. *Lying: Moral Choice in Public and Private Life.* New York: Vintage Books, 1978.

Bowra, C. M. *The Greek Experience.* New York: Mentor, 1957.

Byrd, Robert E. *Losing America: Confronting a Reckless and Arrogant Presidency.* New York: W. W. Norton & Company, 2004.

Casey, John. *Pagan Virtue: An Essay in Ethics.* Oxford: Clarendon Press, 1990.

Chadwick, Henry. *Early Christian Thought and the Classical Tradition.* New York: Clarendon Press, 1984.

Claire, Roger W. *Raid on the Sun.* New York: Broadway Books, 2004.

Clancy, Tom, Tony Zinni, and Tony Koltz. *Battle Ready.* New York: G.P. Putnam Books, 2004.

Clark, Wesley K. *Waging Modern War: Bosnia, Kosovo, and the Future of Combat.* New York: Public Affairs, 2001.

———. *Winning Modern Wars: Iraq, Terrorism, and the American Empire.* New York: Public Affairs, 2003.

Clausewitz, Carl. *On War.* Princeton, NJ: Princeton University Press, 1976.

Deane, Herbert A. *The Political and Social Ideas of St. Augustine.* New York: Columbia University Press, 1963.

Deane, Michael J. *Strategic Defense in Soviet Strategy.* University of Miami: Advanced International Studies Institute, n.d.

Dorrien, Gary. *Imperial Designs Neoconservatism and the New Pax Americana.* New York: Routledge, 2004.

Douglass, Joseph D. and Amoretta M. Hoeber. *Soviet Strategy for Nuclear War.* Stanford University: Hoover Institution Press, 1979.

Elshtain, Jean Bethke. *Just War Against Terror: The Burden of American Power in a Violent World.* New York: Basic Books, 2003.

Encyclopedia of Russian History. New York: MacMillan Reference USA, 2003, 4 volumes.

Finnis, John. *Aquinas: Moral, Political, and Legal Theory.* New York: Oxford University Press, 1989.

Frum, David. *The Right Man: An Inside Account of the Bush White House.* New York: Random House, 2003.

Gaddis, John Lewis. *Surprise, Security, and the American Experience.* Cambridge, MA: Harvard University Press, 2004.

Gordon, Michael and Gen. Bernard Trainor. *Cobra II: The Inside Story of the Invasion and Occupation of Iraq.* New York: Pantheon Books, 2006.

Gorkii, A. P., et al. *Voennii Entsiklopedicheskii slovar'* (*Military Encyclopedia Dictionary*), Moscow: Ministerstvo Oborony Rossiiskoi Federatsii Institut Voennoi Istorii (Ministry of Defense of the Russian Federation, Institute of Military History), 2001, vol. 1-2. (Articles on "preventive war" and "preemptive attack" in this basic, post-Soviet Russian military reference book.)

Gray, Colin S. *Modern Strategy.* New York: Oxford University Press, 1999.

Hamilton Edith and Huntington Cairns. *The Collected Dialogues of Plato: Including the Letters.* Princeton, NJ: Princeton University Press, 1989.

Hargis, Jeffrey W. *Against the Christians: The Rise of Early Anti-Christian Polemic.* New York: Peter Lang Publishing, Inc., 1999.

Herodotus. *The Histories.* New York: Penquin Classics, 1983.

Hoffman, Stanley. *The Ethics of Humanitarian Intervention.* South Bend, IN: Notre Dame University Press, 1996)

Homer. *The Iliad* and *The Odyssey.* Mineola, NY: Dover Publications, 1999.

Johnson, Chalmers. *The Sorrows of Empire: Militarism, Secrecy, and the End of the Republic.* New York: Henry Holt and Company, 2004.

Johnson. James T. *Morality and Contemporary Warfare.* New Haven: Yale University Press, 1999.

Johnson, Loch K. and James J. Wirtz. *Strategic Intelligence: Windows into a Secret World: An Anthology.* Los Angeles: Roxbury Publishing Co., 2004.

Johnson, Paul. *A History of Christianity.* New York: Simon and Schuster, 1995.

Kagan, Donald. *On the Origins of War and the Preservation of Peace.* New York: Anchor Books, 1995.

Kahn, Herman. *On Thermonuclear War.* Princeton, NJ: Princeton University Press, 1961.

Kant, Immanuel. *Perpetual Peace, and Other Essays on Politics, History, and Morals.* Indianapolis: Hackett Publishing Co., 1983.

Keegan, John. *The Iraq War.* New York: Alfred A. Knopf, 2004.

Kennan, George F. *American Diplomacy 1900–1950.* New York: New American Library, 1951.

Kuhn, Hans. *On Being a Christian.* New York: Doubleday, 1984.

Kokoshin. Andrei A. *Soviet Strategic Thought, 1917–1991*. Cambridge, MA: The MIT Press, 1998.

Leebaert, Derek, ed. *Soviet Military Thinking*. London: George Allen & Unwin, 1981.

Leonhard, Robert. *The Art of Maneuver: Maneuver-Warfare Theory and AirLand Battle*. New York: Ballantine Books, 1991.

Lewy, Guenter. *America in Vietnam*. New York: Oxford University Press, 1978.

Liddell Hart, B. H. *Strategy*. New York: Faber & Faber, 1991.

Lockwood, Joanthan S. *The Soviet View of U.S. Strategic Doctrine: Implications for Decision Making*. New Brunswick, NJ: Transaction Books, 1983.

Lucas Jr., George R. *Perspectives on Humanitarian Military Intervention*. Berkeley, CA: University of California, 2001.

Lucas Jr.,George R. and Robert Wertheimer, eds. *Moral Matters and Military Might: New Essays on Ethics and the Military Profession*. Albany: State University of New York Press, 2004.

MacGregor, Douglas A. *Transformation Under Fire: Revolutionizing How America Fights*. New York: Praeger, 2003.

Mann, James. *Rise of the Vulcans: The History of Bush's War Cabinet*.New York: Viking, 2004.

McKeon, Richard. *The Basic Works of Aristotle*. New York: Random House, 1941.

McNeill, William H. *The Rise of the West A History of the Human Community*. Chicago: University of Chicago Press, 1991.

Mead, Walter Russell. *Power, Terror, Peace, and War: America's Grand Strategy in a World at Risk*. New York: Alfred A. Knopf, 2004.

Middleton, Drew. *Retreat from Victory*, New York: Hawthorne Books, 1973.

Minucius Felix. *Octavius*. Cambridge, MA: Loeb Classical Library, 1998.

Momigliano, Arnaldo. *On Pagans, Jews, and Christians*. Hanover: Wesleyan University Press, 1985.

Morgenthau, Hans J. *In Defense of the National Interest: A Critical Examination of American Foreign Policy*. Washington, D.C.: University Press of America Inc., 1982.

Murray, Douglas J. *The Defense Policies of Nations*. Baltimore: Johns Hopkins University Press, 1994.

Nichols, Thomas N. *Winning the World: Lessons for America's Future from the Cold War*. Westport, CT: Praeger, 2004.

Nojeim, Michael J. *Gandhi and King: The Power of Nonviolent Resistance*. Westport, CT: Praeger, 2004.

O'Brien, William V. *The Conduct of Just and Limited War*. New York: Praeger Publishers, 1981.

———. *U.S. Military Intervention: Law and Morality*. Washington, D.C.: Center for Strategic and International Studies, 1979.

Packer, George. *The Assassins' Gate America in Iraq*. New York: Farrar, Straus and Giroux, 2005.

Pollack, Kenneth M. *The Threatening Storm*. New York: Random House, 2002.

Purdum, Todd S. *A Time of Our Choosing: America's War in Iraq*. New York: Times Books, 2003.

Record, Jeffrey. *Dark Victory: America's Second War Against Iraq*. Annapolis, MD: Naval Institute Press, 2004.

Rosen, Gary (ed). *The Right War? The Conservative Debate on Iraq*. New York: Cambridge University Press, 2005.

Scott, Harriet Fast and William F. *Soviet Military Doctrine*. Boulder, CO: Westview Press, 1988.

——, eds. *The Soviet Art of War: Doctrine, Strategy, and Tactics*. Boulder, CO: Westview Press, 1982.

Sun Tzu. *The Art of War*. New York: Oxford University Press, 1963.

Swaim, J. Carter. *War, Peace, and the Bible*. Maryknoll, NY: Orbis Books, 1982.

Sweeney, J. M., et al. *The International Legal System Cases and Materials*, 2nd edition, University Casebook Series, The Foundation Press Inc., U.S. Government Printing Office, 1982.

Tertullian. *Apology. De Spectaculis,Minucius Felix: Octavius*. Cambridge, MA: Loeb Classical Library, 1998.

Thomas Aquinas, *Summa Theologica*. Westminster, MD: Christian Classics, 1981, 5 volumes.

Thucydides. *The Peloponnesian War*. New York: Penguin Classics, 1978.

Vasquez, John A. *Classics of International Relations*. Upper Saddle River, NJ: Prentice Hall, 1996.

Venant, Jean-Pierre. *The Origins of Greek Thought*. Ithaca, NY: Cornell University Press, 1982.

Veyne, Paul. *Did the Greeks Believe in Their Myths? An Essay on the Constitutive Imagination*. Chicago: University of Chicago Press, 983.

Vigor, P. H. *The Soviet View of War, Peace and Neutrality*. London: Routledge & Kegan, 1975.

Weeks Albert L. *Stalin's Other War: Soviet Grand Strategy 1939–1941*. Lanham, MD: Rowman & Littlefield, 2002.

Wilson, Joseph. *The Politics of Truth: Inside the Lies that Led to War and Betrayed My Wife's CIA Identity: A Diplomat's Memoir*. New York: Carroll & Grafs Publishers, 2004.

Woodward, Bob. *Plan of Attack*. New York: Simon & Schuster, 2004.

Zampaglione, Gerardo. *The Idea of Peace in Antiquity*, Notre Dame, IN: Notre Dame Press, 1973.

Zinni, Tony. *The Battle for Peace: A Frontline Vision of America's Power and Purpose*. New York: Palgrave Macmillan, 2006.

ARTICLES AND DOCUMENTS

Albright, Madeleine K. "Bridges, Bombs, or Bluster?" *Foreign Affairs* (September/October, 2003).

Arbatov, Alexei. Russian Military Doctrine and Strategic Nuclear Forces to the Year 2000 and Beyond, Conference, March 26–27, Naval Postgraduate School, Monterey, CA.

Articles by various scolars. "Future Implications of the Iraq Conflict." *American Journal of International Affairs* (January 2004).

Barnett, Thomas P. M. and Henry H. Gaffney Jr. "The Top Ten Rules of the New American Way of War." *Naval Institute Proceedings*, U.S. Naval Institute online document (January 2003).

Brzezinski, Zbigniew. "Hegemonic Quicksand." *The National Interest* (Winter 2003–04): 5–16.

Cordes, Hanni. "Does an Ounce of Prevention Really Bring a Pound of Cure? The Debate Over Preventive War Doctrine." National Defense University, National War College, debate, n.d., http://www.ndu.edu/library/n4/n035605f.pdf.

Crawford, Neta C. "The Slippery Slope of Preventive War." Carnegie Council and Ethics and International Affairs, online document (2004).

Godzimirsky, Jacob. "Russia's New Military Doctrine?" Norwegian Atlantic Community document, No. 8 (2003): 1–4.

Heisbourg, Francois. "A Work in Progress: The Bush Doctrine and Its Consequences." *Washington Quarterly*, Vol. 26, No. 2 (Spring 2003): 75–88.

Ivanov, Sergei. "*Aktual'niye zadazhi razvitiya vooruzhennikh sil Rossiiskoi Federatsii*" ("Timely Tasks for the Development of the Armed Forces of the Russian Federation"). Moscow (October 2003).

Kagan, Frederick W. "War and Aftermath." *Policy Review* (August–September 2003): 1–24.

Krepinevich, Andrew. "Preemption in Iraq: Rationale, Risks, and Requirements." Center for Strategic and Biudgetary Assessments, Washington, D.C. (2003): 1–37.

Lampman, Jane. "Mixing Prophecy and Politics: Christian Zionists Are Growing in Influence." *Christian Science Monitor* (July 7, 2004): 15–16.

Lewis, Bernard. "Freedom and Justice in the Modern Middle East." *Foreign Affairs* (May/June 2005): 36–51.

Lopez, George A. and David Cortright. "Containing Iraq: Sanctions Worked." *Foreign Affairs* (July–August 2004): 90–103.

McPeak, Merrill A. "The Kosovo Result: The Facts Speak for Themselves." *Armed Forces Journal International* (September 1999): 64.

———. "A Neater Way to Win." *Foreign Affairs* (September–October 2004): 160–162.

National Security Strategy of the United States of America, submitted to Congress by President George W. Bush (September 2002).

National Security Strategy for a Global Age, submitted to Congress by President William Jefferson Clinton (December 2000).

Nichols, Thomas M. "Just War, Not Prevention." Carnegie Council on Ethics and International Affairs (document issued May 23, 2004).

Nye Jr., Joseph S. "U.S. Power and Strategy After Iraq." *Foreign Affairs* (July/August 2003).

O'Connell, Mary Ellen. "The Myth of Preemptive Self-Defense." The American Society of International Law, Online document (Autumn 2003).

O'Hanlon, Michael E., *et al.* "The New National Security Strategy and Preemption." Bookings Institution Policy Brief #13 (June 24, 2004).

Perl, Raphael. "Expert Sees More Proactive U.S. Policy Against Terrorism." Address to the German Council on Foreign Affairs, distributed by the Office of International Information Programs, U.S. Department of State (July 2, 2002).

Powers, Gerald. "Would an Invasion of Iraq Be a 'Just War'?" United States Institute of Peace, Special Report 98, online document (2002): 1–21.

Raymond, John (Bro.). "The Just War Theory." www.monksofadoration.org.

Rivkin, David B. and Lee A. Casey. "Leashing the Dogs of War." *The National Interest*: 57–69.

Rumsfeld, Donald M. "Transforming the Military." *Foreign Affairs*. (May/June 2002).

Sapolsky, Robert M. "A Natural History of Peace." *Foreign Affairs* (January/February 2006): 104–120.

Schmitt, Michael N. "Preemptive Strategies in International Law." *Michigan Journal of International Law*, Vol. 24 (Winter 2001): 13–549.

Schroeder, Paul W. "Iraq: The Case Against Preemptive War." *The American Conservative.*, online, n.d.

Shournikhin, Andrei. "The Russian Military's New 'Open Doctrine,'" National Institute for Public Policy, autumn 2003, p. 1-5.

Steele, Max D. "One Roman Catholic's Perspective on Preemptive War." Institute for Global Engagement, document (May 2, 2003).

Weeks, Albert L. "When 'Grenada-type' Intervention May Be Legitimate." *Crossroads*, No. 14 (1985): 43–56.

———. "Soviet Military Doctrine." *Global Affairs* (Winter 1988): 170–187.

———. "Current Soviet Military Strategy." *Global Affairs* (Fall 1987): 168–179.

———. "Russia Unfurls Its New/Old Military Doctrine."*ROA National Security Report* (January 1994): 30–35.

Welsh, Steven C. "Preemptive War and International Law." CDI document (December 5, 2003).

Wolfowitz, Paul. "Building Coalitions of Common Values." Address to the International Institute for Strategic Studies, London(December 2, 2002).

PERIODICALS

The Christian Science Monitor
The Economist
The London Times
Moskovskiye Novosti
Newsweek
The New York Times
Time

Index

About the Author

ALBERT L. WEEKS, Professor Emeritus of NYU, is the author of some eight books dealing with international affairs. His experience has been in the military (USAF), journalism (*Newsweek*), and in Academe (University of Chicago, Columbia University, and other schools). He has published many articles in the civilian press (*The New York Times*, *The Christian Science Monitor*, *Foreign Affairs* quarterly; in two periodicals in post-Soviet Russia, and elsewhere) as well as in several U.S. military and intelligence journals. Dr. Weeks is an amateur astronomer and a "Sunday" watercolor painter.